Lecture Notes in Economics and Mathematical Systems

Managing Editors: M. Beckmann and W. Krelle

352

Onno van Hilten

Optimal Firm Behaviour in the Context of Technological Progress and a Business Cycle

Springer-Verlag
Berlin Heidelberg New York London
Paris Tokyo Hong Kong Barcelona

Author

Dr. Onno van Hilten
Netherlands Energy Research Foundation ECN
P.O. Box 1, NL-1755 ZG Petten, The Netherlands

ISBN 3-540-53563-2 Springer-Verlag Berlin Heidelberg New York
ISBN 0-387-53563-2 Springer-Verlag New York Berlin Heidelberg

Printing and binding: Druckhaus Beltz, Hemsbach/Bergstr.
2142/3140-543210 – Printed on acid-free paper

ACKNOWLEDGEMENTS

Writing this thesis has been a great pleasure. Many people contributed to this pleasure. The first one to be mentioned in this respect is Paul van Loon, who lead me into the world of economics and dynamic optimisation. His creativity with regard to generating ideas and solving the many 'small' problems that occurred, has continued to amaze me in the last four years. Our cooperation was in many ways optimal.
With many colleagues at the University of Limburg I have had interesting discussions on all kinds of subjects. Especially with my 'collega proximus' Kees Cools, who is not a specialist of optimal control theory, but, to me, a specialist of life.
I would also like to thank: Raymond Gradus, Peter Kort, Piet Verheyen (all University of Tilburg) and Jan de Jong (University of Eindhoven) for many discussions on almost every part of the thesis; and Richard Hartl (Technical University of Vienna), who helped me writing Appendix 4 and who patiently and accurately answered the many letters I wrote him.
Appendix 4 has been written during a three weeks stay at the Technical University of Vienna. This stay has been financially supported by the Netherlands Organisation for Scientific Research (NWO).
Many errors have been removed by Peter Kort, who scrupulously read the manuscript with expert eyes, and Mieke Lettink, who improved my use of the English language. All remaining errors are mine.
Finally I want to thank two persons who are almost completely unknowing of the contents of this book, but whose contribution is nevertheless invaluable: my mother, from whom I not only inhereted the need for (too) much sleep, but also a talent for mathematics and a (apparently sufficient) degree of perseverance, and Ankie, who taught me the irrelevance of a long distance and who (mostly unaware of it) took my mind off this book at the right times.

CONTENTS

NOTATION

General remarks

In this thesis small Latin letters are used to denote exogeneous parameters and functions. Latin capitals are used to denote endogeneous variables. Greek letters are used to denote auxilliary variables (for instance, shadow prices). Below is a list of symbols, which is used throughout the thesis. If a symbol is not explained in the text, it should be in this list.
The figures in this thesis are only rough sketches, mainly to indicate whether a particular function is increasing, decreasing or constant.
A dot above a letter (as in $\dot{K}$) denotes the total time derivative. In general total derivatives are denoted by d, partial derivatives by ∂.
If a reference is made to a formula, table or figure in a different chapter, the number of the chapter is added. For instance, Figure 5.3 refers to Figure 3 of Chapter 5; equation (26) refers to equation (26) of the current chapter; equation (4.30) refers to equation (30) of Chapter 4. The formulas in the appendices are denoted as follows: (A3.14) refers to formula (14) in Appendix 3.

List of symbols

<u>Endogeneous variables</u>

D(t)	dividends (dollars/time)
I(t)	investments (dollars/time)
K(t)	number of capital goods
L(t)	number of units of labour
X(t)	equity (dollars)
Y(t)	debt (dollars)
Q(t)	output (numbers/time)
S(t)	revenue (dollars/time)
R(K)	marginal return on investment
$R_e(K,X)$	marginal return on equity
N(t)	birth date of oldest capital goods still in use at time t
V(t)	scrapping date of capital installed at time t
M(t)	lifetime of capital installed at time t (=V(t)-t)

T(t)	lifetime of capital scrapped at time t (=t-N(t))
B(t)	derivative of V

Exogeneous parameters and functions

a	rate of depreciation
b	maximal debt-equity ratio
c	price of capital goods
d(t)	fiscal depreciation scheme
e	price elasticity of demand
f	corporation profit tax rate
g	growth rate of the demand function
h	growth rate of the labour productivity
i	discount rate (required return of the shareholders)
k	capital to output ratio
l	labour to output ratio
m	m-g is the rate of decrease of the demand function
n_0	initial time in models with technological progress
p	price per unit of output
r	rate of interest
t_0	beginning of the recession
t_1	end of the recession
v	fiscal lifetime of a capital good
w	wage rate
y	demand
z	end of the planning period

1
INTRODUCTION

This thesis is a theoretical study of the optimal dynamic policies of a, to some extent, slowly adjusting firm that faces an exogeneously given technological progress and an exogeneously given business cycle. It belongs to the area of mathematical economics. It is intended to appeal to mathematical economists in the first place, economists in the second place and mathematicians in the third place. It entails an attempt to stretch the limits of the application of deterministic dynamic optimisation to economics, in particular to firm behaviour.

A well-known Dutch economist (and trained mathematician) recently stated in a local university newspaper[1] that mathematical economists give economics a bad reputation, since they formulate their problems from a mathematical point of view and they are only interested in technical, mathematical problems. At the same time, however, "profound as economists may be, when it comes to extending or modifying the existing theory to make it applicable to a certain economic problem, an understanding of optimal control theory (which is the mathematical theory used in this thesis, ovh) based solely on heuristic arguments will often turn out to be inadequate" (Sydsæter [1978]). So if one is convinced of the possible usefulness of mathematics in economics, one has to sail between the Scylla of being accused of dealing with technical, economically uninteresting problems, and the Charybdis of being accused of a careless, "inadequate" use of mathematics. This thesis is meant to deal with economically interesting problems in a mathematically adequate way. It is up to the reader to decide whether it does so.

The economic problem addressed can be summarised as the behaviour of a relatively slowly adjusting firm in a changing environment. This thesis belongs to a tradition of books and articles (Lesourne [1973], Ludwig [1978], Leban & Lesourne [1980, 1983], Leban [1983], Van Loon [1983, 1985], Van Schijndel [1988], Kort [1988, 1989]) that use a dynamic optimisation technique called the 'Maximum Principle' to study the optimal behaviour of

---

[1]Van der Ploeg in "Univers", vol. 25, no. 25, 11-3-1988)

a firm in a deterministic context. Most of these books and articles are primarily concerned with the optimal policy towards some stationary state, of which the existence is guaranteed by the stationarity of the environment. Maintaining the deterministic context, this thesis extends the analysis by studying the optimal investment, financing and dividend policies of the firm while the environment is changing in two specific ways:

1) the firm is confronted with a *business cycle*, represented by an exogeneously given fluctuating demand function. If the firm could quickly and costlessly change its size, a changing demand for its product would not cause real problems. If however the firm can only adjust the volume of the capital and/or labour stock relatively slowly (represented in particular by the irreversibility of investments), this 'slowness' may cause that the firm cannot perfectly adjust itself to the changing circumstances.
2) if newer machines are better than old ones, due to an exogeneously given *technological progress*, the firm not only has to decide on the *volume* of the capital goods stock, but also on the optimal *mix* in respect of the age of the individual capital goods. Moreover, if the firm can replace old machines by new ones, part of its 'slowness' with regard to changing its size has been removed. However, if the technological progress is embodied in new capital goods, the firm is slow with regard to changing the technology of its entire capital goods stock.

If these subjects are to be studied in a dynamic optimisation framework, three mathematical problems arise:

a) the models involve more than one state variable. Pitchford [1977] argues that problems with more than one state variable are often very difficult to solve. The popular 'phase-space analysis' is not applicable in this case. The only general, consistent method to deal with such problems is the path connecting procedure developed by Van Loon [1983].
b) the models involve so-called pure state constraints, that is, constraints which do not contain control variables. These constraints may cause the 'costate variables', which can usually be interpreted as the shadow prices of the state variables, to jump (to be discontinuous). This not only complicates the mathematics, but also the economic interpretation of these costate variables as shadow prices.

c) (and most important in this thesis) the models are non-autonomous. This means that time not only appears as an argument of the control and state variables, but also explicitly as an independent variable. This is caused by the changing environment. In the first place this complicates the application of the path connecting procedure mentioned under a). In the second place, with regard to technological progress, it leads to a type of model to which the standard Maximum Principle cannot be applied.

Treating the economic problems mentioned, dealing adequately with the mathematical problems above, leads to an exploration of the interplay of economics and mathematics.
Chapter 2 gives a survey of relevant 'predecessors' of the models in Chapters 5, 7 and 8. Chapter 3 goes deeper into the nature of the class of dynamic optimisation models to which the models in this thesis belong and it derives some methodological advices (guidelines) for the rest of the thesis. Chapter 4 treats the model which forms the basis for the models in the following chapters. Chapter 5 discusses a model in which the firm is confronted with a business cycle. Chapter 6 belongs to "that twilight zone of semantical interpretations of previously developed mathematical structures" (Mirowski [1986]). It extends the interpretation of costate variables as shadow prices. Chapter 7 discusses a model with technological progress. Chapter 8 extends the analysis in Chapter 7 and tries to combine Chapter 5 and Chapter 7. Chapter 9 summarises the thesis and gives the main conclusions.
The order of the appendices is dictated by the order of the chapters in the main text. Appendices 1, 2 and 5 treat the mathematical details of respectively Chapters 4, 5, and 7 and 8. Appendices 3 and 4 are of a different character. They contain independent results of a general character. Appendix 3 derives a shadow price interpretation of the multipliers of the pure state constraints, which is used in Chapter 6. Appendix 4 derives an extension of the Maximum Principle, which is applied to the model in Chapters 7 and 8.

2

A SELECTIVE LITERATURE SURVEY

2.1 Introduction

This chapter discusses some relevant predecessors of the models in the following chapters. All the models in this chapter are dynamic optimisation models, which are in most cases solved by means of the Maximum Principle[1]. Lesourne & Leban [1982] state: "In the last ten years, control theory has proved to be a very efficient tool to study the dynamics of the firm" (p.1). Indeed, many dynamic models of the firm using optimal control theory have appeared in literature. Surveys can be found in Lesourne & Leban [1982], Van Loon [1983], and Sethi [1978]. For a wider range of economic applications of optimal control theory, see, for instance, Feichtinger [1982,1985,1988]. The survey in this chapter discusses some models which have the same basic structure as the models in the following chapters and models which in some way incorporate technological progress or a business cycle. Only those aspects which seem relevant for this thesis are considered.

As already stated in Chapter 1, the models in this thesis are theoretical models, aimed at the derivation of analytical principles, such as "marginal revenue equals marginal cost", and "the level of X only depends on parameters $y_1,\ldots, y_n$".

The fact that these models are theoretical does not mean that they cannot be used in empirical work. Testing this kind of models would require, for instance, the modelling of expectations and the incorporation of possible lags between investment decisions and investment realisations (see Arrow [1968]; for a nice example see Malcomson [1983]). In general, the models in this thesis and most of the models discussed in this chapter only give a very broad outline of "the" firm.

Since theoretical results are asked for, the analytical solution of the optimisation problem involved must be found. As stated in Chapter 1, the

---

[1]In this thesis "Optimal Control Theory" and "The Maximum Principle" are treated as synonyms. The Maximum Principle is explained in Chapter 4.

mathematical complexity of the models in this thesis comes from the non-autonomity, the number of constraints and the number of state variables. This complexity is one of the reasons to work with deterministic instead of stochastic models[2] (see also Chapter 3).

In the following sections a number of models is discussed. All the models are deterministic and time is represented by a continuous variable. The economic problem in these models can be summarised as follows: the firm described is engaged in the production of a homogeneous output using capital and labour. It earns money by selling this output, the costs are mainly expenditures on capital goods and labour costs. The goal of the firm is maximisation of the properly discounted stream of profits or dividends (Leland [1980] shows that the assumption of profit maximisation is useful in many cases). The emphasis lies on the amount and timing of investments, and on the optimal combination of capital and labour. The financial structure of the firm is considered only in a few cases. And last but not least, in most cases the firm is, in one way or another, faced with an exogeneously given technological progress, or with a business cycle.

Section 2.2 discusses some models which use the same framework as the models in this thesis. Section 2.3 examines some models in which the firm faces a business cycle. Section 2.4 reviews some models in which the firm is confronted with technological progress. In Chapter 3 more will be said about the nature and the use of this kind of models.

2.2 The predecessors of the models in this thesis

The model serving as a framework for the models in this thesis is discussed extensively in Chapter 4. In mathematical form, the model is:

$$\underset{I,D}{\text{Max}} \int_0^z e^{-it} D(t)\, dt + e^{-iz} X(z) \tag{1}$$

$$\dot{K}(t) = I(t) - aK(t) \tag{2}$$

$$\dot{X}(t) = (1-f)\,\{S[Q(t)] - wL(t) - aK(t) - rY(t)\} - D(t) \tag{3}$$

$$Q(t) = K(t)/k, \qquad L(t) = lQ(t) \tag{4}$$

---

[2]Maccini [1984] states on this problem: "...intertemporal models appear to be mathematically intractable when uncertainty may enter in a complex fashion and when closed form solutions for choice variables are sought..." (p.46).

$$K(t) = X(t) + Y(t) \tag{5}$$

$$Y(t) \geq 0 \tag{6}$$

$$Y(t) \leq bX(t) \tag{7}$$

$$0 \leq I(t) \leq I_{max} \tag{8}$$

$$0 \leq D(t) \leq D_{max} \tag{9}$$

$$K(0) \text{ and } X(0) \text{ are given} \tag{10}$$

Equation (1) gives the objective of the firm: the firm wants to maximise the discounted value of future dividends plus the discounted value of equity at the end of the planning horizon. The instruments which the firm uses to achieve this (the control variables) are dividends and investments. If the firm invests now, the capital goods stock grows, which may lead to higher revenues and dividends in the future. So the decision problem of the firm is clearly dynamic. Equations (2) and (3) give the development over time of the stock of capital goods and the book value of equity. K and X are the 'state variables'. Together they contain all relevant information from the past: the only things the firm has to know at time t to make an optimal plan for the future are the values of K(t) and X(t). The initial values of K and X are given by (10). Equation (2) shows that the capital goods stock increases through investment and decreases through depreciation. It is assumed that the price of a capital good equals one. Equation (3) denotes that 'after tax profits' (profits equal revenue minus wage costs, depreciation costs, and interest costs) are used to pay out dividends or added to the stock of equity. Equation (4) gives the relation between the factor inputs (capital and labour) and output. Equation (5) is the balance sheet equation: the firm has two sources of funds, equity and debt. Equations (6) and (7) give a lower and an upper bound on the amount of debt. Equations (8) and (9) determine the region from which the control variables must be chosen.

This model goes back to Van Loon [1983]. Van Loon distinguishes *two* linear production activities. He studies the optimal choice of production activities, the optimal dividend policy, and the optimal investment policy (with emphasis on the influence of investment grants, see also Van Loon [1985]). He develops a procedure to derive the optimal policy for the entire planning period, for all possible initial conditions (10). This 'path connecting procedure' (or 'coupling procedure') is used throughout this thesis and it is exemplified in Chapter 4 and Appendix 1. Using this procedure one can obtain pictures like Figure 1, which sketches the optimal development over time of the relevant variables for a growing firm, while equity is cheaper than debt. In this case the firm uses debt to grow quickly in the beginning of the planning period. After reaching a certain size, the firm pays back the expensive debt and only uses retained earnings to grow further. For an extensive discussion of this optimal policy, see Chapter 4.

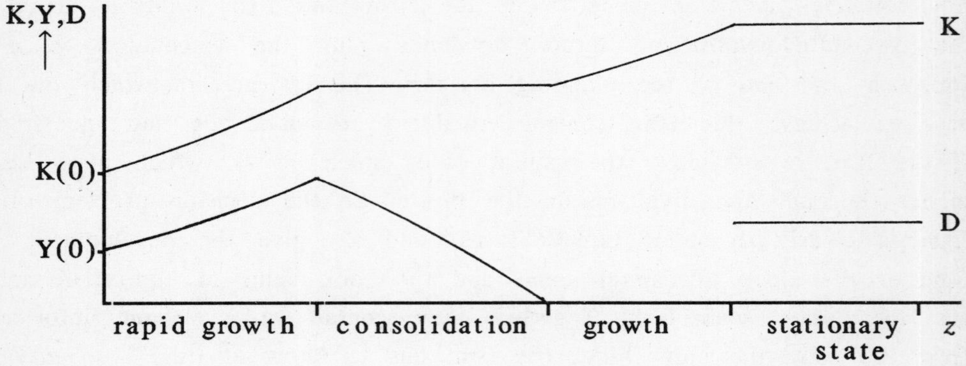

Figure 1: An optimal trajectory

The thesis of Van Loon has been extended in several directions. Van Schijndel [1988] uses the above model to study the optimal behaviour of a firm under personal taxation. Kort [1989] uses the model (without debt and taxes) to study the influence of adjustment costs (see also Kort [1988]) and he derives 'net present value'-rules for the model and several extensions.

More or less related models can be found in Steigum [1983] (rate of interest depends on the leverage ratio), Krouse & Lee [1973], Sethi [1978], and Senchak [1975] (emphasis on financial policies; Krouse & Lee concentrate on the optimal financing mix of retained earnings and external equity, Senchak adds debt financing), Hayashi [1985] (a stochastic model linking the Q theory on investment with the theory of optimal capital structure), Auerbach [1984] (an empirical analysis of financial policies, based on a deterministic dynamic model), Auerbach [1979] (a study of the impact of personal income and capital gains taxes on firm value and the cost of capital).

2.3 Optimal behaviour of a firm facing a business cycle

There are two approaches to study the behaviour of a firm faced with a business cycle with the aid of dynamic optimisation models. This section discusses both approaches.

2.3.1 An explicit business cycle

The first approach is taken by Leban & Lesourne [1980, 1983], Leban [1982], and Nickell [1974][3]. In these articles, the firm faces a given fluctuating demand curve, looking as follows:

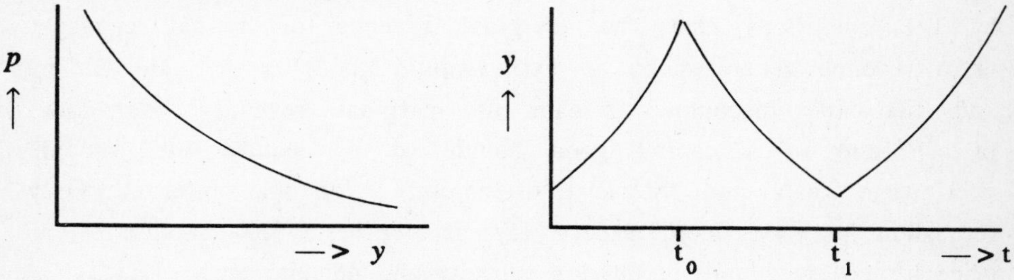

Figure 2: The demand function

The left hand side figure shows the demand curve at a given point of time. In the right hand side the price of output is given. The model of the firm in this case contains the restriction that production must be larger than or equal to demand:

$$Q(t) \geq y(p,t) \tag{11}$$

The optimal behaviour of a firm facing a business cycle is now studied by examining the (optimal) evolution through time of important variables like production, price, investment, recruitment and firing.

In Nickell [1974] and Leban & Lesourne [1980] the price of output is a control variable, whereas in Leban [1982] and Leban & Lesourne [1983], the price of output is fixed. In all these models the financial policy of the firm is not considered. The firm maximises the discounted value of future cash-flows, and investment is irreversible[4].

---

[3]Other articles studying aspects of firm behaviour during a business cycle (especially the demand for labour) are Nickell [1978a], and Van Long & Siebert [1983].

[4]The reasons to assume that investment is irreversible are discussed in

Nickell [1974] studies the optimal policy of a firm during a business cycle in a model with a fixed coefficient production technology (which means that there is only one combination of capital and labour which leads to a given amount of output) and with investments and the price of output as control variables. He finds the "rather natural result, that if wage costs, capital costs and the rate of discount are fixed, then the firm will not invest if demand is falling at least as fast as capacity is depreciating, and there will be no investment over and above replacement unless demand is growing" (p.4). So if during a slump demand decreases at a rate which is larger than the rate of depreciation, a 'zero investment'-period will occur. The dates when the firm stops and resumes investment (n_0 and n_1) are implicitly given by the conditions that the marginal revenue of capital goods (i.e. the extra revenue generated by an extra capital good) is the same in n_0 and n_1 and that the discounted stream of marginal revenues over the interval $[n_0,n_1]$, due to a capital good bought at n_0, equals the discounted cost (i.e. wage costs and the cost of capital) over that interval. Only if the recession is very deep, excess capacity occurs. For 'moderate' recessions, price is used to equate production capacity and demand.
Leban & Lesourne [1980, 1983] study the optimal investment, recruitment and firing policies of the firm, with a Cobb-Douglas production function and linear hiring and firing costs. It is assumed that the recession is 'hard', implying that the firm will, for some time, stop investment and recruitment during the recession, and will possibly fire employees. The conditions for the dates when the firm stops and resumes investment are the same as in Nickell [1974]. The dates when the firm stops and resumes recruiting (n_0' and n_1') and the dates at which firing begins and stops (n_0'' and n_1'') are determined analogously. A typical development of the relevant variables over time is shown in Figure 3, which is taken from Leban & Lesourne [1980].

Chapters 4 and 5. There is a considerable amount of literature on irreversibility of investment in deterministic models in the context of the optimal allocation between investment and consumption on a macro-level. See for instance Majundar & Nermuth [1982], Mitra & Ray [1983] and Mitra [1983].

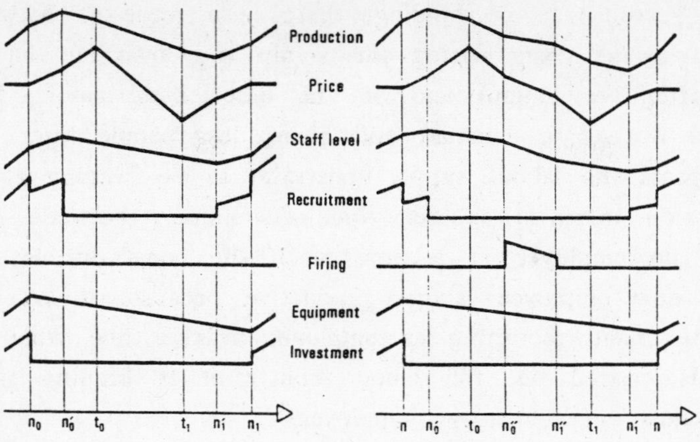

Figure 3: Optimal policy 'over the cycle'

If the firm can manipulate its output price (Leban & Lesourne [1980]), it doesn't allow excess capacity. This is contrary to Nickell [1974]. Since the specification of the business cycle is the same, the difference must lie in the different production technology. In Leban & Lesourne [1980] the firm does not fire people if the firing costs are "high". In the model without price manipulation (Leban & Lesourne [1983]) excess capacity occurs and the firm will use firing as a substitute for price manipulation, even if the firing costs are "high". In a "mild" recession, however, the firm will not fire people. In this case employment fluctuations are small, but the excess-capacity-period will be longer. In general the firm stops recruitment and investment before the start of the recession and will resume them after the end of the recession, thereby aggrevating the recession.

Leban [1982] simplifies the model in Leban & Lesourne [1980,1983] to concentrate completely on wage and employment strategies. Now labour is the only production factor, the number of applicants and the natural quit rate depend on the wage rate, and price policy, investment policy and financial restrictions are excluded. In this situation firing is never optimal, even if it is free of cost. After all, it is always better to lower the wage rate instead, because then the number of employees is reduced (due to a higher quit rate) and at the same time the wage bill for each of the employees is lowered. If the firm does not expect the labour supply constraint (i.e. the number of applicants must be larger than or equal to the number of recruits) to be binding, there is a trade-off between on the one hand saving wage costs during the slump (by lowering the wages and hiring people after the slump) and on the other hand saving hiring costs (by keeping the wage rate constant and hiring less people after the slump). If the firm expects the labour supply constraint to be binding at some time after the recession there is another trade-off, namely between on the one hand recruiting an employee at a time when the constraint is not binding (but when the new employee is not productive because of excess capacity) and on the other hand recruiting an employee at the time when the excess capacity has disappeared but the labour constraint is binding (so that the firm has to increase wages to attract employees).

2.3.2 An implicit business cycle

In the second approach to study the behaviour of a firm during a business cycle, the business cycle is not explicitly modelled. Given a constant environment, the steady state solution (implying constant values for the state variables; cf. the last part of Figure 1) is derived, and it is assumed that the firm has reached this steady state. A business cycle is then represented by an exogeneous change of the demand conditions, leading to different steady state values. As a consequence, the firm will try to adjust the values of the state variables, in order to reach the new steady state. The behaviour of a firm during a business cycle is then studied by linearising the model in the neighbourhood of the 'new' steady state and deriving 'adjustment paths' from this.

An example of this approach is Rossana [1984]. He studies the relationship between labour demand and inventories, which is "widely regarded to be a prominent feature of business cycles" (p.731). The number of employees L and the stock of finished goods inventories F are state variables. If all parameters are assumed to be constant, steady state values L^* and F^* can be derived. Linearisation of the model in the neighbourhood of these values gives:

$$\dot{L}(t) = A_{11}\{L(t)-L^*\} + A_{12}\{F(t)-F^*\} \tag{12}$$

$$\dot{F}(t) = A_{21}\{L(t)-L^*\} + A_{22}\{F(t)-F^*\} \tag{13}$$

These equations give approximations for the optimal paths of L and F towards the steady state values, if the deviations from the steady state values are small. Next it is assumed that during a business cycle L and F will deviate from their steady state values, and that these deviations are small, permitting to use (12) and (13) to analyse the optimal policy. In many optimal control problems it is relatively easy to determine the signs of the 'adjustment parameters' A_{ij}, and there are many technical results concerning the stability of the steady state solution (i.e. do the state variables indeed converge to the steady state or not). Samuelson showed that the comparative statics with respect to the steady state values is intimitely related with the stability properties of the steady state (the famous 'correspondence principle').

Salop [1973] discusses "the behaviour of a profit-maximizing firm (over a business cyle,ovh) in a market characterised by uncertain wage differentials for a homogeneous occupation" (p.321) in a similar way. Maccini [1984] studies the interrelationship between price and output decisions and investment (in capital and inventories of finished goods) decisions. He discusses (a.o.) the optimal reactions of the firm to changes in demand using the same method as Rossana.

2.4 Optimal behaviour of a firm facing technological progress

This section treats some models in which the firm is faced with a given exogeneous technological progress. Models incorporating technological progress are an important issue in the modern theory of economic growth (see, for instance, Stiglitz and Uzawa [1969], Van den Goorbergh, De Groof and Peer [1979]), and since 1974 they have played an important role in the economic models of the Dutch Central Planning Bureau (for a review see Den Hartog [1984]). These models are not discussed here. In the following some optimisation models are discussed in which the effects of exogeneous technological progress on the behaviour of an individual firm are studied.

One can discern six different types of exogeneous technological progress. The following table is taken from Wan [1971].

	Disembodied	Embodied
Output-augmenting	$Q(t,v)=A(t)F\{K(t,v),L(t,v)\}$	$Q(t,v)=A(v)F\{K(t,v),L(t,v)\}$
Labour-augmenting	$Q(t,v)=F\{K(t,v),A(t)L(t,v)\}$	$Q(t,v)=F\{K(t,v),A(v)L(t,v)\}$
Capital-augmenting	$Q(t,v)=F\{A(t)K(t,v),L(t,v)\}$	$Q(t,v)=F\{A(v)K(t,v),L(t,v)\}$

At time t $Q(t,v)$ products are produced on machines of vintage v, using $K(t,v)$ machines and $L(t,v)$ units of labour. F is the production function. The function A measures the technological progress and it is assumed that A

is an increasing function. The difference between embodied and disembodied technological progress is that embodied progress at time t only affects capital goods bought at time t, while disembodied progress affects all capital goods installed in the past. For instance, consider the labour-augmenting type. Suppose $K(t_1,v)=K(t_2,v)$ and $L(t_1,v)=L(t_2,v)$. Then production with capital goods installed at time v is the same at t_1 and t_2 $(Q(t_1,v)=Q(t_2,v))$ if there is only embodied technological progress. If there is only disembodied progress, production at t_2 is larger than at t_1 (provided $t_2>t_1$), because the disembodied technological progress for $t>t_1$ positively affects production at $t=t_2$.
It is assumed that capital goods installed at the same time are identical and that the disembodied type of technological progress affects all capital goods in the same way. Thus the set of capital goods installed at a certain time can be treated as a homogeneous set, named a *vintage*. Models in which technological progress works in this way are called vintage models.
Moreover, in the models to be discussed it is assumed that, after a vintage of capital goods has been installed, there is no substitution possible between labour and capital (i.e. ex post the production technology is of the 'clay' type). Regarding ex ante substitutability, the production technology may be of the 'putty' or of the 'clay' type. In the 'putty' case the firm can choose different combinations of capital and labour to generate a given amount of output. In the 'clay' case there is only one combination of capital and labour that generates a given amount of output.
In the vintage models to be discussed now the necessary conditions for optimality are derived and interpreted. However, the development over time of the relevant variables, like in section 2.2 and 2.3.1, is not given. One of the reasons is the mathematical complexity of vintage models. In Chapter 8 the optimal policy for the entire planning period is given for a (relatively simple) vintage model.
Virmany [1976] discusses a putty-clay vintage model (i.e., the ex ante production technology is of the 'putty' type, the ex post technology is of the 'clay' type) with disembodied output augmenting technological progress. Virmany points out that, whereas in a neo-classical non-vintage model the firm reacts to price changes by adjustments of the capital and labour stock, in his model adjustments are made through the level of investment and the capital-labour ratio of the new vintage.
Virmany assumes that a capital good depreciates exponentially, but that it is never scrapped. This is not a harmless assumption in the presence of

embodied technological progress. Since in that case newer machines are better than older ones, it may be profitable to scrap old machines and buy new ones even if the scrap value is zero. From a technical point of view, the possibility to scrap old vintages is the central problem of vintage models. The capital good stock in such a vintage model is given by:

$$K(t) = \int_{t-T(t)}^{t} K(t,v)\, dv \tag{14}$$

Technically, this is a constraint of the optimisation problem. Unfortunately, the standard Maximum Principle does not deal with constraints like (14) (note that differentiation of (14) does not give a differential equation like (2)). Nickell [1975] gives a set of conditions which are sufficient conditions for optimality, but he does not tell how he derived these conditions. Malcomson [1975,1983] 'derives' necessary conditions, but he does not explain why his method is correct, and his models do not involve pure state constraints. In Appendix 4 a set of optimality conditions is derived (using in fact the same 'tric' as Malcomson does) for a rather general vintage model with pure state constraints, and a formal sufficiency proof is given. These conditions are used in the vintage models in Chapters 7 and 8.

Malcomson [1975] and Nickell [1975] concentrate on replacement investment in a clay-clay vintage model (i.e. the ex ante as well as the ex post production technology are of the 'clay' type). In Malcomson [1975] capital is the only production factor and the firm maximises profits (revenues minus operating costs and investment expenditures) over an infinite horizon:

$$\max_{I,Y,T} \int_0^{\infty} e^{-it} \left\{ p(Y(t),t)Y(t) - \int_{t-T(t)}^{t} c(v,t)I(v)dv - c(t)I(t) \right\} dt \tag{15}$$

$$Y(t) = \int_{t-T(t)}^{t} b(v,t)I(v)dv \tag{16}$$

$$Y(t)\geq 0,\ I(t)\geq 0,\ T(t)\geq 0,\ \dot{T}(t)\leq 1, \tag{17}$$

where:

b(v,t): units of output of a machine of vintage v at time t

c(v,t): operating costs of a machine of vintage v at time t

Technological progress is represented by the fact that "the operating cost per unit of output is always less on more recent vintages than on older ones" (p.26). He derives an optimal replacement rule which implies that the optimal lifetime of capital goods is bounded by a sequence of lower bounds and a sequence of upper bounds. Unfortunately he is not able to show that these sequences converge to the same limit, which would imply a unique optimal lifetime of capital. In Chapter 7 an optimal replacement rule is derived which is more general than Malcomson's rule and it is shown that the sequences of upper and lower bounds indeed converge to the same limit.

Nickell [1975] discusses a clay-clay vintage model with embodied capital and labour augmenting technological progress. Capital goods do not depreciate but maintenance costs grow with age. He shows that there is a unique optimal lifetime of capital goods if the labour-augmenting technological progress is zero and the rate of capital-augmenting technological progress is constant. Nickell also treats the case of possible 'zero investment'-periods. He states that the optimal scrapping condition (or replacement rule) still holds during the zero investment period, which seems questionable to me. The problems with zero investment periods are discussed in the context of the model of Chapters 7 and 8 in Appendix 5.4.

Nickell also studies the effect of demand variations, but he assumes that the rate of technological progress is zero. During a slump in demand he finds a cyclical pattern for the price of output and investments, with 'backward echo effects' (the cyclical pattern also occurs *before* the slump). This result is discussed further in Chapter 8.

Nickell extensively examines a model with adjustment costs, which is not considered here.

Malcomson [1983] studies the effects of changes in tax incentives for investment in a putty-clay vintage model with disembodied capital- and labour-augmenting technological progress and embodied output augmenting technological progress. Malcomson does not try to find the optimal values for the control and state variables. His aim is to perform simulations with the model to study the effects of a change in investment incentives. One theoretical aspect of this model is interesting in view of Chapters 7 and 8. Malcomson observes that if the tax incentives for investment are increased, existing vintages are scrapped earlier than planned. This creates a spurt in (replacement) investment, which reproduces itself when the vintages installed during the spurt are scrapped themselves. Thus an 'echo-effect' is created. This kind of echo-effects is typical of vintage models.

Broer [1987] uses vintage models to study aggregate firm behaviour. He devotes much attention to the theoretical properties of vintage models. His models do not incorporate the financial side of the firm, but apart from this his models are more general than the models in this thesis, because they, for instance, include various adjustment costs and the possibility to vary the utilisation rates of production factors. Broer proves the existence of a unique steady state solution for a clay-clay model and studies the linearisation of the model in the neighbourhood of the steady state. For a putty-clay model he does not succeed in proving the existence of a steady state because of the "analytical complexity of vintage models" (p.150). Moreover, in the putty-clay case, "general results do not seem to be available outside the steady-state" (p.12). Broer does not use the Maximum Principle to find the optimal solution, since, in his view, a vintage model "cannot easily be formulated as an optimal control problem in the absence of a suitable set of state variables" (p.119). Although in Appendix 4 the vintage model *is* formulated as an optimal control problem, Broer's observation will play an important role in Chapters 7 and 8.

2.5 Summary

This chapter discusses some relevant predecessors of the models in this thesis. The framework of the models in the following chapters is a model by Van Loon [1983], in which the optimal investment, dividend and financial policies are derived simultaneously. This model and some extensions are discussed in section 2.2.

Section 2.3 discusses some models which study the optimal behaviour of a firm during a business cycle. These models do not treat the dividend and financial policies of the firm. The same is true for the vintage models in section 2.4, which involve exogeneous technological progress. In Chapters 5 and 7, the financial side of the firm is incorporated in a business cycle model and a vintage model.

It is shown that there are two ways of studying the behaviour of a firm during a business cycle, of which one will be chosen in Chapter 5.

Section 2.4 shows that vintage models involve technical problems, which make it difficult to derive analytical results. In Chapters 7 and 8 a vintage model of the firm will be discussed. A set of optimality conditions for vintage models, derived in Appendix 4, will be used to generate, as far as possible, analytical results.

3
ON DYNAMIC OPTIMISATION MODELS OF THE FIRM AS A BRANCH OF 'PURE THEORY' AND ON THE USE OF MATHEMATICS

3.1 Introduction

This chapter consists of two parts. Section 3.2 discusses the use of theoretical optimisation models of the firm. In section 3.3 some guidelines are derived for the use of mathematics in the remainder of this thesis.

3.2 Theoretical dynamic optimisation models of the firm: a branch of 'pure theory'

3.2.1 Pure theory

After reading Chapter 2 one might wonder: what is the use of those theoretical optimal control models, as part of an empirical science like economics? An answer can be found in Klant [1984]. Much of what he says on 'pure theory' applies to this thesis. Klant does not give one clear-cut definition of pure theory (the difference between pure and applied is gradual), but he gives several descriptions: 'pure theory' is theory being "entirely free from considerations regarding its practical use" (p.85); "..a theory, which is based on assumptions of an empirical nature but describes formal relations" (p.85); "What economists since Walras understand by 'pure theory' is the general theory on the behaviour of economic agents, who in taking their decisions allow themselves to be guided by certain praxeological principles. Pure theory then consists, at any rate in part, of decision theory - applied logic, in other words" (p.85).
What is the use of a 'pure theory'? Klant states: a pure theory is a tool box. He quotes Robinson (a pure theory is "an essay in the technique of economic analysis.."; p.104) and Hutchison ("pure theory offers us a sharp, clear-cut language or system of definitions with which to approach the problems which the facts of the world raise"; p.108), and he summarises the view of De Vries (p.109): the task of 'pure theory' is to formulate and

define ideas; it produces a conceptional apparatus that can be used in discussing concrete economic problems. However, the ultimate goal of economic science always is "...a working model of the actual world..... To tinker with the tool-box is merely a preliminary to the main attack" (Robinson, quoted by Klant, p. 104). But the essential problem is: "It is difficult to establish to what extent purely formal theories could ever be used in framing theories with empirical content" (p.185).

The distinction between pure theory and empirical economics is similar to the distinction between pure and applied mathematics. Browder [1976] defines: "Pure mathematics is that part of mathematical activity that is done without explicit or immediate consideration of direct application to other intellectual domains or domains of human practice". With regard to possible future applications of pure mathematics, Browder states: "We do not know what will be useful (or even essential) until it has been used".

3.2.2 An illustration

There are many optimal control models of the firm and not all these models are to the same extent 'pure theory'. On the one hand there are optimal control models that are focussed on a micro-economic foundation of macro-economics (e.g., Malcomson [1983], Rossana [1984], Maccini [1984], Vroman [1987]). Using this kind of models, one tries to show that "macroeconomic behavioral relations have a solid microeconomic foundation" (Maccini [1984], p.41). If these models are really tested, on an aggregated level, they <u>are</u> used to frame theories with empirical content, and in that case they are not 'pure theory'.

On the other hand there are models that are explicitly intended to help the management of a firm to solve problems, concerning finance, production and inventory, marketing, machine maintenance and replacement, optimal consumption of natural resources. There are a number of books containing such models, for instance Bensoussan, Hurst and Näslund [1974], Sethi & Thompson [1981], Kamien & Schwartz [1981], Tu [1984], and Feichtinger & Hartl [1986]. Sethi [1978b] gives an extensive survey of management science applications of the deterministic Maximum Principle. Sethi and Thompson state in the introduction of their book (p.xiii): "The emphasis of the book is .... on modelling realistic situations faced in business and management". Tu states (p.331): "Optimal Control has proved a valuable tool in all these areas" (of management science,ovh). So the aim of these books is clear: modelling of realistic situations so that the results can be used by the management of firms. However, although the books are full of 'management science'-examples, there are only a few examples of an empirical application or an actual implementation of an optimal policy. The reason seems quite clear: if a dynamic model of the firm is to be usable for the management, then it has to be solvable and it has to describe the problem at hand adequately. These two demands are almost inevitably conflicting.

Given this state of affairs (the present models lack empirical content), an interesting discussion arises whether these models will, in the terminology of Klant, *ever* be used in framing theories with empirical content. This discussion affects to a lesser degree also many of the models in Chapter 2 (Van Loon [1983,1985], Salop [1973], Leban [1982], Leban & Lesourne [1980, 1983], Kort [1989], Van Schijndel [1988]). (to a lesser degree because their aims are less ambitious with regard to modelling realistic situations and management science applications). Tapiero [1978] formulates the difficulties of optimal control models as part of management science as follows: "Thus, the management scientist must continually assess the relevance of a particular model, as a simplification of reality, versus the possibilities of obtaining useful analytical and computational results". Bensoussan, Hurst and Näslund [1974]) have made an unambiguous choice: "At this stage in the application of control theory to management problems, it is felt preferable to solve exactly the perhaps inexact statements of real problems, using this solution to gain structural insights, rather than to solve approximately an exact statement of the problem, failing in the process to gain any real feeling for the structure of the solution".

With regard to modelling realistically the way people make choices, Simon [1979] states: "There can no longer be any doubt that the micro assumptions of the theory (of the firm, ovh)-the assumptions of perfect rationality-(which are inherent in many optimal control models, ovh) are contrary to fact. It is not a question of approximation; they do not even remotely describe the processes that human beings use for making decisions in complex situations". Moreover: "If our interest lies in descriptive decision theory (or even normative decision theory, (underlining added)), it is now entirely clear that the classical and neoclassical theories have been replaced by a superior alternative that provides us with a much closer approximation to what is actually going on". The central element of that "superior alternative" is the concept of 'bounded rationality'.

Schmidt [1982], who also discusses 'decision theory', especially concerning the use of economic theory for financial management problems, admits that the neo-classical theory at present gives no answers which the financial manager can use, for instance because financial institutions are irrelevant in that theory. Still Schmidt concludes, when judging different approaches on their contributions to the financial management of firms, "I tend to believe that the 'economic approach' is in the long run more succesful than the behavioral approach. Taking for granted that presently (underlining added) behavioral theories give a more 'valid' representation of those parts of reality which matter for financial management, I cannot see a 'hard core'[1] in the behavioral approach. ... The 'economic' approach to the study of institutions, on the other hand, is still in its infancy, but it can be expected to advance rapidly, *because* it is a research programme with the 'hard core' of agents' rationality and market equilibrium. To overcome the sterile irrelevance propositions in financial economics requires drastic changes in the 'protective belt'. They can be made...".
These two opposing opinions show a wide disagreement on the significance of the present lack of realism of a theory. It seems that the dispute cannot be decided on the grounds of objective arguments. A great deal of personal assessment and belief play an important part. This illustrates Klant's point that it is difficult to "establish to what extent purely formal theories could ever be used in framing theories with empirical content".

Another line of criticism of deterministic optimisation models of the firm is to reject the usefulness of *deterministic* models in economics at all. It is clear that economic life is stochastic, take for instance the financial markets. And, with respect of firm behaviour, the firm will try to protect itself against unforeseen calamities by being flexible, which is hard to model in a deterministic way, even when using expectations of uncertain variables instead of 'certain' parameters. So modelling the stochastic elements in economic life brings the models closer to reality. However, for stochastic models Tapiero's problem (assessing the relevance of a particular model, as a simplification of reality, versus the possibilities of obtaining useful analytical and computational results) is probably even bigger.

---

[1]The term 'hard core' is meant in the sense of Lakatos: it is that part of a 'research program' that "is treated as irrefutable by the methodological decision of its protagonists" (Blaug [1980], p.36).

The supporters of stochastic optimisation can point at a tremendous success with respect to the application of theoretical results, namely the Black and Scholes formula (however, this success can not only be contributed to the stochastics, but also to the fact that financial markets are "organized auction markets operating under high information conditions", Teece and Winter [1984]). And, more in general, stochastic optimisation seems to make more of the claim of being useful in management science than deterministic optimisation (Sengupta [1985], Bensoussan, Kleindorfer and Tapiero [1980]). However, there seem to be not many applications at the firm level (see also Tapiero [1988]). Stochastic models which are comparable to the deterministic models in this thesis mostly consist of only a few variables, and consequently they incorporate less aspects of firm behaviour (see Bensoussan & Lesourne [1980], Lesourne & Dominguez [1983], Kort [1989] and section 6.5 of Tapiero [1988]). So the practical use of stochastic optimal control models of the firm seems to be very limited at present. One of the reasons certainly is the difficulty to solve stochastic dynamic optimisation problems, in particular with respect to *constrained* optimisation. Especially *analytical* results are hard to obtain. Deterministic dynamic optimisation (subject to constraints) might serve as a point of reference for the (more difficult) stochastic variant.

3.3 Some guidelines for the use of mathematics

3.3.1 Introduction

The previous section concluded that the dynamic optimisation models of the firm in this thesis can be seen as a tool for economic analysis. The economic conclusions of these models are derived with the aid of a branch of mathematics, called Optimal Control Theory (i.c. the Maximum Principle). So the mathematics of optimisation is, as it were, a tool in a tool. This section derives some guidelines concerning the use of mathematics in the remainder of the thesis. Section 3.3.2 briefly discusses the role of mathematics in economics in general. Section 3.3.3 discusses the status of the economic assumptions in mathematical models. Section 3.3.4 goes further into the mathematical translation of some common economic assumptions and emphasises the importance of interpreting, as much as possible, the mathematical tools.

3.3.2 On the role of mathematics in economics

It is without doubt that mathematics plays an important role in economics nowadays. Mathematics constitutes a substantial part of the education of economists and many economic journals are full of mathematics. What is the reason of this important role of mathematics? It seems that this question is not answered satisfactorily yet. Weintraub [1985] writes: "It is a minor scandal that there is no comprehensive history of either the rise of econometrics or the mathematization of economics" (p.140). One can discern, however, some factors which stimulate the use of mathematics in economics[2].
The most 'basic' of these factors is probably that "two of its central concepts, commodity and price, are quantified in a unique manner, as soon as units of measurement are chosen" (Debreu [1986], p.1261).
Secondly, Pareto, one of the pioneers of the application of mathematics in economics , asserted that the complexity and interdependency of social phenomena are reasons for the successful application of the mathematical language to economics (Klant [1984], p.143). Especially the possibility to express simultaneous relations in mathematical language is important, according to Pareto. Moreover, the consistency of a set of mathematical equations is relatively easy verified (Vermaat [1970], p.11).
A third factor is the fact that mathematics has been successful in other disciplines, especially in physics. The scientific character of physics has often been seen as outstanding by economists, and thus it is tempting to use the same methods in economics as in physics. According to Mirowski [1987], economists did not resist this temptation. On the contrary, in his view "...the early neoclassicals took the model of 'energy' from physics, changed the names of all variables, postulated that 'utility' acted like energy, and then flogged the package wholesale as economics" (p.81). The reason that it is possible to simply apply the same mathematical model to different subjects, is, as Mirowski states, in the nature of mathematics: mathematics is a method of thinking in <u>metaphors</u>. Poincaré once defined mathematics as 'the art of giving the same name to different things' (see also Weintraub [1985], p.37: "Mathematics is a metaphor machine"). But it

---

[2]This list is not meant to be exhaustive. For a more systematic treatment of the advantages and disadvantages of the use of mathematics in economics, see Debreu [1986] and Vermaat [1970].

is not without danger to apply metaphors. Weintraub (p.34) cites Koopmans, who states: "the succes of a mathematical tool or theory in one field (such as physics) creates no presumption either for or against its usefulness in another field (such as economics). But each transfer of a tool between fields is attended by a risk....The test of suitability of a tool of reasoning is whether it gives the most logical and economic expression to the basic assumptions appropriate to the field in question, and to the reasoning that establishes their implications......The difficulty in economic dynamics has been that the tools have suggested the assumptions rather than the other way around".As a fourth factor the work of the Vienna Circle can be mentioned, which has given a strong stimulus to the use of mathematics in twentieth century economics. Weintraub [1985] extensively describes how members of the Vienna Circle, who propagated that mathematics must play the premier role in philosophy and science (Weintraub [1985], p.63), play an important part in the development of general equilibrium analysis.

Finally, part of probably all these factors is the recognition that the use of mathematics has heuristic value: it is a tool to find theories (see, for instance, Vermaat ([1970], p.11) and section 3.3.4).

3.3.3 The status of assumptions

Many articles on dynamic models of the firm start off with a set of (often bold) economically phrased assumptions and their mathematical translations. Musgrave [1981] distinguishes three types of assumptions:

1) negligibility assumptions: these are hypotheses that some factor F has no effect on the phenomenon under investigation. "Now suppose an economist 'assumes that there is no government', meaning thereby to assert that the existence of the government has negligible effects on the phenomena he is investigating. It would be plain silly to object that this assumption is 'unreal' because there is, infact, a government" (p.379).
2) domain assumptions: this kind of assumptions specifies the domain of applicability of a theory. "The more unrealistic domain assumptions are, the less testable and hence less significant is the theory" (p.382).
3) heuristic assumptions: simplifying assumptions, made to develop a theory. "Heuristic assumptions play an important role in developing

> any theory whose logico-mathematical machinery is so complicated that a method of successive approximation has to be used..... The consequences drawn from heuristic assumptions do not represent the precise predictions of the theory in question; rather, they are steps towards such precise predictions" (p.383).

Confusion about the status of an assumption easily arises because "the same form of words" is employed for all three types of assumptions (p.381). Therefore Musgrave states: "Misunderstanding, misguided criticism, and methodological controversy, could be alleviated if this rather prosaic recommendation (i.e. that economists make it clear exactly which sort of assumption they are making at any point in their investigations, ovh) were to be followed".
This advice is especially relevant in empirical work. In a purely theoretical thesis (like this), one could of course ignore the status of assumptions or simply state that all assumptions are heuristic (compare the definition of heuristic assumptions with the statement in section 3.2.1 that pure theory is a "preliminary to the main attack"). But concerning a number of assumptions one can argue: if this model is to be tested one way or another, assumption X will most likely belong to category Y. For instance, the assumption that the wages are constant will probably not be a 'negligibility assumption', and if treated as a 'domain assumption' it will allow only a very small domain. The assumption that the debt-equity ratio is limited by some constant b and the assumption act solely in the interest of shareholders will probably be domain assumptions. In Chapter 4 it is tried to follow Musgrave's recommendation.
More generally, in highly mathematical models like the ones in this thesis, one often wonders whether a certain assumption is economically or mathematically motivated. For instance, in equation (2.8) the assumption $I \geq 0$ is economically motivated (investments are irreversible, see Chapter 4), while the assumption $I \leq I_{max}$ is primarily mathematically motivated (to avoid jumps of the state variables, see Chapter 4). In the remainder of this thesis special attention will be given to the question whether an assumption is mathematically or economically motivated.

3.3.4 On the mathematical translation of economic assumptions and the interpretation of mathematical tools

Another problem connected to the use of mathematics in economics is whether the mathematical tools which are used have an economic interpretation. This interpretation is often a source of confusion. The heuristic use of mathematics in economics can be pictured as follows (Weintraub [1985], p.146):

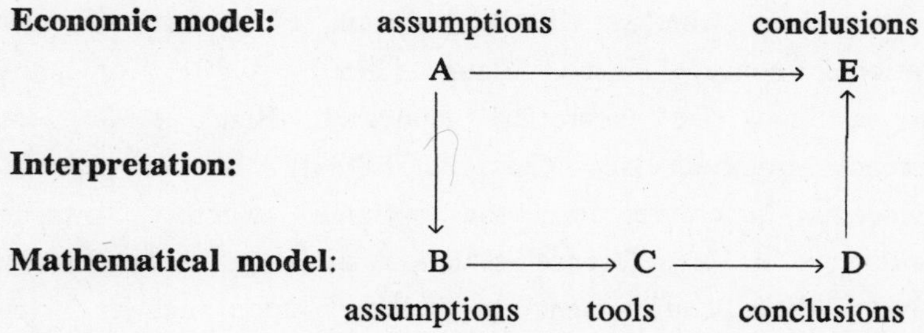

Weintraub writes: "We would like to go from A to E. What we do, in fact, is go from A to E indirectly, identifying A with B, then proceeding from B to D (using C) and reidentifying D with E". It is often said, as in the Koopmans' quote in section 3.3.2, that C determines B and A instead of the other way around. Moreover, the economic interpretation of C is often lacking. This subsection does not focus on the point whether C determines B and A (see for instance Weintraub [1985] or Mirowski [1986]), but concentrates on the difficulties in translating A into B and interpreting C.

As an example, consider the assumption that agents independently optimise subject to constraints, which is an important element of the hard core of neo-classical economics. 'Optimisation subject to constraints' is a 'B-assumption'. The corresponding 'A-assumption' is often unclear. It seems to be very difficult to mark out the set of A-assumptions about economic behaviour that correspond to the B-assumption 'optimisation subject to constraints'. For a discussion, see Van Witteloostuyn [1988]. In this thesis the assumption that firms maximise the discounted value of future dividends is not questioned (it is a 'hard-core' assumption). This thesis can thus be seen as a contribution to the attempts to model firm behaviour on the basis of the maximisation principle.

Another element of the hard core of neo-classical economics is the assumption that: "Observable economic outcomes are coordinated, so they must be discussed with reference to equilibrium states" (Weintraub [1985], p.109)[3]. In economics, the notion equilibrium has many meanings (see, for instance, Hahn [1984]). In optimal control problems the notion equilibrium mostly means a so-called 'steady state' equilibrium, which means (a part of) an optimal solution with *constant* values for the state variables[4]. Very often the analysis of the optimal solution of a model is confined to a discussion of the steady state.

There is much discussion whether this equilibrium is a fact of economic life (an "operational concept", see Blaug [1980], p.101) or only an analytical notion (a "tool for theoretical analysis", Blaug [1980], p.101), used as a reference situation (see Carvalho [1984]). If one favours the latter view, it seems logical to use the optimal trajectory towards the steady state equilibrium as a reference situation as well. Adherents of the first view motivate their confinement to steady state analysis with the argument that the path towards the steady state is subject to noise ("accidental influences", see Carvalho [1984]), and thus not of interest. However, it seems that the same argument applies to the local analysis in the neighbourhood of the steady state, which often accompanies a steady state analysis. This local analysis follows from a linearisation (that is, an approximation!) of the model around the steady state[5]. But why then not study the exact optimal policies in the neighbourhood of the steady state?[6]

One reason certainly is a mathematical one. In many optimal control problems, one can only achieve nice analytical results on the steady state of the problem and on the linearisation of the problem in the neighbourhood of the steady state. Very seldom one encounters a model in which a complete

---

[3]According to Debreu [1986] there is a "perfect fit between the mathematical concept of a fixed point and the social science concept of an equilibrium" (p.1262).

[4]It should be noted that in most optimal control models of the firm the equilibrium is a *partial* equilibrium.

[5]As an example consider the models which use the second method to decribe behaviour during a business cycle, as described in Chapter 2 (Rossana e.a.).

[6]Teece and Winter [1984] state: "While comparative statics is one way to get at dynamic issues, it suffers from inattention to the path to equilibrium, a matter which is usually exceedingly important" (p.118).

solution of the optimisation problem is given, including the exact (as opposed to approximate) optimal trajectory towards the steady state. The reason is that such a complete solution is in most cases very difficult and/or very time consuming to achieve. In spite of this, the analysis in the following chapters will not be restricted to the study of steady states. The entire optimal solution of the models is searched for, including the optimal trajectory towards the steady state (if there is one), using the coupling procedure of Van Loon (see Chapter 4 and Appendix 1).

One of the very nice aspects of Optimal Control Theory with respect to its use in economics is that the necessary conditions it gives for optimality can often be interpreted economically. This is primarily due to the fact that the auxiliary variables appearing in the Maximum Principle can be interpreted as shadow prices. However, a confusion of tongues easily emerges as a consequence of the difference between economical intuition and mathematical formalism. Chapter 6 tries to help resolve this confusion.

The upshot of this section is that if mathematics is widely used in economics, translations of 'economic' statements into 'mathematical' statements and vice versa, are crucial. But that is often where the shoe pinches. After all, one cannot expect from economists that they know the latest developments in mathematics, let alone that they invent suitable mathematics[7]. So if one wants to find out if mathematical techniques exist or can be developed for a certain economic problem (for instance group theory, as mentioned by Mirowski [1986], or the application of Lie groups to the theory of technological change (e.g. Sato [1981])), then there has to be a good communication between mathematicians and economists. Mathematical economists could perform the task of intermediairies.

Given a group of mathematical economists as intermediairs, the communication between this group on the one hand and economists and mathematicians on the other hand should be good. Although, according to Koopmans [1957], "there is substantial agreement that mathematical economists...should do their utmost to communicate the assumptions and

---

[7]Mirowski ([1986], p.200) states: "In fact, since economists are so rarely first-class mathematicians, most of the contributions economists can reasonably aspire to make to their chosen discipline must come in that twilight zone of semantical interpretations of previously developed mathematical structures".

conclusions of their analyses in verbal form...", it seems that the communication between mathematical economists and economists is rather bad. According to Vermaat [1970], the opinion of the economist about mathematical economics reads: "I admit that I do not understand it and I am sure that I do not like it". It is probably even worse. Many economists seem to think: "I admit I do not understand it and I am sure that I will never understand it". Apart from several well-founded objections, many economists seem to have cold feet concerning the use of mathematics. These economists came to the conclusion a long time ago that mathematics was to difficult for them and since that time they do not want to have anything to do with it (out of fear or irritation). To warm their feet, it might help a lot if the mathematical economists would possess more didactical qualities. Nowadays it is popular to teach economists as much mathematics as possible, but it is at least as important to teach mathematically trained persons the ability to translate mathematical theories and techniques into non-mathematical terms. The interaction between economists and mathematicians would greatly benefit from this.[8]

3.4 Summary and Conclusions

Section 3.2 concludes that many optimal control models of the firm can be seen as 'pure theory'. Pure theory consists for a large part of development of tools and, as again Koopmans said ([1957], p.vii) "...tools are of interest more in their promise than in their achievements". However, as Klant concludes, it is hard to determine whether pure theory will ever be used for framing theories with empirical content. One of the reasons of the present lack of empirical content of many optimisation models is that (adapting Koopmans [1957], p.179) "One enters a different, and in many ways poorer and more rigid, world when one examines the mathematically expressed

---

[8]A long time after I had written this, I found out that I am like one of the students in Weintraub's book, who states: "...professional integrity seems to require that the subdiscipline (i.e. mathematical economics, ovh) be opened to all economists so that professional standards can be widely appreciated. For too long our profession has been full of calls by the mathematically literate for higher mathematical literacy rates in the economics profession and calls by the unsophisticated for more surveys and translations of standard mathematical results" (p. 149). In Weintraub's book emphasis is put on the translation between A and B and between D and E (see the scheme on p.27).

literature of economic dynamics".

This is especially apparent with respect to management science models. In the terminology of section 3.3.3: when management problems are concerned, few things are negligible. Thus most assumptions can not be treated as negligibility assumptions. Moreover, if one treats these assumptions as domain assumptions, the field of possible application becomes very narrow. Consequently, most assumptions have to be treated as heuristic assumptions, and thus the present usefulness of dynamic models of the firm is very limited.

The use of dynamic optimisation models of the firm as a branch of pure theory can be compared to what Solow [1985] says on the functions of 'analytical economics', namely: "to organize our necessarily incomplete perceptions about the economy, to see connections that the untutored eye would miss, to tell plausibe -sometimes even convincing- causal stories with the help of a few central principles...".

Section 3.3 discusses the use of the mathematical language in economics in general and in dynamic optimisation models of the firm in particular. Three guidelines are derived with respect to the use of mathematics in this thesis: 1) make clear the motivation of assumptions; 2) consider not only the steady state solution of a model, but the entire optimal solution (that is, the optimal control and state variables as functions of time for the whole planning interval; 3) as a contribution to the interpretation of the mathematical tool which is used (the Maximum Principle), give attention to bringing together economic intuition and mathematical formalism concerning shadow prices in a dynamic context.

The remainder of this thesis can be seen as an exercise in 'pure theory'. There will be a lot of "tinkering with the tool box", meant in a positive sense. And as far as the economic implications are concerned, they should be considered with care, since each model in this thesis will involve some heuristic assumptions.

4
THE BASIC MODEL

4.1 Introduction

The model to be presented in this chapter will serve as the core of the more complicated models in the next chapters. It is in fact also the core of most of the models in Van Loon [1983], Van Schijndel [1988] and Kort [1989]. Their analysis of this model is extended in three directions. Firstly, bringing into practice one of the guidelines of chapter 3 (section 3.3.3), Musgrave's advice concerning the background of assumptions is followed (section 4.2). Secondly, a feedback decision rule is derived (section 4.4), which gives the optimal policy for (almost) all possible initial conditions (the exceptions are treated in section 4.6). It will be argued that this decision rule is a very convenient and useful shorthand way to characterise the optimal solution. In the following chapters it will be investigated if and why this decision rule is still valid in more complicated models. Thirdly, whereas Kort, Van Loon and Van Schijndel are primarily focussed on the analysis of the growth of the firm, section 4.5 also studies how the firm reduces its size in an optimal way (which is used in the next chapter). The necessary and sufficient conditions for optimality are given in section 4.3. Section 4.7 discusses the difference between the 'book value' and the 'market value' of equity in the model. Section 4.8 summarises this chapter and gives conclusions.

4.2 The model and its assumptions

The model which is the core of this thesis is:

$$\max_{I,D} \int_0^z e^{-it}D(t)\,dt + e^{-iz}X(z) \qquad (1)$$

$$\dot{K}(t) = I(t) - aK(t) \qquad (2)$$

$$\dot{X}(t) = (1-f)\left\{S[Q(t)] - wL(t) - aK(t) - rY(t)\right\} - D(t) \qquad (3)$$

$$Q(t) = K(t)/k, \qquad Q(t) = L(t)/l \qquad (4)$$

$$K(t) = X(t) + Y(t) \qquad (5)$$

$$Y(t) \geq 0 \qquad (6)$$

$$Y(t) \leq bX(t) \qquad (7)$$

$$0 \leq I(t) \leq I_{max} \qquad (8)$$

$$0 \leq D(t) \leq D_{max} \qquad (9)$$

$$K(0) \text{ and } X(0) \text{ are given} \qquad (10)$$

Before the specific assumptions of this model are discussed, two general features of the models in this thesis are stressed.

Firstly, time is a continuous variable. If one is primarily interested in analytical results, the use of continuous time is in my opinion most appropriate. The choice to treat time as a continuous variable is thus clearly mathematically motivated. The use of continuous time has many consequences, especially in Chapter 7.

Secondly, all models are deterministic. Uncertainty is kept outside the model in the following way: the firm has certain specific expectations and on the basis of these expectations it makes its plans. If at some time the expectations prove incorrect, the firm reformulates its expectations and computes a new optimal policy (e.g. Nickell [1974])[1]. As already indicated

---

[1]See also Arrow [1968]. Arrow observes that "to determine the empirical implications of this model, it would be necessary to add a second relation, showing how the anticipated profit function and interest rates (or, in general, the anticipated values of all parameters of the model, ovh) shift with time, possibly in response to new observations on market magnitudes" (p.17).

in Chapters 2 and 3, the reason to work with deterministic models in this thesis is the combination of the aim to obtain analytical results and the wish to incorporate more (many) aspects in existing models.
Now the specific assumptions of the model are discussed.
The firm acts solely in the interest of the shareholders (domain assumption). Its goal is to maximise the discounted stream of dividends (D) plus the discounted value of equity (X) at the end of the (finite) planning period (see (1)). This form of the objective function implies unanimity of the shareholders concerning the investment plans of the firm. Therefore it is implicitly assumed that, for instance, the possible existence of personal taxes or borrowing and lending restrictions does not destroy that unanimity. It is assumed that the business risk does not change (domain or heuristic assumption). Moreover, the variability of the financial risk is limited by the constraint $Y \leq bX$. Finally, the interest rate r is assumed to be constant (heuristic assumption). Together these assumptions imply that the discount rate i can be assumed constant.
The firm uses two homogeneous production factors, capital (K) and labour (L), to produce a homogeneous output (Q) (domain or heuristic assumption). The production technology is a fixed coefficients technology, which means that there are linear relationships between capital and labour and between capital and production (domain or heuristic assumption; see (4))[2]. The capital goods stock depreciates at a rate a. It is implicitly assumed that fiscal depreciation equals technical depreciation. This could be a negligibility assumption, but it most likely is an heuristic assumption. Separating technical and fiscal depreciation and describing both in a realistic way would make the model less elegant and would create great difficulties with regard to finding the optimal solution. In the vintage models of Chapter 7 the need, from an economic point of view, to separate fiscal and technical depreciation is even more pressing. Fortunately, the variant of the Maximum Principle, derived in Appendix 4 to cope with the vintage structure, also makes it possible to treat fiscal depreciation in a realistic way. At this point, the economic and mathematical incentives to change a certain unrealistic assumption go hand in hand, by way of exception.

---

[2]Van Loon [1983], Van Schijndel [1988], and Kort [1989] do not impose these simple linear relationships in all their models.

The capital goods stock can be augmented by investments and it is assumed that all prices are normalised in such a way that the price of a capital good equals one. This gives (2). The only costs associated to labour are proportional to the volume of the labour stock: wL (this assumption can be of each of the three types). For simplicity, w is named the 'wage rate'. This wage rate is assumed to be constant (heuristic assumption). The firm sells all goods it produces (heuristic assumption). In this chapter it is assumed that the output price p is only a function of production and it is assumed that this function is such that revenue $S=pQ$ is a concave function of Q (domain assumption[3]):

$$S=S[Q(t)], \quad \frac{dS}{dQ} > 0, \quad \frac{d^2S}{dQ^2} < 0 \tag{11}$$

New issues of equity are not allowed (domain or heuristic assumption). X only increases if retained earnings are positive. Retained earnings are defined as revenue minus costs after taxes and after dividends (see (3)). The costs consist of wage costs, depreciation costs and interest costs[4].

The firm has two sources of funds, equity X and debt Y (with regard to the qualitative properties of the optimal investment and dividend policy, this can be a negligibility assumption). It is assumed that X, Y, and K are book values[5], so that the balance sheet equation assures (5). The amount of debt is limited: debt is assumed to be non-negative (domain assumption; see (6)) and the debt-equity ratio is bounded from above by a certain constant b (domain assumption; see (7)). It may seem odd to distinguish between equity and debt in a deterministic model. The difference between debt and equity is that the suppliers of debt get a fixed reward, whereas the suppliers of equity only have a residual claim on the firm. The value of this residual claim depends on the policy of the firm and, moreover, if the expectations of the firm prove incorrect (see p.34), the shareholders bear the consequences.

---

[3]The assumption of a *concave* revenue function is clearly mathematically motivated. As is well known, for a maximisation problem to have a solution, a concavity is needed. However, in optimal control problems it is not necessary that the *objective function* is concave. For the details, see the sufficiency theorem in Appendix 1.

[4]Note that the revenue at time t and all costs, except the depreciation costs, at time t are cash-flows at time t.

[5]A consequence of this assumption will be discussed in section 4.7.

The restriction $I \geq 0$ means that investments are irreversible (domain assumption). The irreversibility of investments can have several reasons. Appelbaum and Harris [1978] mention technological phenomena and market imperfections in the market for capital goods. Pindyck [1988] argues: "Irreversibility arises because capital is industry- or firm-specific, that is, it cannot be used in a different industry or by a different firm" (p.969). Nickell [1978b] states :"Now it is quite clear that there is a large class of capital goods which are, in reality, almost impossible to sell other than as scrap" (p.39). Given the fixed-coefficients technology, the irreversibility restriction may also reflect a restriction on the rate of change of the labour force. The assumption of irreversibility is crucial if the firm wants to contract. Arrow and Kurz [1970] show that irreversibility influences the optimal strategy in a Ramsey model when the initial capital goods stock is high. For the same reason irreversibility will play an important role in the Chapter 5, since if the firm is confronted with a business cycle, it is likely that situations will occur which force the firm to contract.

As in Nickell ([1975], p.56) it is assumed that labour is employed on all capital goods. An interesting extension of the model would be a model in which idle capital has no labour working on it. However, as Nickell notes, this would lead to "considerable notational and expositional inconvenience" (p.56). Moreover, the assumptions made in this chapter (which lead to a rather 'rigid' firm) accentuate the effects of a fluctuating demand, studied in Chapter 5.

Although the assumptions of full utilisation of capital and no inventory of finished goods can be motivated economically (see also p.62), an other important motivation for these assumptions is to keep the number of (state) variables low (see the remarks on p.2).

Finally, this model will not describe reality equally well for all possible kinds of firms. Assumptions like 'a homogeneous capital stock and production', and 'no access to sources of external equity' seem to make, when considered as domain assumptions, the model most suitable for relatively small firms. Moreover, in the case of small firms the reward for suppliers of debt is not necessarily lower than the reward for suppliers of equity. It is possible that the suppliers of equity (the owner(s) of the firm) only ask a relatively low reward, for instance if their main goal is to stay in business (to survive).

From a technical point of view, note that Q, L and Y can be eliminated from the model (see (4) and (5)). Thus the model has two state variables (K and X) and two control variables (I and D). The upper bounds on I and D are artificial and they are imposed because the model is linear in the control variables. An infinite control variable would imply a discontinuous change (jump) of the state variables affected by this control variable. Imposing upper bounds on the control variables implies that abrupt changes in the state variables are impossible; only gradual changes are permitted. This emphasises that the firm can only slowly adjust its size (see Chapter 1)[6]. A policy where the control variables are on their artificial bounds can be interpreted as: the firm wants to bring about a change of one or more state variables *as quickly as possible*. It is assumed that the upper bounds are very high, so that the firm can only maintain $I=I_{max}$ or $D=D_{max}$ through borrowing the necessary money, implying a rapid rise of the amount of debt[7].

4.3 Necessary and sufficient conditions for optimality

The Maximum Principle is used to find the necessary and sufficient conditions for optimality. All details can be found in Appendix 1. After elimination of Q, L and Y, the model contains two pure state constraints. Pure state constraints, i.e. constraints that do not explicitly contain one or more control variables, complicate the application of the Maximum Principle, since the variables appearing in these constraints can only be manipulated <u>indirectly</u> through the control variables. Feichtinger and Hartl [1986][8] give an excellent exposition of the different ways to handle these

---

[6]The reason to exclude abrupt changes is partly mathematical: abrupt changes (jumps) of the state variables complicate the application of the Maximum Principle.

[7]Kort ([1989], p.13) states that there are implicit financing bounds on the control variables; it seems to me, however, that the firm can *temporarily* finance an arbitrarily high I or D by lending money.

[8]I will refer frequently to this book, although it has been written in German. The reason is that I think it is the most complete book from an applicants point of view: all existing variants of the deterministic

pure state constraints. They advise to use the so-called 'direct adjoining approach' and this advice is followed in this thesis. Now the necessary conditions are presented and explained afterwards.
The Hamiltonian and the Lagrangian are defined as follows:

$$\mathbb{H} = D + \lambda_1(I\text{-}aK) + \lambda_2\{(1\text{-}f)(S\text{-}wL\text{-}aK\text{-}rY)\text{-}D\} \tag{12}$$

$$\mathbb{L} = \mathbb{H} + \mu_1 I + \mu_2(I_{max}\text{-}I) + \mu_3 D + \mu_4(D_{max}\text{-}D) + \upsilon_1(K\text{-}X) + \upsilon_2\{(1+b)X\text{-}K\} \tag{13}$$

When using the 'direct adjoining approach', one has to take into account that the costate variables λ_i, which can usually be interpreted as shadow prices of the state variables, may jump in entry- or exit points of a boundary (i.e. an interval on which a pure state constraint is active[9]). When some appropriate regularity conditions are satisfied (see Appendix 1), the Maximum Principle states that for an optimal (I,D,K,X) there exist piecewise continuously differentiable functions λ_i, piecewise continuous functions μ_i and υ_i, constants γ_i, and for each timepoint τ where λ is discontinuous a vector $\eta(\tau)$, such that for all timepoints t where (I,D) and λ are continuous:

---

optimal control problem are treated systematically. Less extensive references in the English language are Seierstad and Sydsaeter [1987] (mathematically precise), Kamien and Schwartz [1981], and Sethi and Thompson [1981].

[9]For a precise definition of a boundary, see Appendix 1, p.151.

$$\frac{\partial \mathbb{L}}{\partial I} = 0 \iff \lambda_1 + \mu_1 - \mu_2 = 0 \tag{14}$$

$$\frac{\partial \mathbb{L}}{\partial D} = 0 \iff 1 - \lambda_2 + \mu_3 - \mu_4 = 0 \tag{15}$$

$$\dot{\lambda}_1 = -\frac{\partial \mathbb{L}}{\partial K} + i\lambda_1 = (i+a)\lambda_1 + \lambda_2(1-f)\{\frac{wl}{k} + a + r - \frac{dS}{dK}\} - \upsilon_1 + \upsilon_2 \tag{16}$$

$$\dot{\lambda}_2 = -\frac{\partial \mathbb{L}}{\partial X} + i\lambda_2 = (i-(1-f)r)\lambda_2 + \upsilon_1 - (1-b)\upsilon_2 \tag{17}$$

$$\mu_1 I=0,\ \mu_2(I_{max}-I)=0,\ \mu_3 D=0,\ \mu_4(D_{max}-D)=0,\ \ \mu_i \geq 0,\ i=1,2,3,4 \tag{18}$$

$$\upsilon_1(K-X)=0,\ \upsilon_2\{(1+b)X-K\}=0,\ \upsilon_1\geq 0,\ \upsilon_2\geq 0 \tag{19}$$

$$\lambda_1(z) = \gamma_1 - \gamma_2,\quad \lambda_2(z) = 1 - \gamma_1 + (1+b)\gamma_2 \tag{20}$$

$$\gamma_1\{K(z)-X(z)\}=0,\ \gamma_2\{(1+b)X(z)-K(z)\}=0,\ \gamma_1\geq 0,\ \gamma_2\geq 0 \tag{21}$$

If λ is discontinuous in τ, then:

$$\lambda_1(\tau^+) = \lambda_1(\tau^-) - \eta_1(\tau) + \eta_2(\tau) \tag{22}$$

$$\lambda_2(\tau^+) = \lambda_2(\tau^-) + \eta_1(\tau) - (1+b)\eta_2(\tau) \tag{23}$$

$$\eta_1(\tau)\{K(\tau)-X(\tau)\} = 0,\ \eta_2(\tau)\{(1+b)X(\tau)-K(\tau)\} = 0,\ \eta_1(\tau)\geq 0,\ \eta_2(\tau)\geq 0 \tag{24}$$

Equations (14) and (15) constitute the heart of the Maximum Principle. From the definition of the Hamiltonian (12) and the Lagrangian (13), it is clear that (14) and (15) state that the Hamiltonian is maximised with regard to the control variables, subject to the control constraints (8) and (9). The Hamiltonian can be interpreted as follows: λ_1 is interpreted as the shadow price of capital and λ_2 as the shadow price of equity. This means that λ_1 (λ_2) measures the rate at which the objective function grows if the capital (equity) stock grows. The Hamiltonian (12) is equivalent to:

$$\mathbb{H}(K,X,I,D,t) = D(t) + \lambda_1(t)\dot{K}(t)+\lambda_2(t)\dot{X}(t) \tag{25}$$

At time t the firm can use the control variables to generate direct contributions to the objective function (i.e. pay out dividends) or it can use the control variables to generate contributions to the objective function in the future. These indirect contibutions at time t are measured, due to the shadow price interpretation of λ_1 and λ_2, by $\lambda_1(t)\dot{K}(t)+\lambda_2(t)\dot{X}(t)$! So, maximising the Hamiltonian with regard to the control variables at each point of time means maximising the *total* contribution (the sum of immediate and future contributions) to the objective function *at each point of time*. This implies that the *dynamic* optimisation problem is split up in infinitely many *static* optimisation problems. Of course, these static optimisation problems are not independent. Their interdependency is captured by equations (16) and (17), which give the developement over time of the shadow prices λ_1 and λ_2. Chapter 6 is devoted to the interpretation of λ_1 and λ_2, especially with regard to the interpretations of the possible jumps (see (22)-(23)). For a more elaborate intuitive derivation of the Maximum Principle, see for instance Dorfman [1969] or Intriligator [1971].

Equations (18) and (19) are the complementary slackness conditions for the inequality constraints (like in linear programming). Equations (20) and (21) constitute the transversality conditions, which determine the values of λ_1 and λ_2 at the end of the planning period.

In Appendix 1 it is shown that these necessary conditions are also sufficient, but that there may be more than one solution. Also in Appendix 1 one finds an elaboration of the so-called 'coupling procedure' (or path connecting procedure), which is an iterative procedure, developed by Van Loon [1983], to find the optimal policy for the entire planning period $[0,z]$. The idea of this procedure is as follows: the optimal policy is determined by answering the question: which constraints are active at each point of time. It is most likely that a constraint is only active during one or more subintervals of $[0,z]$. Consequently, the set of active constraints at a certain point of time will change over time: at time t_1 other constraints are active than at time t_2. Now a *path* is defined as an interval of time on which the set of active constraints does not change. The optimal policy will in general consist of a succession (a *string*) of paths. The coupling procedure is a systematic way to find the optimal string for every initial situation (given by K(0) and X(0)).The relevant properties of the feasible paths are summarised in table 1. See Appendix 1 for the details[10].

---

[10]The borderline case $i=(1-f)r$ is excluded. For a motivation, see van Loon ([1983], p.48).

path	I	D	$\dot{Y}$	$\dot{X}$	$\dot{K}$	Y	dS/dK
1	aK	+	0	0	+	0	$= \frac{wl}{k}+a+\frac{i}{1-f}$
2	aK	+	+	0	+	bX	$= \frac{wl}{k}+a+\frac{br+i/(1-f)}{1+b}$
3	+	0	0	+	+	0	
4	aK	0	-	+	0	+	$= \frac{wl}{k}+a+r$
5	0	+	0	-	-	0	
6	0	+	-	-	-	bX	
7	0	0	±	±	-	+	
8	aK	D_{max}	+	-	0	+	$= \frac{wl}{k}+a+r$
9	I_{max}	D_{max}	+	±	+	+	
10	I_{max}	0	+	±	+	+	
11	0	D_{max}	+	-	-	+	
12	+	0	+	+	+	bX	

Table 1: The optimal paths

Path 1 and path 5 are only feasible if $i<(1-f)r$. Path 2 and path 6 are only feasible if $i>(1-f)r$. Since dS/dK denotes marginal revenue[11], one expects that the right hand sides in the 'dS/dK-column' in the table denote some marginal costs. It is clear that wl/k and a are respectively the wage costs and the depreciation costs per unit of capital. The only other costs are financing costs. If an extra unit of capital is entirely financed with equity, before tax financing costs equal $i/(1-f)$ (N.B. the price of a capital good equals one). If this extra unit is entirely financed with debt, the financing costs are r. If the firm has maximal debt (i.e. $Y=bX=b/(1-b)K$), an extra unit of capital will be financed with $b/(1-b)$ units of debt and $1/(1+b)$ units of equity. Total financing costs per unit of capital are therefore:

$$\frac{b}{1+b}\,r + \frac{1}{1+b}\,\frac{i}{1-f}$$

So on path 1,2,4 and 8, marginal revenue indeed equals marginal costs for different financing situations.

[11]A more precise (but longer) name would be: marginal revenue product of capital.

4.4 A feedback decision rule

This section gives a feedback decision rule which characterises the optimal policy in economic terms. It is good to realise that this rule was in fact derived *ex post*: the optimal policy was first found mathematically and economically interpreted afterwards.

The decision rule uses a few well known economic concepts. The marginal return on assets, R(K), is defined as the extra income generated by one extra unit of capital, divided by the expenses made to acquire that capital good. The price of a capital good equals one, so that:

$$R(K) = (1\text{-}f) \left\{ \frac{dS}{dK} - \frac{wl}{k} - a \right\} \qquad (26)$$

Note that, since S is a concave function of K, R is a decreasing function of K. This R(K) is an important quantity, but for the shareholders the crucial quantity is the return on equity, denoted by $R_e(K,X)$. The following leverage formula can be used to derive the marginal return on equity:

$$R(K) = R_e(K,X) * \frac{X}{K} + (1\text{-}f)r * \frac{Y}{K} \qquad (27)$$

And thus, using (5):

$$R_e(K,X) = R(K) + \{R(K)\text{-}(1\text{-}f)r\} * \frac{Y}{X} \qquad (28)$$

Given the values of the state variables K and X (implying Y) at a certain time t, there is a net cash-flow equal to:

$$(1\text{-}f)\{ S(K/k) - (\frac{wl}{k})K - aK - rY \} + aK \qquad (29)$$

Equation (29) is usually named 'accounting cash-flow' (after tax profits plus depreciation). In this chapter and Chapter 5 the term 'accounting cash-flow' always denotes the quantity in (29). The problem facing the firm at every instant of time can now be phrased as follows:

> How should it spend this 'accounting cash-flow' to obtain the highest possible value for (1)?

From (2), (3), (5) and (29) it follows that:

$$\text{'accounting cash-flow' at time } t = I(t) + D(t) - \dot{Y}(t) \qquad (30)$$

So to reach its goal, the firm can choose between three activities:

a) invest in capital goods

b) pay back debt or borrow

c) pay out dividend

In fact, the firm can choose two activities freely; together with (30) this fixes the third activity. The firm will now make a comparison between the returns on each of these activities. The minimum return required by the shareholders equals i. The marginal return on paying back debt equals $(1\text{-}f)r$ and the marginal return on investment equals R(K). The marginal cost of borrowing equals $(1\text{-}f)r$. Note that $(1\text{-}f)r$ and i are constants, but R(K) and $R_e(K,X)$ are not.

For the moment it is assumed that (29) is always a positive amount. To see how the firm should optimally act, three different situations have to be distinguished:

A) $R_e(K,X) > i$

The marginal return on equity the firm can achieve exceeds the required return on equity, so in this situation it is certainly not optimal to pay out dividend. It is better to keep the money inside the firm. But how should the 'accounting cash-flow' be spent?

If $R(K) > (1\text{-}f)r$, the firm invests as much as possible and borrows the necessary money. If debt is already maximal, the firm maintains $Y=bX$; together with $D=0$ and (30) this determines the level of investments. Borrowing is profitable, since the marginal return on investment exceeds the cost of debt. Or, putting it differently, as long as $R(K) > (1\text{-}f)r$ the firm has a positive leverage (see (28)) and therefore borrows as much as possible to finance investments. If $R(K) < (1\text{-}f)r$, the firm has a negative leverage, so if it has debt, it is optimal to spend all its 'accounting cash-flow' to pay back debt (the marginal return on paying back debt exceeds the marginal return on investment); if it has no debt, it invests its 'accounting cash-flow'. Finally, if R(K) equals $(1\text{-}f)r$, the firm invests to maintain this equality and uses the remaining 'accounting cash-flow' to pay back debt: if it would invest more, R(K) would fall below $(1\text{-}f)r$ which would call for an end to investment; if it would invest less, R(K) would become larger than $(1\text{-}f)r$ and this would call for maximal investment.

B) $R_e(K,X) < i$

The marginal return on equity the firm can achieve is less than the required return on equity. Now it is tempting to say that the firm should use all its 'accounting cash-flow' to pay out dividend. But that does not have to be optimal. Suppose $i<(1-f)r$. $R_e(K,X)$, the marginal return on equity, is in fact the extra return a shareholder gets if the firm *invests* an extra unit of equity, *given* the debt-equity ratio at that moment. But the firm has more opportunities for spending its money than just investing. It can easily be seen from (28) that $R_e(K,X)<i$ implies $R(K)<(1-f)r$. So if the firm has debt, the leverage effect is negative. Therefore, if $i<(1-f)r$, it is more profitable for the firm to lower its debt-equity ratio by paying back debt than to pay out dividend.

The decision rule in this situation is: do not invest in capital goods; if $i>(1-f)r$, borrow to pay out dividends at a maximal rate; if debt is already maximal, maintain maximal debt and use the remaining 'accounting cash-flow' to pay out dividend; if $i<(1-f)r$, use all 'accounting cash-flow' to pay back debt if there is debt, otherwise pay out dividend.

C) $R_e(K,X) = i$

If $(1-f)r<i$, then this is the optimal situation, provided debt is at its maximum (since debt is cheap now). So the optimal policy is: invest to maintain $R_e(K,X)=i$ and use the rest of the 'accounting cash-flow' to pay out dividends. This means that if debt is not yet at its maximum, the firm pays out dividends at a maximal rate and borrows the necessary money.

If $i<(1-f)r$, debt is expensive. When the firm has debt, it can easily be seen that $R(K)<(1-f)r$ and thus it is most profitable to use the 'accounting cash-flow' to pay back debt. If debt is already zero, the situation is optimal and the firm invests to maintain $R_e(K,X)=i$ and uses the rest of the 'accounting cash-flow' to pay out dividend.

In summary, the decision rule for the firm is:

IF $R_e > i$ THEN $D=0$;

IF $R > (1\text{-}f)r$ THEN IF $Y<bX$ THEN $I=I_{max}$

IF $Y=bX$ THEN maintain $Y=bX$ and invest

IF $R = (1\text{-}f)r$ THEN maintain $R=(1\text{-}f)r$ and pay back debt

IF $R < (1\text{-}f)r$ THEN IF $Y>0$, $I=0$ and pay back debt

IF $Y=0$, invest the 'accounting cash-flow'

IF $R_e < i$ THEN $I=0$;

IF $i < (1\text{-}f)r$ THEN IF $Y>0$, $D=0$ and pay back debt

IF $Y=0$, pay out the 'accounting cash-flow'

IF $i > (1\text{-}f)r$ THEN IF $Y<bX$ THEN $D=D_{max}$

IF $Y=bX$ THEN maintain $Y=bX$ and pay dividends

IF $R_e = i$ THEN

IF $i < (1\text{-}f)r$ THEN IF $Y>0$, $D=I=0$ and pay back debt

IF $Y=0$, maintain $R_e=i$ and pay dividends

IF $i > (1\text{-}f)r$ THEN maintain $R_e=i$ and $D=D_{max}$

In the next section it is illustrated that this decision rule exactly explains the optimal strategy of the firm for every possible initial (K(0),X(0)), assuming that (29) is always positive.

It is important to note that this decision rule implies that for this model the optimal control is *synthesised*, which means that the optimal (I(t),D(t)) is given as a function of (X(t),K(t)). (see Seierstad and Sydsaeter [1987], p.161). This is an extremely useful property, especially with regard to the way uncertainty is treated (see p.34). If the expectations of the firm prove wrong, it does not have to solve a new optimisation problem. The firm can simply apply the decision rule to the changed circumstances!

In general, such a synthesised control can not be found (cf. Feichtinger and Hartl [1986], p.62). Feichtinger and Hartl suggest that if one succeeds to apply the coupling procedure of Van Loon, one can also find a synthesised control (see p.365). In the next chapter however, the coupling procedure is applied, but a synthesised control is not found. The reason seems to be that the model in Chapter 5 is no longer autonomous. The model in this chapter is autonomous (i.e., the time argument only appears as argument of the control and state variables, and nót as a separate variable (except in the discount factor); in other words: the parameters do not depend on the time variable) and time does not explicitly appear in the decision rule. In other words, the optimal (I(t),D(t)) is expressed as a function of (X(t),K(t)) instead of (X(t),K(t),*t*). One can imagine that in a model with a business cycle, not only X(t) and K(t) determine I and D, but also t (that is, the position in the cycle).

This decision rule has a different structure than the decision rules in Van Loon [1983]. Van Loon divides the optimal decision into three 'sub-rules', where each subrule is concerned with a different decision: production (choice of production techniques), finance (borrowing or not) and the distribution on the financial means between investments and dividends. There is a hierarchy in these rules. They have to be applied in a specific order: first 'production', then 'finance' and finally 'investments/dividends'. This rule has a 'management science' character: each 'division' of the firm has its own (sub-)rule. The rule derived in this chapter has a 'systems theory' character: the optimal controls are given as functions of the state variables. Of course, the rules are equivalent in that they lead to (are based on) the same optimal policies. It is a matter of taste which formulation one prefers.

4.5 Illustrations of the decision rule

Two cases have to be distinguished: $i<(1\text{-}f)r$ and $(1\text{-}f)r<i$.

<u>The case $i\leq(1\text{-}f)r$</u>

From (26) it is easily seen that:

$$dS/dK=wl/k+a+r \iff R(K)=(1\text{-}f)r \tag{31}$$

$$dS/dK<wl/k+a+r \iff R(K)<(1\text{-}f)r \tag{32}$$

$$dS/dK=wl/k+a+i/(1\text{-}f) \iff R(K)=i \tag{33}$$

$$dS/dK>wl/k+a+i/(1\text{-}f) \iff R(K)>i \tag{34}$$

Moreover, Y=0 and $dS/dK=wl/k+a+i(1\text{-}f)$ together imply $R_e(K,X)=R(K)=i$. This is the optimal situation for this case, according to the decision rule. This suggests that the firm will try to reach path 1 (see Table 1). In Appendix 1 it is shown that path 1 indeed satisfies the transversality conditions at time z. Note that K is constant on path 1, because dS/dK is constant. The initial condition is given by K(0) and X(0), which immediately give dS/dK(0) and Y(0). The decision rule, however, is phrased in terms of R, R_e, i and $(1-f)r$. Therefore it is necessary to take a closer look at the relations between dS/dK, Y/X, R_e, R, i, and $(1-f)r$. It can easily be seen that if Y/X grows from zero to b, the corresponding value of dS/dK that maintains the equality of R_e(K,X) and i, increases from $wl/k+a+i/(1-f)$ to $wl/k+a+br/(1+b)+i/((1-f)(1+b)$. Together with (31)-(34) this leads to the following picture:

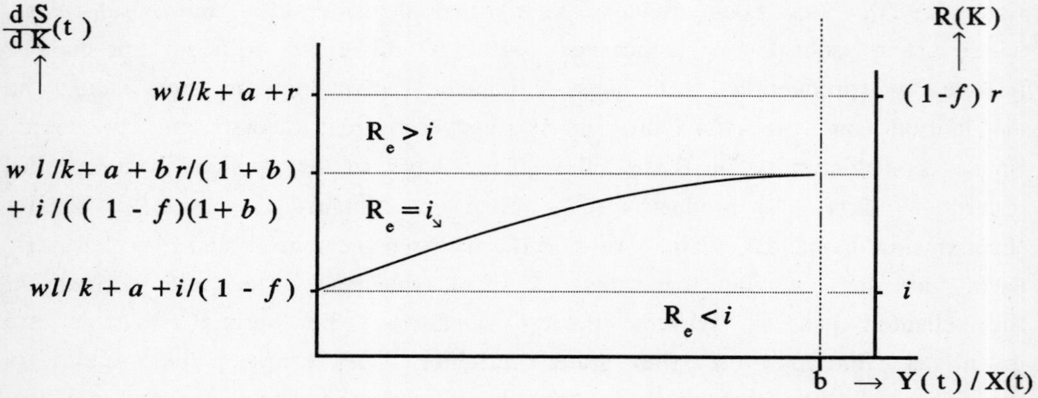

Figure 1: The relation between marginal revenue, the debt equity ratio, the marginal return to assets and the marginal return to equity.

Together with Figure 1, the decision rule gives the optimal solution for each (K(0),X(0)), since K(t) and X(t) determine Y(t) and dS/dK(t). Figure 2 gives the optimal solution if the initial level of the capital goods stock is much lower than the 'desired' level on path 1. Figure 3 gives the optimal solution if the initial level of the capital goods stock is larger than the 'desired' level. Note that dS/dK is a decreasing function of K. This implies that the firm grows (K increases) if and only if dS/dK decreases.

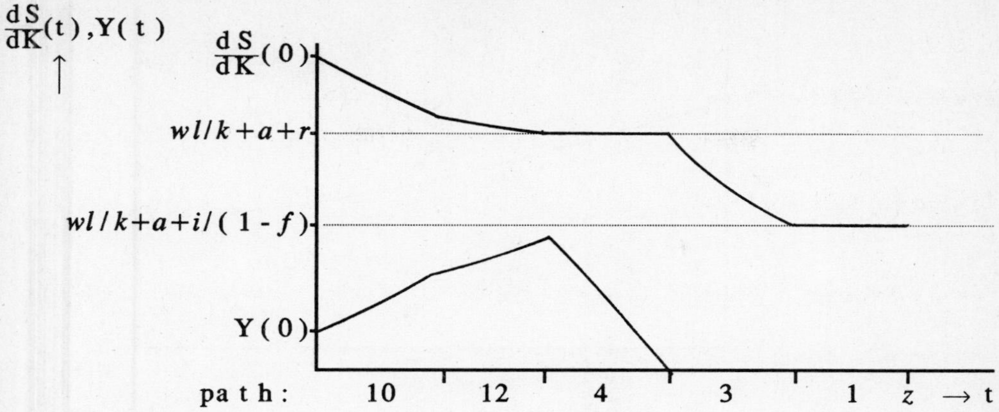

Figure 2: The optimal policy if the initial capital goods stock is 'low'

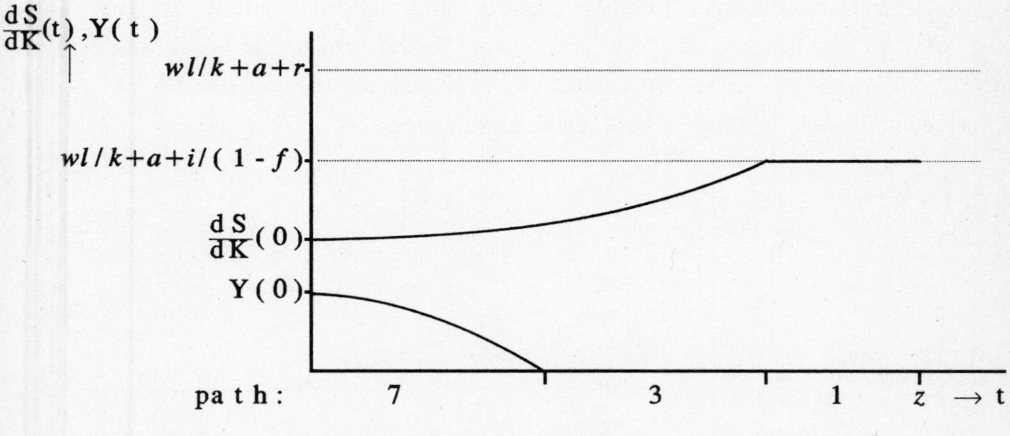

Figure 3: Optimal policy if the initial capital goods stock is 'high'.

<u>The case $(1\text{-}f)r \leq i$</u>

Equations (31)-(34) are still valid. Moreover, $Y=bX$ and $dS/dK=wl/k+a+br/(1+b)+i/((1\text{-}f)(1+b))$ imply that $R_e(K,X)=i$. This suggests that the firm will try to reach path 2 (see Table 1). For this case, the following figure corresponds to Figure 1:

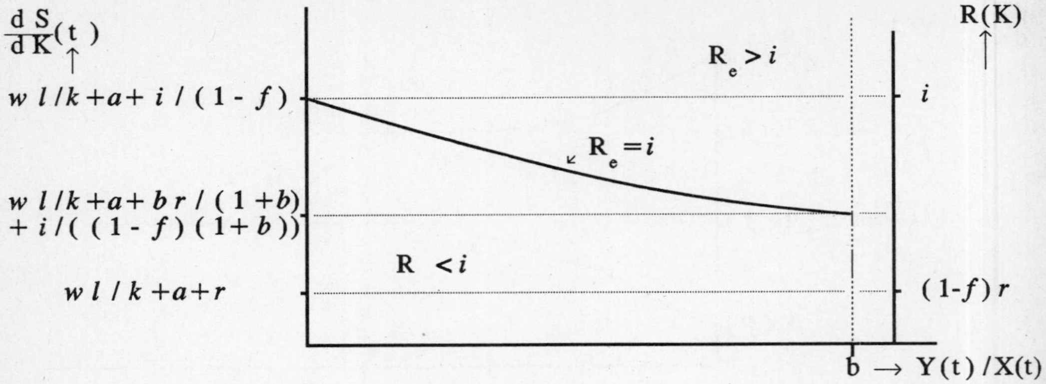

Figure 4: The relation between marginal revenue, the debt equity ratio, the marginal return to assets and the marginal return to equity.

Together with Figure 4, the decision rule gives the optimal policy for each set of initial conditions. Figure 5 gives the optimal policy if the initial level of the capital goods stock is much lower than the desired level on path 2. Figure 6 gives the optimal solution if the initial level of the capital goods stock is larger than the desired level.

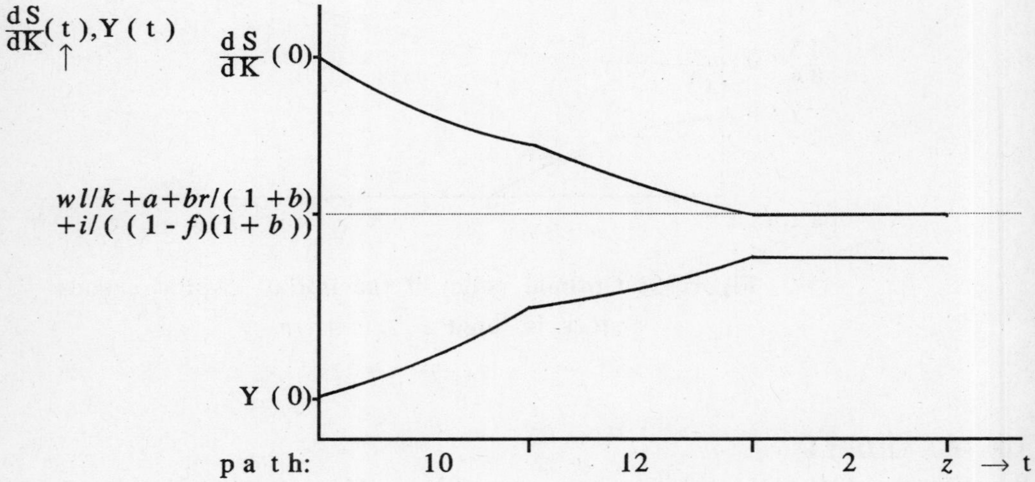

Figure 5: The optimal policy if the initial capital goods stock is 'low'.

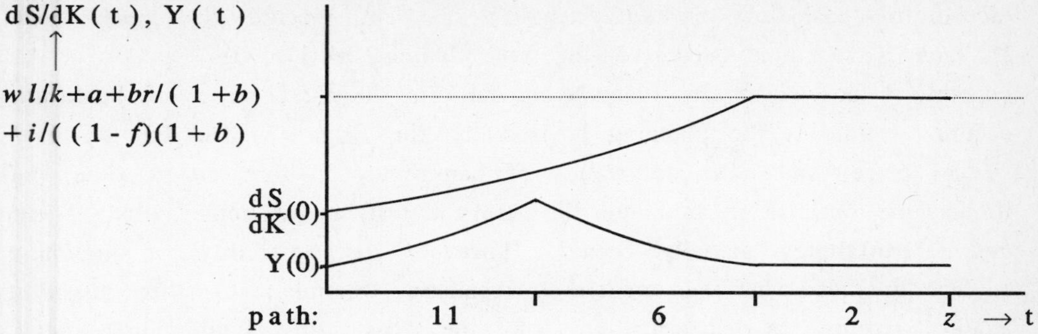

Figure 6: The optimal policy if the initial capital goods stock is 'high'.

4.6 Limitations of the decision rule

Until now it was assumed that (29) is always positive. This section relaxes this assumption. Figure 7 shows the sign of the 'accounting cash-flow' for all possible combinations of K and Y.

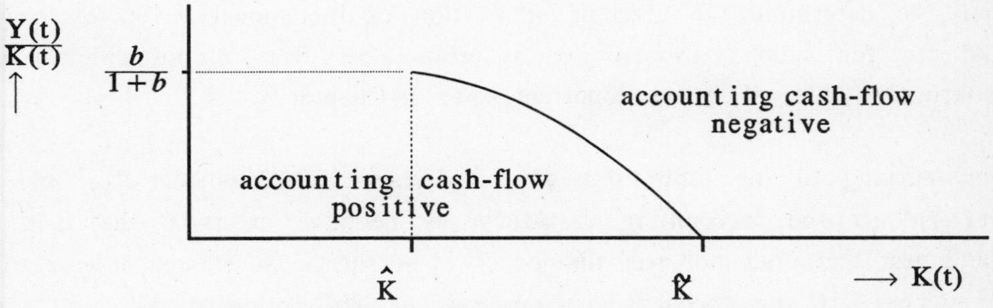

Figure 7: The relation between the accounting cash flow, debt and capital

The levels of K on the final paths 1 and 2 lie to the left of $\hat{K}$ in Figure 7. This reveals that (29) is only negative if the capital goods stock is extremely large. The reason to be interested in such situations, is that a change of the environment may lead to a change of the 'equilibrium ('final path'-) value' of marginal revenue. With regard to this new 'equilibrium value' the 'old' optimal K may be far too large in the new circumstances.

Before explaining the limitations of the decision rule, it is useful to discuss the meaning of *bankruptcy* in the model. Bankruptcy occurs if the

'accounting cash-flow' is still negative as debt reaches its upper bound. If such a situation occurs during the planning period, the model of this chapter is no longer an adequate model. In the first place, if bankruptcy occurs at time t, the planning horizon for the firm is not z but t. In the second place, since the occurrence of bankruptcy is foreseen at time $t=0$, it may be optimal to liquidate the firm at $t=0$ or at some point of time *before* bankruptcy actually occurs. However, the possibility of liquidation is not included in the model. A realistic treatment of this possibility would require a specification of the cost of liquidation and a specification of the *market* value of the capital goods.
Now there are two important implications for the models in this thesis. Firstly, an optimal solution of the model is by definition a *feasible* solution (i.e. an investment and dividend policy for the interval $[0,z]$ satisfying (2)-(9)). This implies that the existence of an optimal solution means that the firm will not go bankrupt (except possibly at time z; see Appendix 1, p.156). So, *if* the firm can avoid bankruptcy, it will do so (in an optimal way). Secondly, if the firm can *not* avoid bankruptcy, the model is not appropriate.
Thus, to determine the area of application of the model it is important to find out for which parameter configurations the firm is not able to avoid bankruptcy. This will be an important issue in Chapter 5.

Now turning to the limitations of the decision rule, consider the case that $i<(1-f)r$. If the 'accounting cash-flow' is negative at $t=0$, the firm does not invest and does not pay dividends. It borrows just enough money to pay the wages. If the 'accounting cash-flow' is still negative as debt reaches its upper bound, the firm is bankrupt. If this is not the case, the decision rule can be applied beginning at the moment that the 'accounting cash-flow' becomes positive. So the decision rule can easily be adjusted in this situation: as long as 'accounting cash-flow' is negative, do not invest and do not pay dividends.
The situation is more complex when $i>(1-f)r$.
In this case the cost of debt is smaller than the cost of equity, no matter how large the capital goods stock is. So it seems optimal to reach $Y=bX$ as soon as possible. If the initial level of the capital goods stock is high, this would mean: $I=0$ and $D=D_{max}$. In Figure 7 this means an almost vertical upward movement (Y increases rapidly, K decreases relatively slowly;

remember the assumption that $D=D_{max}$ requires massive borrowing). This implies that even if the 'accounting cash-flow' is positive at t=0, this policy ($I=0, D=D_{max}$; path 11) may lead the firm into the "negative 'accounting cash-flow'-region", and eventually into a bankruptcy. The only way to avoid bankruptcy in this case is to leave path 11 and to stop paying dividends in time (i.e. switch to path 7). So the firm will start on path 11; at a certain time, when the 'accounting cash-flow' is negative but Y is not yet maximal, the firm switches to path 7. This 'switch' is timed in such a way that when the debt-equity ratio reaches its upper bound, the firm can continue on path 6 (or path 2). This phenomenon (the firm uses path 7 to avoid bankruptcy) will be discussed in detail in Chapter 5. The important point to note now is that the decision rule does not tell *when* to switch from path 11 to path 7. The answer to this question seems to depend crucially on the specific form of the revenue function S and on the values of the parameters. For instance, given some initial conditions K(0) and X(0), the firm will go bankrupt for a low b and it will survive for a large b. Moreover, the value of b is one of the determinants of the point of time at which the firm switches from path 11 to path 7. So the firm cannot simply look at the values of the state variables. In other words, the feedback decision rule breaks down.

4.7 Book value and market value

In section 4.2 X and Y have been defined as the *book values* of equity and debt. The book value of X appears in the objective function (1). To be in accordance with the theoretical finance literature, the objective function should be: the discounted dividend stream plus the *market* value of equity at the end of the planning period. The question is whether the approach using book values leads to different result, compared to an approach using market values. This question can be partially answered by examining a result in Hartl [1988]. Hartl compares the optimal solutions of two models which only differ with regard to the objective function. The two objective functions are:

$$\max \int_0^z e^{-it} D(t)\, dt + e^{-iz} X(z), \qquad \text{and} \qquad \max \int_0^\infty e^{-it} D(t)\, dt. \tag{34}$$

He finds that for both models the optimal policy is the same, provided z is large enough. So the 'book value approach' apparently does not lead to biased results. However, he also finds that

$$\int_0^z e^{-it}D(t)\ dt + e^{-iz}X(z) < \int_0^\infty e^{-it}D(t)\ dt \tag{35}$$

The same result can be easily derived for the model in this chapter. Equation (35) implies that the book value of equity at time z, $X(z)$, is less than the market value of equity, $\int_z^\infty e^{-i(t-z)}D(t)\ dt$.

This can be understood in the following way. "z is large enough" means: the firm reaches the final path before time z. So at time z the firm is on path 1 (if $i<(1-f)r$) or on path 2 (if $i>(1-f)r$). Consider the case $i<(1-f)r$. The firm is on path 1 and on path 1 dividends are constant (use (3)), say $\hat{D}$. This implies that the market value of equity at time z, MVE(z), equals $\hat{D}/i$.

The next step is to realise that on path 1 *marginal* revenue equals *marginal* costs:

$$\partial S/\partial K = wl/k + a + i/(1-f) \tag{36}$$

The right hand side of (36) is a constant, so *total* costs are a linear function of K. Moreover, it is assumed that total revenue S is a concave function of K. Finally for K=0, total revenue and total costs are zero. This leads to the following picture:

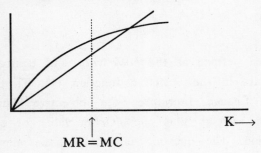

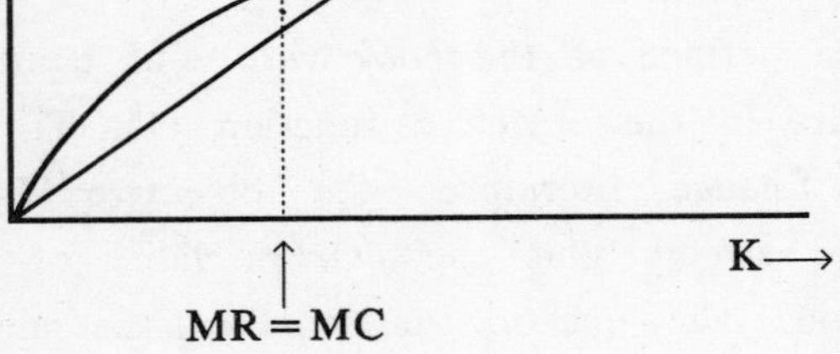

Figure 8: Total revenue and total costs

Figure 8 implies that if *marginal* revenue equals *marginal* costs (as on path 1), then *total* revenue exceeds *total* costs. So on path 1:

$$S(K) > \left\{wl/k + a + i/(1-f)\right\} K \tag{37}$$

The important point to observe now is that total costs include a reward iX for the suppliers of equity. Thus (37) implies that after covering all costs, including the required reward for the shareholders, there is still some revenue left, to which these shareholders are entitled. The conclusion is that, although on a *marginal* dollar the return is exactly i, the return on the *total* amount of dollars supplied to the firm by the shareholders exceeds i! In other words, the market value of equity exceeds the book value. Indeed, it can easily be seen (using (3)) that (37) is equivalent to:

$$\hat{D} > iX \Rightarrow X < \hat{D}/i = MVE \tag{38}$$

4.8 Summary and conclusions

In this chapter the optimal solutions of the basic model of this thesis are discussed. Emphasis is laid on the assumptions of the model and on the derivation of a feedback decision rule which gives the optimal policy for almost all possible initial conditions, including conditions which imply an initial capital goods stock which is too large. This decision rule breaks down if there is a chance of bankruptcy, while $i > (1\text{-}f)r$. In the following chapters the model of this chapter is extended in several ways.

5
MODELS WITH A BUSINESS CYCLE

5.1 Introduction

The models discussed thusfar in this thesis are *dynamic* models: the objective function is defined on an interval consisting of many periods of time (in models with continuous time even infinitely many), the state and control variables are functions of time, the development in time of the state variables is given by differential equations, and, generally spoken, decisions taken by the firm today have consequences for the decisions of tomorrow. In these models, the environment is stationary. This often implies the existence of some 'steady state' (final path), which implies constant values for the capital goods stock, equity, dividends and investments. In the models of Van Loon, Van Schijndel and Kort it is mainly studied *how* the firm reaches this steady state in an optimal way. In this chapter the environment is no longer stationary: the firm faces an exogeneously given business cycle, represented by a fluctuating demand curve. This leads to another kind of dynamics: the model is *non-autonomous* (see p.46). In a non-autonomous model it is difficult to apply the path connecting procedure and the existence of a decision rule is doubtful.
If the demand curve changes 'smoothly' over time (that is, there are no abrupt changes) and the firm is not restricted with regard to changing its size (except that it can only change its size smoothly, since K must be continuous), then the firm would simply maintain the equality of marginal revenue and marginal costs (or the equality of marginal return on equity and the cost of equity), as on path 1 and 2 in Chapter 4. However, if investments are irreversible and labour is working on all capital goods (see section 4.2), the firm cannot quickly reduce the size of the capital goods stock and labour stock, which only diminish due to depreciation. So in the context of a changing environment, irreversibility of investments is a crucial element of the model. Arrow [1968] states: "...at a time at which investment is still profitable as far as current calculations are concerned, the firm may refrain from investment if it anticipates that in

the relatively near future it would have disinvested if it could" (p.3). Before this problem is analysed in detail, several preliminary remarks have to be made.

In economics one discerns several cyclical patterns in economic activity, mainly determined by demand factors. The 'business cycle' in this chapter is not meant to refer to a particular kind of cycle. It is only meant to designate that the demand curve exhibits an up and down going movement.

The bulk of the literature on business cycles concentrates on the *explanation* of those cyles: why does a cycle occur?. There is much less literature on how firms react when they are confronted with a variability in economic activity. It is of course an important issue whether a business cycle is simply the sum of all actions taken by individual economic subjects, or whether there is some phenomenon on an aggregate level to which individual economic subjects can only react. The same phenomenon can be observed concerning growth theories, as indicated by Marris [1971]: "...but most of these theories have left open the question of whether we should best see the growth of the system as a direct aggregation of the growth of the parts, or whether the parts mainly respond passively to underlying forces pervading the whole" (p.1).

In its macro-economic models, the Dutch Central Planning Bureau identifies 'demand expectations' as one of the explanatory variables for the level of investments. And when businessmen are interviewed about their investment behaviour, they often mention the expectations on economic activity in general and on the demand for their products in particular as an important factor, which they can only partly influence. When economic activity is going up, the firm expects to be able to sell more in the future and thus it invests. Thus businessmen *react* to fluctuations in economic activity, considering these fluctuations as given. This especially holds in an open economy like the Dutch economy, where the economic situation, the trend of the market, is largely exogeneous. So there seems to be reason enough to study the optimal behaviour of firms as they react to fluctuations in economic activity. In this chapter it is assumed that these fluctuations are captured by a cyclical movement of the demand function of the firm in question.

In the literature on business cycles, the study of irreversibility of investments is (again) primarily concerned with the explanations of business cycles: it is shown that the combination of irreversibility and

uncertainty about the profitability of investments may lead to cyclical movements of the capital goods stock (Bernanke [1983]).
This chapter concentrates on the consequences of an exogeneously given business cycle for the optimal policies of a firm, while investments are irreversible. Section 5.2 discusses the model and gives the necessary and sufficient conditions for optimality. Section 5.3 discusses the optimal policy for different degrees of severeness of the recession if equity is cheaper than debt ($i<(1-f)r$). Section 5.4 does the same for the opposite case ($i>(1-f)r$). In section 5.5 this chapter is summarised and the main conclusions are presented.

5.2 The model and the optimality conditions

5.2.1 The model

In the literature survey in Chapter 2 it has been noted that there are two approaches to handle business cycles in a dynamic model of the firm. One approach explicitly models the fluctuations in economic activity, the other approach studies the behaviour of firms during business cycles by assuming that the steady state of the model changes exogeneously and studying the adaptive process of reaching the new steady state. In this chapter the first approach is applied.
The models in this chapter are partly based on three articles (Leban & Lesourne [1980,1983], Nickell [1974]) in which a firm faces a business cycle (for a discussion of these articles, see Chapter 2). Nickell studies the investment behaviour of the firm over a business cycle and concludes that the expectations of the firm on the demand function are a crucial determinant of that investment behaviour. Leban & Lesourne sum up the means a firm has at its disposal to face economic fluctuations: "it can try to influence the market through pricing or products differentiation; it can create manufacturing capacities, finance research-development projects, invest or disinvest, recruit, let its staff decrease through voluntary quits, bear labour hoarding, fire, distribute more or less dividends, increase or not increase its equity, borrow or pay back its current debt" (p.201-202). In their articles, they concentrate on investing behaviour when there is irreversibility of investments, and on recruiting and firing policies. The last three items of their list of means, all concerning

financial policies, are not adressed in their articles, nor in the article by Nickell. Introduction of a business cycle in the basic model of Chapter 4 makes it possible to study these financial policies, within the same framework as used by Nickell and Leban & Lesourne.
The only thing to change in the model of Chapter 4 is the specification of the revenue function S(Q). From now on this revenue function will also be a function of time. To be more precise, let p(t,Q(t)) be the price per unit of output at time t if the total output at time t is Q(t). Now S(Q,t) = p(t,Q(t))Q(t). The specification of the price function is the same as in Nickell and Leban & Lesourne:

$$
\begin{aligned}
p(Q,t) &= \left[e^{-gt} Q(t) \right]^{-1/e} && \text{for } t \le t_0, \\
&= \left[e^{(m-g)t} e^{-mt_0} Q(t) \right]^{-1/e} && \text{for } t_0 < t \le t_1, \qquad (1) \\
&= \left[e^{-gt} e^{m(t_1 - t_0)} Q(t) \right]^{-1/e} && \text{for } t > t_1 .
\end{aligned}
$$

It is assumed that $e > 1$ and $m > g$[1].
In graphical form:

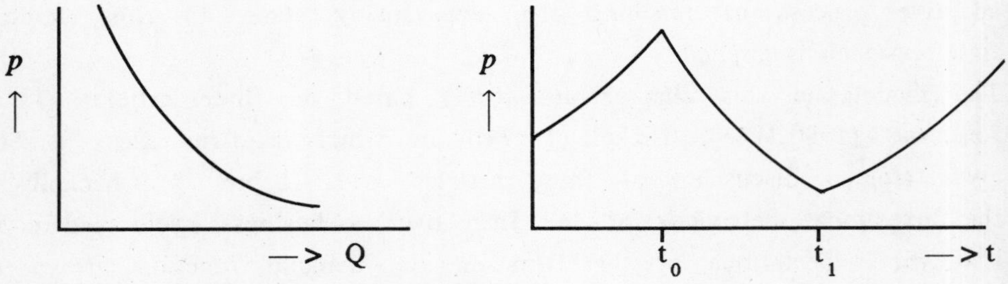

Figure 1: The demand function

In the left-hand figure, t is fixed, in the right-hand figure , Q is fixed. The left-hand figure shows the demand curve at a particular point of time, the right-hand figure shows how the demand curve changes over time. It can easily be derived from the algebraic formulation of p that for fixed Q the

[1]Note that p is not differentiable in t_0 and t_1. The Maximum Principle requires that all functions appearing in the model are continuously differentiable, but in Appendix 2 it is shown that the discontinuities of $\partial p/\partial t$ do not cause any trouble.

price elasticity of the demand curve is $-e$. So the price elasticity is constant over time. This implies that the so-called degree of monopoly ($1/e$) is also a constant. This reflects that the market conditions for the firm do not change; the business cycle affects its competitors in the same way.

Deliberately, only *one* recession is modelled. It is assumed that the expansion period following the recession is long enough for the firm to recover from the recession, so that the behaviour of the firm will be the same if it faces another recession.

The given specification of p leads to a linear relationship between marginal revenue and price and to relatively easy expressions for the rate of change of marginal revenue:

$$\partial S/\partial K(t) = (1/k)(1-1/e)*p(Q,t) \quad \text{for all t} \tag{2}$$

$$\frac{d\ \partial S/\partial K}{dt}(t) = \left\{ \frac{(g+a)K(t)-I(t)}{eK(t)} \right\} \partial S/\partial K(t) \text{ for } t<t_0 \text{ and } t>t_1, \tag{3}$$

$$\frac{d\ \partial S/\partial K}{dt}(t) = \left\{ \frac{(g+a-m)K(t)-I(t)}{eK(t)} \right\} \partial S/\partial K(t) \text{ for } t_0<t<t_1. \tag{4}$$

The complete model is:

$$\max_{I,D} \int_0^z e^{-it}D(t)\,dt + e^{-iz}X(z) \tag{5}$$

$$\dot{K}(t) = I(t) - aK(t) \tag{6}$$

$$\dot{X}(t) = (1-f)\ \{S[Q,t] - wL(t) - aK(t) - rY(t)\} - D(t) \tag{7}$$

$$Q(t) = K(t)/k, \qquad L(t) = lQ(t) = \frac{wl}{k} K(t) \tag{8}$$

$$K(t) = X(t) + Y(t) \tag{9}$$

$$Y(t) \geq 0 \tag{10}$$

$$Y(t) \leq bX(t) \tag{11}$$

$$0 \leq I(t) \leq I_{max} \tag{12}$$

$$0 \leq D(t) \leq D_{max} \tag{13}$$

Note that again Q, L, and Y can be eliminated. It is assumed, as before that i, a, r, k, l, b and f are constant and that $z>t_1$.

In the context of a business cycle it would be interesting to introduce the possibility to keep an inventory of finished goods. The reason to exclude this possibility is partly a heuristic assumption (it can of course also be a domain assumption, for instance in the case of perishable goods). An economic justification for not including inventories is given by Nickell [1974]: "It is reasonable to assume that one of the major roles of inventories is to protect the firm against inevitable small random fluctuations in demand. Since this model is focused on broad changes in demand, I do no think that their exclusion is a matter of very vital importance" (p.17)[2].

Another assumption of the model is that labour is employed on all capital goods. It would be interesting to study a model in which capital goods can be idle, with no labour working on it (see also p.37) In such a model, excess capacity may occur during a business cycle. Nickell [1974] shows that such excess capacity periods only occur if the recession is very long and/or steep.

The assumptions made in this chapter (no inventory, no idle capital) accentuate the effects of a business cycle on the investment and dividend policy of the firm. So, although they are partly mathematically motivated, for the purposes of this chapter these assumptions are reasonable.

The problem for the firm is clear: if in a recession marginal cost becomes larger than marginal revenue, it can try to shift along the demand curve by diminishing the capital goods stock and production. But this is only possible to a limited extent due to the irreversibility of investments. The capital goods stock can only diminish through depreciation. Thus there are two competing effects during a recession: price tends to increase as a consequence of a leftward shift *along* the demand curve, but it tends to decrease as a consequence of a downward shift *of* the demand curve.

5.2.2 The conditions for optimality

The necessary conditions for optimality are (14)-(24) of Chapter 4, with dS/dK replaced by $\partial S/\partial K$, since S is now a function of K and t. The

---

[2] For a deterministic continuous time optimal control inventory model, see Feichtinger and Hartl [1985]. In their model a firm chooses the optimal production and price paths, while demand is given. They make some remarks on the case of a cyclical demand.

definition of the feasible paths is also the same as for the basic model. However, the implications of this definition for the values of dK/dt, dX/dt and dY/dt are not the same. For instance, if $\partial S/\partial K$ is constant, it can no longer be concluded that K is constant. For the details and an enumeration of all feasible strings, see Appendix 2.1.

5.3 The optimal solution in case $i<(1\text{-}f)r$

5.3.1 Introduction

As in Chapter 4, a distinction has to be made between $i<(1\text{-}f)$r ('equity is cheaper than debt') and $i>(1\text{-}f)r$ ('debt is cheaper than equity'). This section studies the case $i<(1\text{-}f)r$. In Chapter 4 it is shown how the firm reaches the final, 'desired' path (in this case path 1). Now suppose that the firm is on path 1 when the message is received that a recession is likely to occur, beginning t_0 time periods later. To study the consequences of such a forecasted recession on the optimal policy of the firm, it is assumed that the time at which the message is received is time zero. So the magnitude of t_0 can be seen as a measure of how early the recession is anticipated. Since the firm is on path 1 at time zero:

$$Y(0) = 0 \quad \text{and} \quad \frac{\partial S}{\partial K}(0) = \frac{wl}{k} + a + \frac{i}{(1\text{-}f)} \tag{14}$$

Because the central feature in this model is the business cycle, the parameter m has a special role: for arbitrary but fixed values of all other parameters the optimal string is studied for different values of m. Note that for given g, the magnitude of m is a measure for the severeness of the recession. Remember that m must be larger than g (see (1)). During the recession, marginal revenue tends to decrease, due to the downward shift of the demand curve (see (4)). Consequently, the profitability of investments prior to and during the recession is reduced, as is the 'accounting cash-flow'. This indicates that two crucial aspects of the optimal policy will be:

1) Does the reduced profitability of investments lead to a complete (temporary) stop of investments (I=0)?; if so, when does the firm stop investments and when does it resume investments?

2) Does the reduced 'accounting cash-flow' lead to liquidity problems (that is, will the cash-flow become negative), forcing the firm to borrow during the recession?; if so, will it be able to pay it back?; if so, when?

In the following subsections the optimal policies are given for increasing values of m, and the crucial values of m, for which the optimal policy qualitatively changes, are derived. For each optimal policy, the development over time of marginal revenue ∂S/∂K, capital goods stock K, equity X, debt Y, investments I and dividends D is given.

5.3.2 A 'light' recession ($g < m \leq g+a$)

At t=0 the firm is on path 1. Staying on path 1 for t>0 implies maintaining both equalities in (14) and using the remaining 'accounting cash-flow' to pay dividends. During an expansion, (3) gives the rate of change of ∂S/∂K:

$$\frac{d\ \partial S/\partial K}{dt}(t) = \left\{ \frac{(g+a)K(t)-I(t)}{eK(t)} \right\} \frac{\partial S}{\partial K}(t) \qquad (15)$$

Maintaining the equality of marginal revenue and marginal costs implies keeping ∂S/∂K constant, since marginal costs

$$\frac{wl}{k} + a + \frac{i}{(1-f)} \qquad (16)$$

are constant. From equation (15) it is clear that this implies $I(t)=(g+a)K(t)$. Thus K grows at an exponential rate g. So during an expansion the firm can stay on path 1[3].

During a recession (4) gives the rate of change of ∂S/∂K:

$$\frac{d\ \partial S/\partial K}{dt}(t) = \left\{ \frac{(g+a-m)K(t)-I(t)}{eK(t)} \right\} \frac{\partial S}{\partial K}(t) \text{ for } t_0 < t < t_1 \qquad (17)$$

(17) reveals that keeping marginal revenue constant during a recession asks for $I(t)=\{g+a-m\}K(t)$. Thus the firm is able to keep marginal revenue (and price) at a constant level without violating the irreversibility of investment constraint if and only if $g+a-m \geq 0$. As long as $m-g$, the 'rate of decrease' of the demand function is smaller than or equal to the rate of depreciation a, the firm can compensate the downward shift of the demand curve with a leftward shift along the curve (note that the value of the price elasticity does not matter in this respect). Thus, for $m \in (g, g+a]$, the

---

[3]It is assumed that path 1 is a feasible path during an expansion, which means that there is enough 'accounting cash-flow' to invest $(g+a)K(t)$ and to pay out dividend. It is easily derived that for $t<t_0$ this assumption implies: $(wl/k+a)/e + (i-g(1-1/e))/(1-f) \geq 0$.

optimal policy is to stay on path 1 during the recession. Figure 2 shows the development over time of the relevant variables.

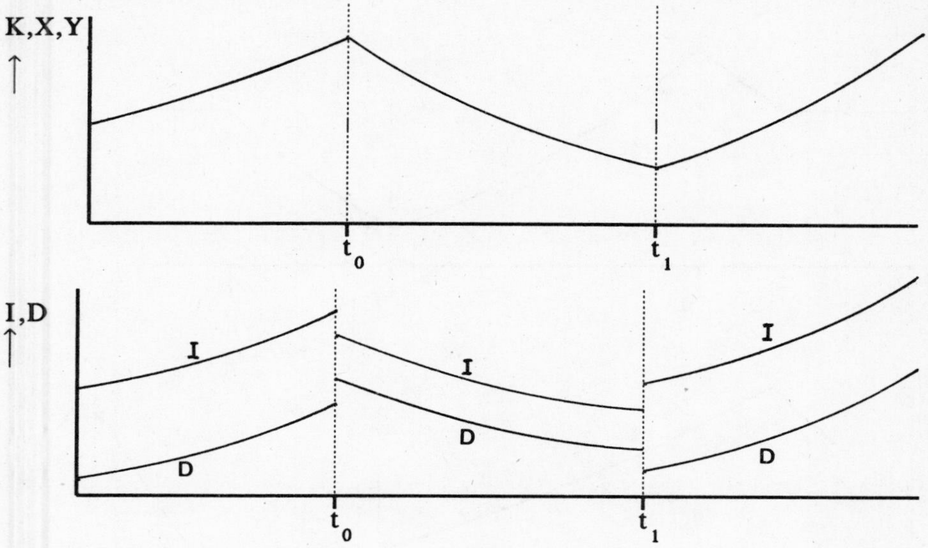

Figure 2: The optimal policy if $m \in (g, g+a]$

Staying on path 1 implies a cyclical movement of the capital goods stock, investments, equity, and dividends, following the movement of the economic activity: K, I, X, D increase until t_0, decrease between t_0 and t_1, and increase again after t_1.
In fact, the optimal solution of the model in this case ($g+a-m>0$) for *arbitrary* initial conditions is to reach path 1 as quickly as possible, just like in the basic model. The 'extra' dynamics does not influence the structure of the solution : the optimal decision at time t does not depend on t, but only on K(t) and X(t). The decision rule can be used to find the optimal solution.

5.3.3 A 'moderate' recession ($g+a<m\leq m^*$)

The previous subsection shows that to keep marginal revenue constant during the recession, investments must equal $\{g+a-m\}$K(t). So if $m>g+a$, the firm will not be able to keep marginal revenue constant (and equal to marginal cost), due to the irreversibility of investments constraint. In this case the optimal string is 1-5-1. Figure 3 shows the optimal development over time of the relevant variables if $m \in (g+a, m^*]$, where the critical value m^* is explained later on.

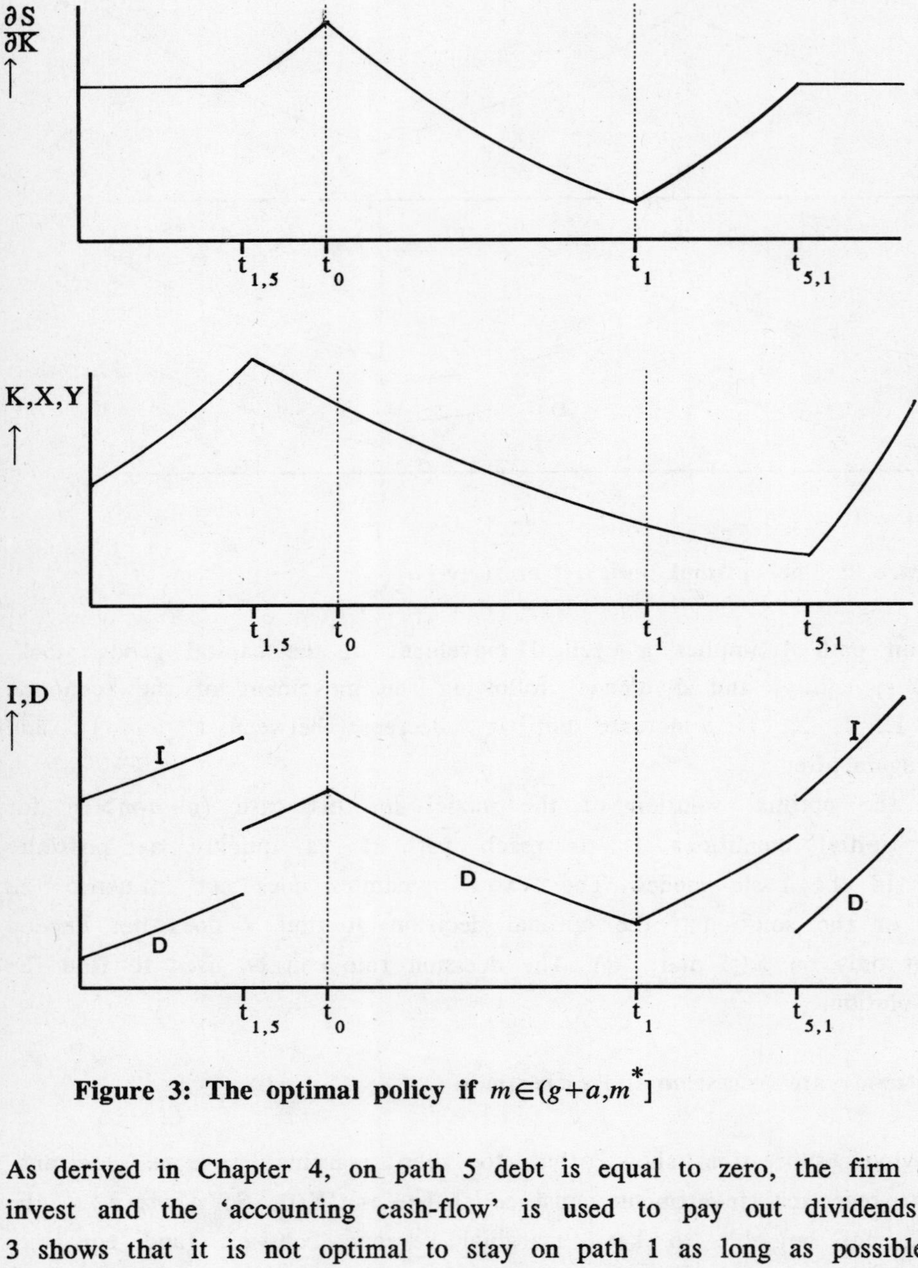

Figure 3: The optimal policy if $m \in (g+a, m^*]$

As derived in Chapter 4, on path 5 debt is equal to zero, the firm does not invest and the 'accounting cash-flow' is used to pay out dividends. Figure 3 shows that it is not optimal to stay on path 1 as long as possible (which would mean up to t_0). At $t_{1,5}$ the firm decides to give up the remaining growth opportunities: it stops investment and consequently marginal revenue

grows and becomes larger than marginal costs (which are constant). During the recession price and marginal revenue decrease. At a certain time during the recession, marginal revenue falls below marginal cost: the firm is too large, given the circumstances. The firm will continue to contract its capital goods stock after t_1 until marginal revenue equals marginal cost again. As Leban & Lesourne [1980] observe, the fact that $t_{1,5}$ is smaller than t_0 indicates that "an anticipation of a recession may be sufficient to generate a recession" (p.69). The reason that the firm stops investing *before* the recession starts is that it seeks an optimal balance between 'leaving path 1 as late as possible during the first expansion' and 'returning to path 1 as quickly as possible during the second expansion'.
As in the case of the light recession, K and X show a cyclical pattern, but their 'downswing' is now longer than the expected length of the recession. Dividends jump upward when the firm switches from path 1 to path 5, since the 'accounting cash-flow' that is no longer spent on investments can be paid out as dividends. During the recession dividends decrease rapidly, since both p and K decrease (implying a rapid decrease of revenue S).
The two conditions determining the switching points $t_{1,5}$ and $t_{5,1}$ are:

a) since $\partial S/\partial K = wl/k + a + i/(1\text{-}f)$ on path 1 and $\partial S/\partial K$ is continuous, this equality must hold at $t_{1,5}$ as well as at $t_{5,1}$. This is equivalent to:

$$\int_{t_{1,5}}^{t_{5,1}} \frac{d}{dt}\frac{\partial S}{\partial K}(\tau)\, d\tau = 0 \tag{18}$$

In Appendix 2 it is shown that (18) is equivalent to:

$$t_{5,1} - t_{1,5} = \frac{m}{g+a}(t_1 - t_0) \tag{19}$$

(19) shows that the heavier the recession (i.e. the larger m-g), the longer the 'zero investment'-period. Leban & Lesourne and Nickell, who use the same specification of the demand function, also find equation (19). So, the introduction in the model of financial variables does not lead, at this point, to different conclusions concerning the length of the 'zero investment'- period.

b) $\lambda_1(t_{1,5}) = \lambda_1(t_{5,1}) = 0$ and $\lambda_1(t) < 0$ for $t \in (t_{1,5}, t_{5,1})$. (20)

Appendix 2 shows that this implies:

$$\int_{t_{1,5}}^{z} e^{-(i+a)(\tau - t_{1,5})} \left\{\frac{\partial S}{\partial K} - \left[\frac{wl}{k} + a + \frac{i}{1\text{-}f}\right]\right\} d\tau = 0 \tag{21}$$

$$\int_t^z e^{-(i+a)(\tau-t)} \left\{\frac{\partial S}{\partial K} - \left[\frac{wl}{k} + a + \frac{i}{1-f}\right]\right\} d\tau < 0 \text{ for } t \in (t_{1,5}, t_{5,1}) \tag{22}$$

This can be interpreted as follows: during the 'zero investment'-period (path 5) the present value of future revenues due to an extra unit of investment is less than the present value of future costs. To understand this, note that one unit of capital bought at time t depreciates at rate a; thus at time τ this unit leads to marginal revenue equal to

$$e^{-a(\tau-t)} \partial S/\partial K,$$

and marginal costs equal to

$$e^{-a(\tau-t)} \left\{\frac{wl}{k}+a+\frac{i}{(1-f)}\right\}$$

Thus the integrals in (21) and (22) denote the discounted value of the revenues minus costs generated by one unit of capital over the remanining part of the planning horizon. In other words, the 'net' present value.[4]

Similar conditions are found by Nickell and Leban & Lesourne.

Equations (19) and (21) constitute two equations with two unknowns, $t_{1,5}$ and $t_{5,1}$. Table 1 gives the derivatives of $t_{1,5}$ and $t_{5,1}$ with regard to the parameters. If possibe, they were derived analytically, otherwise numerically.

	w	k	l	r	f	t_0	t_1	i	g	m	a	e
$dt_{1,5}/d..$	0	0	0	0	0	+	-	+	+	-	+	-
$dt_{5,1}/d..$	0	0	0	0	0	-	+	+	-	+	-	-
method	A	A	A	A	A	N	N	N	N	N	N	N

Table 1: Sensitivity analysis for $t_{1,5}$ and $t_{5,1}$

"A" stands for analytic, "N" for numeric.

When reading this table it is important to keep in mind that the derivation

---

[4]Note that the *revenues* and *costs* are discounted. For an extensive treatment of the use, in dynamic models of the firm, of the net present value rule based on *cash-flows*, see Kort [1989].

of $t_{1,5}$ and $t_{5,1}$ uses (14). So if *w,k,l,a,i* or *f* change, $\partial S/\partial K(0)$ automatically changes, and thus the initial values of the state variables change. Consequently, the value of the marginal cost $(wl/k+a+i/(1-f))$ does not influence $t_{1,5}$ and $t_{5,1}$. This explains the derivatives with regard to *w,k,l,* and *f*. So, the wage costs per unit of capital and the level of the corporate tax rate do not influence the length and the position of the 'zero investment'-period, *given* the fact that at time zero marginal revenue equals marginal cost.
The parameters *a* and *i* have an additional effect on $t_{1,5}$ and $t_{5,1}$. A higher *a* means that the firm can diminish its size more quickly during the recession. For a given value of *m*, this means that the firm can stop investments later and resume investments earlier. If *i* is large, events close to $t=0$ get more important, so the firm will try to benefit more from the growth of the economy before t_0 and thus it will postpone the 'zero investment'-period.
The derivatives of $t_{1,5}$ and $t_{5,1}$ with regard to *e* are negative. To understand this remember that during the 'zero investment'-period, the firm tries to decrease the capital goods stock as quickly as possible to offsett the consequences of the downward shift of the demand curve. If *e*, the price elasticity of demand, is large, a relatively large decrease of the capital goods stock is necessary to bring about a certain increase in price. To compensate this, the firm will stop growing earlier.
The remaining derivatives in Table 1 are self-evident.

The string 1-5-1 is optimal as long as $t_{1,5}$ is positive and the firm has enough 'accounting cash-flow' on path 5 to pay a positive or zero dividend during the whole recession. Table 1 shows that the heavier the recession (the larger *m*), the smaller $t_{1,5}$. It is assumed that t_0 is 'large', so that $t_{1,5}$ is positive ($dt_{1,5}/dt_0>0$, see table 1)[5]. This means that the firm starts on path 1.
It is obvious that for a 'large' *m*, marginal revenue is small during the recession and thus there is not much 'accounting cash-flow' available to pay a positive dividend. For a certain crucial value of *m* (named m^*), dividends on path 5 become zero during the recession. For values of *m*

---

[5]In Appendix 2 strings beginning with path 5 are also studied and it is shown that 1-5-1 and 5-1 cannot both be optimal for the same set of parameters.

larger than this m^*, the optimal policy qualitatively changes. In Appendix 2 it is shown that this m^* equals:

$$m^* = \frac{(g+a)(t_1 - t_{1,5}) - e\ln\Phi}{t_1 - t_0} \tag{23}$$

where $\Phi = (1-1/e) * (wl/k - fa/(1-f)) \,/\, (wl/k + a + i/(1-f))$[6].

The timepoint at which the 'accounting cash-flow' becomes negative is named t^*. It is interesting to see how the parameters influence t^*. The following table gives the derivatives of t^*, partly derived analytically, partly numerically.

	w	k	l	r	f	t_0	t_1	i	g	m	a	e
$dt^*/d\ldots$	-	+	-	0	+	+	+	-	+	-	+	±
method	A	A	A	A	A	N	N	N	N	N	N	N

Table 2: Sensitivity analysis for t^*

"A" stands for analytic, "N" for numeric.

To analyse this table note that the characteristics of path 5 (see Chapter 4 or Appendix 1) imply that dividends become zero when

---

[6]Note that (23) only makes sense if $\Phi > 0$, that is, if

$$\frac{wl}{k} - \frac{fa}{(1-f)} > 0$$

If the left hand side of this expression is negative, the wage costs per unit of capital are less than the tax deductions per unit of capital due to depreciation. In that case dividends would never become zero during the recession, and consequently liquidity problems would not occur, irrespective of the value of *m*! However, in the model it is implicitly assumed that if profits (S(Q)-*w*L-*a*K) are negative, the government 'pays taxes' to the firm (see for instance (7)). In practice, losses can be 'carried back or forward' to reduce the tax bill in other years. In the model the firm in fact receives this reduction at the moment that it incurs a loss. It is clear that a realistic treatment of these 'carry back and forward' opportunities would complicate the model considerably, but it would not change the message: liquidity problems occur if the value of *m* is 'high enough'. So, although the precise value of m^* has no real meaning, it is reasonable to assume that m^* does make sense. Moreover, even within the context of the model, parameter configurations for which $wl/k - fa/(1-f)$ is negative are extreme.

$$\frac{\partial S}{\partial K} = (1\text{-}1/e)\left\{wl - \frac{fak}{(1\text{-}f)}\right\} \tag{24}$$

Note that the right hand side of (24) is a constant, and that ∂S/∂K decreases during the recession. The higher the right hand side of (24) or the lower the right hand side, the earlier ∂S/∂K reaches the right hand side of (24).

The level of ∂S/∂K during the recession is determined by m, g, e, a (see (3) and (4)), the value of $t_{1,5}$, and the value of ∂S/∂K at $t=t_{1,5}$ which is:

$$\frac{wl}{k} + a + \frac{i}{(1\text{-}f)} \tag{25}$$

This implies that w, l, k, f, a, and e influence the right hand side as well as the left hand side of (24), and i influences the left hand side of (24) in a complicated way. The derivatives in Table 2 measure the net effect of the different influences. As an example consider the derivative of t^* with regard to e, which is negative for e close to 1 and positive for large e. Note that e affects t^* in two ways: a larger e diminishes the difference of the marginal revenue at the beginning of path 5 and marginal revenue at t^* (compare (24) and (25)); this tends to make t^* smaller; and a larger e decreases the rate at which ∂S/∂K decreases during the recession, $(m\text{-}g\text{-}a)/e$; this tends to make t^* larger. Thus there are two opposing effects of e plus the effect of e on t^* through $t_{1,5}$, and apparently the net result depends on the value of e.

5.3.4 A 'severe recession' ($m^* < m \leq m^{**}$)

If cash-flow problems occur during the recession, the firm has no other choice than to borrow money to meet its obligations (to pay wages). If the firm survives the recession it will pay back the debt as soon as possible, since debt is expensive ($i < (1\text{-}f)r$). Borrowing means entering path 7. On path 7 dividends and investments are zero and the 'accounting cash-flow' equals -dY/dt (see Appendix 1). This means that if the 'accounting cash-flow' is negative, exactly that amount will be borrowed and Y will rise, while if the 'accounting cash-flow' is positive, it is used to pay off debt. It can easily be seen that Y increases during the recession, so at time t_1, at the end of the recession debt is positive and (as in the previous subsection) marginal revenue is less than marginal cost. For $t > t_1$ the decision rule of Chapter 4 can be applied to find the optimal trajectory towards the final path 1. For values of m sufficiently close to

m^*, Figure 4 shows the optimal policy:

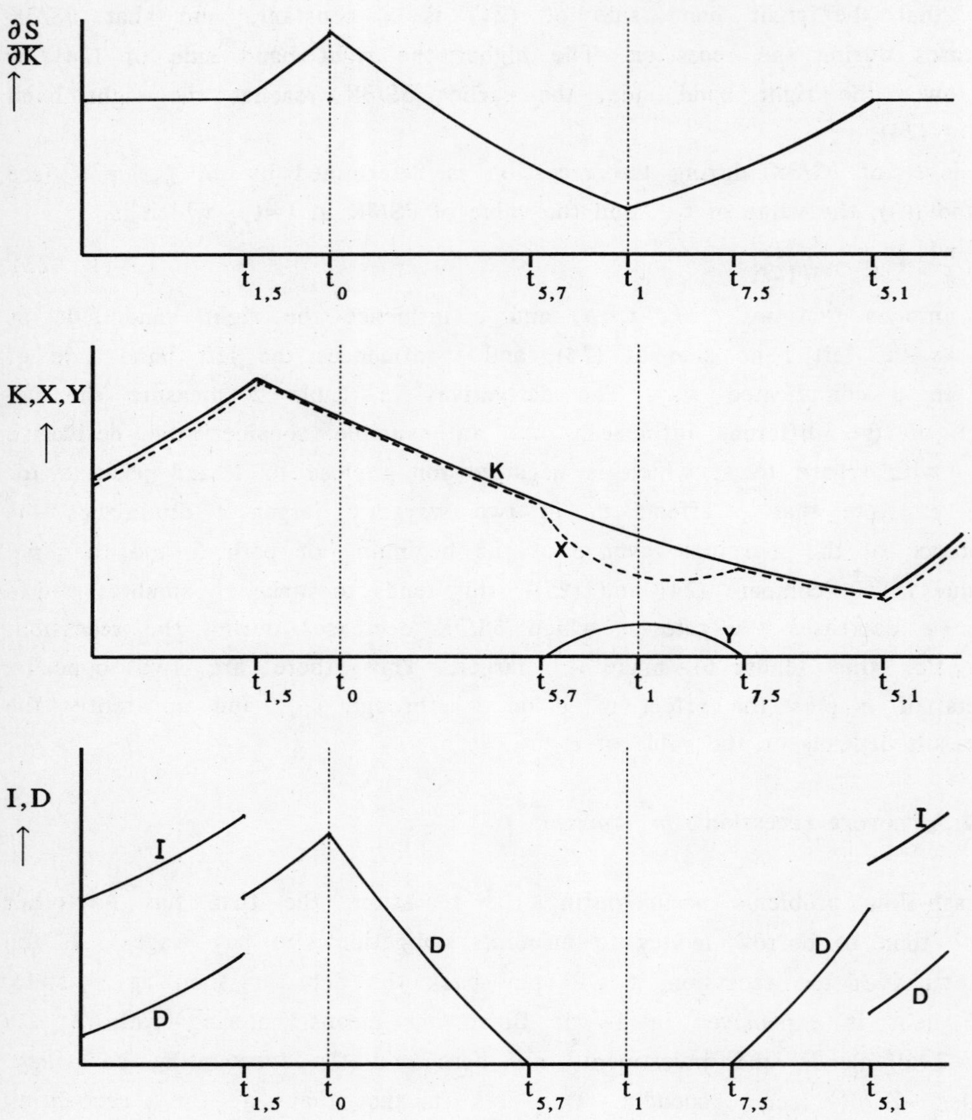

Figure 4: The optimal policy for *m* close to m^*

The development of ∂S/∂K and K, as well as the length of the 'zero investment'-period are the same as for the string 1-5-1. During the 'debt period' no dividends are paid and the stock of equity decreases to a lower level than it does on string 1-5-1.

There are four conditions to determine the switching points $t_{1,5}$, $t_{5,7}$, $t_{7,5}$, and $t_{5,1}$ [7]. These conditions are discussed in detail in Appendix 2. The first condition is (see (24)):

'accounting cash-flow' equals zero at the end of path 5 (at $t_{1,5}$) (26)

The second condition is:

debt equals zero at $t_{5,7}$ and at $t_{7,5}$ $\Rightarrow$ $\int_{t_{5,7}}^{t_{7,5}} \frac{dY}{dt}(\tau)\, d\tau = 0$ (27)

The third condition is the same as (18):

$$\int_{t_{1,5}}^{t_{5,1}} \frac{d}{dt}\frac{\partial S}{\partial K}(\tau)\, d\tau = 0 \tag{28}$$

This implies, since the differential equation for $\partial S/\partial K$ is the same on path 5 and path 7, that (19) is again valid, which means that the length of the 'zero investment'-period is the same for string 1-5-7-5-1 as for 1-5-1.

The fourth condition is the same as (20):

$$\lambda_1(t_{1,5}) = \lambda_1(t_{5,1}) = 0 \text{ and } \lambda_1(t) < 0 \text{ for } t \in (t_{1,5}, t_{5,1}). \tag{29}$$

This condition is now more complicated since λ_1 is discontinuous at time $t_{5,7}$ (see the end of Appendix 1). The analog of (21) is:

$$\int_{t_{1,5}}^{t_{5,7}} e^{-(i+a)(\tau-t_{1,5})} (1-f)\left\{\frac{\partial S}{\partial K} - \left[\frac{wl}{k} + a + \frac{i}{1-f}\right]\right\} d\tau \; +$$

$$\int_{t_{5,7}}^{t_{7,5}} e^{-(i+a)(\tau-t_{1,5})} (1-f)\lambda_2(\tau)\left\{\frac{\partial S}{\partial K} - \left[\frac{wl}{k} + a + r\right]\right\} d\tau \; +$$

$$\int_{t_{7,5}}^{z} e^{-(i+a)(\tau-t_{1,5})} (1-f)\left\{\frac{\partial S}{\partial K} - \left[\frac{wl}{k} + a + \frac{i}{1-f}\right]\right\} d\tau \; +$$

$$e^{-(i+a)(t_{5,7}-t_{1,5})} * \eta_1 = 0, \tag{30}$$

where η_1, the magnitude of the jump of λ_1 at $t_{5,7}$ equals:

---

[7]Note that, $t_{1,5}$ and $t_{5,1}$ are now switching times of the string 1-5-7-5-1 which in general will not coincide with the switching times of the string 1-5-1, even though $t_{5,1}$-$t_{1,5}$ is the same for both strings!

$$\eta_1 = \int_{t_{5,7}}^{t_{7,5}} \{(1-f)r-i\}\ \lambda_2(\tau)\ d\tau \tag{31}$$

Equation (30) can, in the same way as (21), be interpreted as: the 'net present value' of an investment at $t_{1,5}$ equals zero.

The first and the third integral are similar to (21): they denote the discounted value of the marginal revenue minus marginal costs due to a unit of capital bought at time $t=t_{1,5}$ during the interval $[t_{1,5},t_{5,7}]$ resp. $[t_{7,5},z]$. Marginal costs include wage costs, depreciation costs and financing costs. Financing costs are $i/(1-f)$, the cost of equity. In the second integral two things are different: λ_2 appears and the financing costs are r instead of $i/(1-f)$. The appearance of r is not difficult to understand: on path 7 the 'accounting cash-flow' is zero, thus an additional unit of capital can only be financed with debt; this implies that the marginal financing costs of investment are r. The appearance of λ_2 is more difficult to understand. An extra capital good installed at time $t_{1,5}$ leads to an extra revenue

$$e^{-a(\tau-t_{1,5})}\ \partial S/\partial K(\tau),$$

at time τ. This implies that $\dot{X}$ rises with this amount (see (7)). The contribution, at time τ, of this rise of $\dot{X}$ to the objective function is measured by $\lambda_2(\tau)$ (see also (4.25)). So the contribution, at time τ, to the objective function of an extra capital good installed at time $t_{1,5}$ equals

$$e^{-a(\tau-t_{1,5})}\lambda_2(\tau)\frac{\partial S}{\partial K}(\tau).$$

Likewise for the extra costs. So

$$\int_{t_{5,7}}^{t_{7,5}} e^{-(i+a)(\tau-t_{1,5})}\ (1-f)\lambda_2(\tau)\left\{\frac{\partial S}{\partial K} - \left[\frac{wl}{k} + a + r\right]\right\} d\tau$$

measures the total contribution to the objective function during the interval $(t_{5,7},t_{7,5})$ generated by an extra unit of capital installed at time $t_{1,5}$, discounted to time $t_{1,5}$.

Now the obvious question is of course: why does λ_2 not appear in the first and third integral of (30) and in (21-22)? In fact, it does occur, but on path 5 $\lambda_2 = 1$[8].

There are two differences with regard to the interpretation of (21-22) and (30), compared to Leban & Lesourne and Nickell. In the first place, in Leban & Lesourne and Nickell the financing cost is, in all cases, simply the discount rate. In the model of this chapter, the financing cost depend on the source of funds used, which in turn depends on the financial situation of the firm. In the second place, the objective function of Leban & Lesourne and Nickell is the discounted value of revenues minus expenses; the effects of extra unit of capital have the same 'dimension'. In this thesis, however, these effects (revenues and costs) have to be translated in terms of dividends (that is, multiplied by the shadow price of equity). If λ_2 is larger than one, marginal costs and revenues are valued higher, because equity is 'extra' valuable (more equity would mean less expensive debt).

To complete the interpretation of (30) the appearance of the jump has to be explained. Note that η_1 is positive, so that the 'jump-term' in (30) has the same sign as marginal revenue. Apparently the upward jump of the shadow price of equity may be seen as a revenue. I have not found a satisfactory explanation of the magnitude of the jump from an economic point of view.

The analogue of (22) has to be split in two seperate conditions, one for $t < t_{5,7}$ and one for $t > t_{5,7}$:

$$\int_{t}^{t_{5,7}} e^{-(i+a)(\tau-t)} (1-f) \left\{\frac{\partial S}{\partial K} - \left[\frac{wl}{k} + a + \frac{i}{1-f}\right]\right\} d\tau \ +$$

$$\int_{t_{5,7}}^{t_{7,5}} e^{-(i+a)(\tau-t)} (1-f)\lambda_2(\tau) \left\{\frac{\partial S}{\partial K} - \left[\frac{wl}{k} + a + r\right]\right\} d\tau \ +$$

$$\int_{t_{7,5}}^{z} e^{-(i+a)(\tau-t)} (1-f) \left\{\frac{\partial S}{\partial K} - \left[\frac{wl}{k} + a + \frac{i}{1-f}\right]\right\} d\tau \ +$$

$$e^{-(i+a)(t_{5,7}-t)} * \eta_1 < 0, \quad \text{for } t < t_{5,7} \qquad (32)$$

[8]In Chapter 6 it is explained *why* $\lambda_2 = 1$ on path 5.

$$\int_{t}^{t_{7,5}} e^{-(i+a)(\tau-t)} (1-f)\lambda_2(\tau) \left\{\frac{\partial S}{\partial K} - \left[\frac{wl}{k} + a + r\right]\right\} d\tau \quad +$$

$$\int_{t_{7,5}}^{z} e^{-(i+a)(\tau-t)} (1-f) \left\{\frac{\partial S}{\partial K} - \left[\frac{wl}{k} + a + \frac{i}{1-f}\right]\right\} d\tau < 0 \text{ for } t>t_{5,7} \quad (33)$$

Together (32) and (33) denote that the net present value of an investment at time $t \in (t_{1,5}, t_{5,1})$ is negative.
Of the four equations for the 'switching-points' of the string 1-5-7-5-1, two are very large and complicated non-linear equations (see (A2.22) and (A2.26)). It is impossible to solve these equations analytically for the four timepoints. In Appendix 2 the results of a numerical solution of the set of equations are summarised.

For larger values of *m*, debt Y will reach a higher level. Provided that Y does not reach its upper bound, this means that it will take the firm longer to pay back the debt. So the 'contraction process' after t_1 (which can be derived using the decision rule, as said before) gets more complicated. The string 1-5-7-5-1 is replaced by 1-5-7-3-1, which in turn is replaced by 1-5-7-4-3-1. The details of these strings can be found in Appendix 2. The contraction process 7-4-3-1 is pictured in Figure 3 of Chapter 4. It is interesting to note that for the strings 1-5-7-3-1 and 1-5-7-4-3-1, the 'zero investment'-period is *longer* than for the strings 1-5-1 and 1-5-7-5-1. So if the recession is very hard, the liquidity problems of the firm influence the length of the 'zero investment'-period. This is a nice example of how financing decisions and investment decisions are related. Note that it is not true that the mere presence of a 'debt period' leads to a longer 'zero investment'-period, since for 1-5-7-5-1 it has the same length as for 1-5-1 (see page 73).

5.3.5 A fatal recession

In the previous subsection it was assumed that debt does not reach its upper bound. If debt is on its upper bound *b*X and the 'accounting cash-flow' is negative, the firm is bankrupt. If the firm goes bankrupt at a certain time t, the model of this chapter is not an adequate model, as explained in section 4.6. This subsection studies the circumstances under which the firm goes bankrupt.

The firm will certainly go bankrupt if the amount of debt explodes. The interest expenses rise as long as Y rises. It might happen that after t_1 the rise of the interest expenses dominates the rise of the 'accounting cash-flow', which implies that the firm has to borrow more, etcetera. To decide whether Y explodes or not, the differential equation of Y on path 7 is solved in Appendix 2. The results are:

If

$$(g+a)/e-a-r(1-f) > 0, \tag{34}$$

debt will not explode. Note that since I=0 on path 7, K decreases at rate a, and thus total revenue, pK increases during an expansion at rate $(g+a)/e-a$. The interest expenses increase at rate $(1-f)r$. So (34) implies that total revenues increase faster than interest expenses. It is understandable that in this case debt does not explode.

If

$$(g+a)/e-a-r(1-f) < 0, \tag{35}$$

whether debt explodes or not, depends on the level of debt at the moment that the 'accounting cash-flow' before interest becomes positive. If the level of debt is relatively low at that point of time, the firm succeeds in paying back this debt, despite the fact that interest expenses increase faster than total revenue. If Y is relatively large, debt explodes. In other words, since the interest expenses rise fast, the firm only survives if it can pay back the debt quickly. Appendix 2 gives some numerical examples.

Even if debt does not explode the firm can go bankrupt, namely if debt is still increasing as it reaches its upper bound. It is clear that the firm can try to avoid bankruptcy by stopping investment immediately at t=0. So if the firm goes bankrupt (that is, there is no solution to our model obeying all constraints), it must be that the restriction $Y \leq bX$ is even violated for strings beginning with path 5, followed by path 7. For a string beginning with 5-7, the value of m can be computed, for which the firm is at one moment on the brink of bankruptcy but does not go bankrupt. This value of m is named m^{**}. In Appendix 2 it is shown how m^{**} can be derived.The firm will certainly go bankrupt if $m > m^{**}$.

5.4 The optimal solution in case $i > (1\text{-}f)r$

5.4.1 Introduction

This section treats the case $(1\text{-}f)r < i$. It will be much shorter than section 3, since many aspects of the optimal solution for the case $(1\text{-}f)r < i$ are similar to their counterparts for the case $i < (1\text{-}f)r$.
If $(1\text{-}f)r < i$, debt is cheap. In Chapter 4 it was argued that if S is not a function of t, the optimal strategy for almost all situations is: whatever the investment/dividend decision is, attract maximal debt as quickly as possible and maintain $Y = bX$ for the rest of the planning period. The only exception was the case where maximal debt leads to bankruptcy. The same phenomenon appears in this section. Again it is assumed that at $t=0$ the firm is in its desired position, that is, path 2. This implies (see Chapter 4):

$$Y(0) = bX(0) \quad \text{and} \quad \frac{\partial S}{\partial K}(0) = \frac{wl}{k} + a + \frac{b}{1+b}\, r + \frac{1}{1+b}\,\frac{i}{1\text{-}f} \qquad (36)$$

Note that the last equality in (36) implies that marginal revenue equals marginal cost, where the financing costs are a weighted average of the cost of equity and the cost of debt (note that maximal debt implies $Y = \frac{b}{1+b}K$ and $X = \frac{1}{1+b}K$; see also p.42).

5.4.2 A 'light' recession ($g < m \leq g+a$)

This situation is completely analogous to the situation described in section 5.3.2, with path 2 instead of path 1.

5.4.3 A 'moderate' recession ($g+a < m \leq \hat{m}$)

If $g+a < m$, path 2 is not feasible during the recession. The firm is not able to keep $\partial S/\partial K$ on its desired level, since this would require a negative investment (see (4) or (17)). $\partial S/\partial K$ will decrease during the recession. To keep the 'damage' limited, the firm will stop investment during the recession and possibly even longer. The optimal string is 2-6-2 and the development of $\partial S/\partial K$, K, I and D over time has a similar pattern as in Figure 2. The only difference is that the firm maintains maximal debt. Path 6 is the analogue of path 5: investments equal zero, the firm maintains maximal debt and the remaining 'accounting cash-flow' is used to pay out dividends. The two conditions determining the switching points $t_{2,6}$ and $t_{6,2}$ are:

a) $$\frac{\partial S}{\partial K}(t_{2,6}) = \frac{\partial S}{\partial K}(t_{6,2}) = \frac{wl}{k}+a+\frac{b}{1+b}\,r+\frac{1}{1+b}\,\frac{i}{1-f} \qquad (37)$$

and thus:

$$\int_{t_{2,6}}^{t_{6,2}} \frac{d}{dt}\frac{\partial S}{\partial K}(\tau)\, d\tau = 0. \qquad (38)$$

This leads to:

$$t_{6,2}-t_{2,6} = \frac{m}{g+a}\,(t_1-t_0) \qquad (39)$$

Note that the length of the 'zero investment'- period is exactly the same as in the case $i<(1-f)r$ for the string 1-5-1.

b) $\lambda_1(t_{2,6})=\lambda_1(t_{6,2})=0$ and $\lambda_1(t)<0$ for $t\in(t_{2,6},t_{6,2})$ (40)

This is equivalent to:

$$\int_{t_{2,6}}^{z} e^{-(i+a)(\tau-t_{2,6})} \left\{\frac{\partial S}{\partial K} - \left[\frac{wl}{k} + a + \frac{b}{1+b}\,r + \frac{1}{1+b}\,\frac{i}{1-f}\right]\right\} d\tau = 0. \qquad (41)$$

$$\int_{t}^{z} e^{-(i+a)(\tau-t)} \left\{\frac{\partial S}{\partial K} - \left[\frac{wl}{k} + a + \frac{b}{1+b}\,r + \frac{1}{1+b}\,\frac{i}{1-f}\right]\right\} d\tau < 0, \text{ for } t\in(t_{2,6},t_{6,2}) \qquad (42)$$

These formulas can be interpreted in exactly the same way as (21) and (22). The 'net present value' of an investment is negative during the 'zero investment'-period. Only the financing costs are different now.

Equations (39) and (41) constitute two equations with two unknowns, $t_{2,6}$ and $t_{6,2}$. The derivatives of $t_{2,6}$ and $t_{6,2}$ are the same as in Table 1, and also b does nót influence $t_{2,6}$ and $t_{6,2}$.

If the recession is 'severe' (m is 'large'), it may happen, since marginal revenue decreases steadily, that the 'accounting cash-flow' becomes negative. In that case 2-6-2 is no longer a feasible strategy. The analogue of (23) is: the string 2-6-2 is no longer possible (since the 'accounting cash-flow' would become negative during the recession) if $m>\hat{m}$ (see Appendix 2, p.173).

$$\hat{m} = \frac{(g+a)(t_1 - t_{2,6}) - e\ln\Psi}{t_1 - t_0}, \tag{43}$$

where

$$\Psi = (1-1/e) * \frac{wl/k + a + br/(1+b) - a/((1-f)(1+b))}{wl/k + a + br/(1+b) + i/((1-f)(1+b))}$$ [9]

In section 5.3.3 a sensitivity analysis has been performed with regard to the timepoint where the 'accounting cash-flow' becomes negative. For the string 2-6-2 this timepoint is named $\hat{t}$. The derivatives of $\hat{t}$ with regard to the parameters have the same sign as the partial derivatives in Table 2, with the difference that $\hat{t}$ also depends on b and r.

1) $d\hat{t}/dr > 0$. If the rate of interest increases, the marginal costs per unit of capital increase, so one would expect that $\hat{t}$ would decrease. But if r increases, marginal revenue on path 2 increases and apparently this more than offsets the increase of marginal costs.

2) The effect of b on $\hat{t}$ depends on the value of b: $d\hat{t}/db > 0$ if $0 < b < (r - wl/k - a)/(r + wl/k + a)$, and $d\hat{t}/db < 0$ otherwise. This is intuitively not clear. A larger b means more debt and thus a lower marginal financing cost, since $(1-f)r < i$. But a higher b also means a lower marginal revenue on path 2. The total effect on $\hat{t}$ depends on the actual value of b. Note that $d\hat{t}/db < 0$ if $b > 1$.

5.4.4 A 'severe' recession ($m > \hat{m}$)

Suppose the firm stays on path 6 during the recession: the firm carries maximal debt, does not invest and pays out dividends; K, X and Y decrease at rate a; at a certain moment the 'accounting cash-flow' becomes insufficient to keep the debt-equity ratio constant, even if dividends are zero: to keep the debt equity ratio constant, the firm has to pay back debt: $\dot{Y}(t) = -aY(t)$; from (4.30) it can be seen that this implies that the 'accounting cash-flow' at time t must be at least as large as $aY(t)$. If this is no longer the case, maintaining the cash-flow identity (4.30) would require paying back debt at a lower rate, but this would raise the debt-equity ratio. But since this debt-equity ratio is already maximal, the

---

[9] See footnote 6.

firm would be bankrupt! However, if the firm foresees this, it will try to take precautionary measures. The firm will *not* employ the myopic strategy of maintaining maximal debt, come what may. It will pay back debt while it is still possible (at the cost of dividends!) to create a borrowing buffer for the 'hard times'. The optimal policy will now be: 2-6-7-6-2, which is depicted in Figure 5.

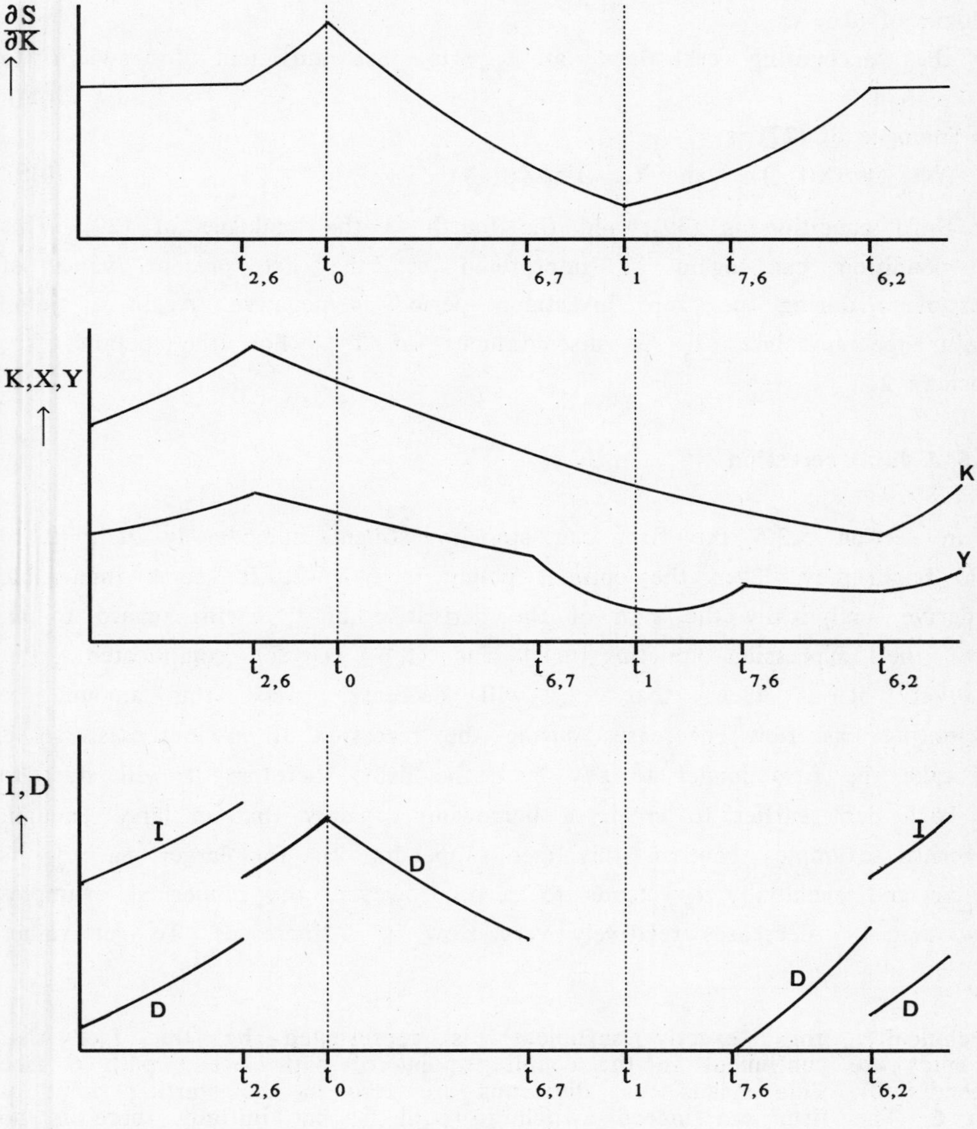

Figure 5: The optimal policy if $m > \hat{m}$

From $t_{6,7}$ onwards the firm stops paying out dividends and uses the available 'accounting cash-flow' to pay back debt in order to lower the debt-equity ratio. The firm will postpone $t_{6,7}$ as long as possible. In fact, it will time $t_{6,7}$ in such a way that at the moment that Y reaches its upper bound bX (at $t_{7,6}$), the 'accounting cash-flow' is exactly sufficient to switch back to path 6![10]. The string 2-6-7-6-2 is the analogue of 1-5-7-5-1. Again four conditions are needed for the 'switching times'. The analogue of (26) is:

the 'accounting cash-flow' at $t_{7,6}$ is just sufficient to switch to path 6 (44)

The analogue of (27) is:

$$Y(t_{6,7})=bX(t_{6,7}) \quad \text{and } Y(t_{7,6})=bX(t_{7,6}). \tag{45}$$

The third condition is (39), and the fourth is the analogue of (29). This last condition can again be interpreted as: the net present value of investments during the 'zero investment'-period is negative. Again a 'jump term' appears, since λ_2 is discontinuous at $t_{7,6}$. For the details, see Appendix 2.

5.4.5 A fatal recession

As in section 5.3.5 the firm can stop investment immediately at $t=0$ to avoid bankruptcy. Then the optimal policy is 6-7-6-2. It seems impossible to derive analytically the sign of the derivative of $t_{6,7}$ with regard to m, since the expression relating $t_{6,7}$ and $t_{7,6}$ is so complicated. But intuitively it is clear that $t_{6,7}$ will decrease, since the amount of 'accounting cash-flow' decreases during the recession if m increases, so it will take the firm longer to pay back the debt; therefore it will start to pay back debt earlier to create a borrowing capacity that is large enough. Numerical examples confirm this (see Appendix 2): for larger m, $t_{6,7}$ is smaller and eventually $t_{6,7}$ tends to zero. However, the numerical examples show that $t_{6,7}$ decreases relatively very slow if m increases. To get values

---

[10]Technically, this 'exactly sufficient' is represented by the fact that dividends are continuous in the coupling point of path 7 and path 6 (see Appendix 2). This means that dividends are zero in the starting point of path 6. The firm can indeed switch to path 6, but initially there is no money left to pay out dividends

of $t_{6,7}$ close to zero, one has to take unrealistically high values of *m*. The firm is bankrupt if $t_{6,7}$ is smaller than zero, because this means that even if the firm starts redeeming debt immediately at t=0, liquidity problems during the recession force the firm to accumulate debt at such a rate that the debt-equity ratio exceeds *b*. This happens when $m > \hat{\hat{m}}$, where $\hat{\hat{m}}$ is the analogue of m^{**}.

5.5 Summary and conclusions

This chapter discusses a model in which the firm faces a temporary recession. Section 5.3 treats the case where debt is expensive, section 5.4 treats the case where debt is cheap. For different values of 'severeness' of the recession the optimal policy is presented. Due to the sluggishness of the firm, represented by the irreversibility of investment constraint, during 'moderate' and 'severe' recessions the firm cannot painlessly adapt its size to the decreasing demand. The firm stops investment already before the recession begins and resumes investments some time after the end of the recession. During this 'zero investment'-period marginal revenue does not equal marginal cost. For 'severe' recessions, an additional problem for the firm is the possibility of a negative 'accounting cash-flow'. For the case of expensive debt this forces the firm to borrow, in order to meet its obligations. For the case of cheap debt this forces the firm to create a borrowing buffer for the 'hard times'. In both cases the liquidity problems may even cause bankruptcy, which may occur *after* the recession is over. For the case of cheap debt however, numerical examples show that bankruptcy only occurs for unrealistically high values of *m-g* (*m-g* indicates the severeness of the recession).

With regard to the length of the 'zero investment'-period, the same results have been found as in Nickel [1974] and Leban & Lesourne [1980,1983] (who do not include financial variables in their models), except for very severe recessions. Careful interpretation of the costate variables as shadow prices makes it possible to interpret the 'zero investment'-period as the period in which the net present value of investments is negative. Unfortunately, no economic interpretation has been found for the magnitude of the jump of the shadow price of equity.

Sensitivity analysis is performed for the starting and ending point of the 'zero investment'-period and the time point at which the 'accounting cash-flow' becomes negative on the strings 1-5-1 and 2-6-2. One of the results is that the wage costs do not influence the starting and ending point of the 'zero investment'-period, but they do influence the time point at which the accounting cash-flow becomes negative: higher wage costs force the firm to leave the 'desired' level of debt (i.e zero resp. maximal) for smaller values of m. The sensitivity analysis with regard to many parameters can only be performed numerically, since these parameters have different, opposite effects. Especially the effect of the price elasticity is complicated.

From a technical point of view the most interesting feature of the model in this chapter is the fact that the model is non-autonomous: time enters the problem explicitly (that is, not only through the state and control variables) because of the cyclical movement of the demand function. As a consequence, the optimal solution cannot be described with the decision rule derived in Chapter 4: the optimal choice of the control variables at a certain point of time not only depends on the values of the state variables at that point of time; it also depends on the rate of change of the demand function at that point of time (is it shifting upwards or downwards) and on the entire future development of the demand function.

Interesting extensions of the model would be models in which: the firm has the possibility to vary the utilisation rates of the production factors; the firm has the possibility to keep an inventory of finished goods; the cyclical movement of the demand function is accompanied by cyclical movements of parameters (for instance the interest rate or the discount rate).

6

SHADOW PRICES IN A MODEL WITH PURE STATE CONSTRAINTS

6.1 Introduction

The concept of 'shadow prices' is often used in economic analysis. Many books and articles appeared on the existence of shadow prices in dynamic optimisation models (e.g., Maurer [1984], Peterson [1973]) and their usefulness in economics (e.g., Intriligator [1971]). Of course, the most prominent feature of dynamic shadow prices is that they are functions of time. In Optimal Control Theory, especially the shadow prices belonging to the state variables play an important role in the economic interpretation of optimal solutions (e.g., Dorfman [1969]). The shadow price of a state variable, which in technical terms is the value of the costate variable (see p.39), is the rate of change of the maximum attainable value of the objective function as a consequence of a marginal change of the state variable.[1]

However, in a dynamic context the interpretation of these costates is often not intuitively clear. Especially in models with pure state constraints, where it has been shown that the costates may jump. Moreover, there are rather strong theorems concerning the timepoints of these possible jumps, but there is no theorem which states: "The costates jump if and only if ....". In short, as Feichtinger and Hartl [1986] state in their reference work on the Maximum Principle (p.179), a full economic interpretation of the costates and multipliers in problems with pure state constraints is still missing. This chapter can be seen as a contribution to the attempts to find such a full economic interpretation. The aim is to shed more light on the shadow price interpretation of the costates and to study the question: when and why does a costate jump.

A crucial element in that attempt is a shadow price interpretation for the

---

[1] Note that the costate can be seen as a kind of Lagrange multiplier of the equality constraint $dx/dt=f(x,u,t)$. This suggests that the interpretation of the costates is similar to the interpretation of Lagrange multipliers in linear programming problems.

multipliers associated with the pure state constraints, which is also of interest in itself. The proof of that interpretation, which presupposes a thorough understanding of functional analysis, can be found in Appendix 3. Section 6.3 states the result and gives a sketch of the proof.
The immediate cause for this chapter are the jumps of the costate variables in the model of the previous chapter. In section 6.2, a model is formulated which is a slightly modified version of that model and which will be used as a stepping stone for the presentation of the results in this chapter. Section 6.4 gives an interpretation of the costate variables. Section 6.5 explains the jumps of the costates which occur in the model. Section 6.6 gives some general guidelines concerning the shadow price interpretation of costates in models with pure state constraints. Section 6.7 summarises this chapter and gives some conclusions.

6.2 The model

In this chapter the model of Chapter 5 is used, with one modification[2]: it is assumed that the demand over time for the products of the firm is given by a cyclical function *y*, independent of the outputprice:

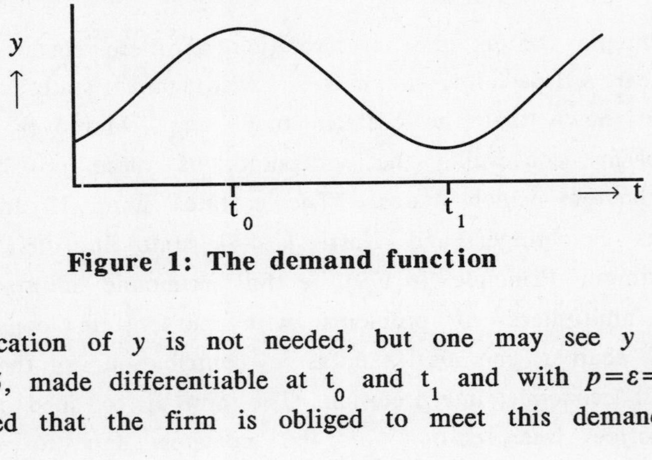

Figure 1: The demand function

A specification of *y* is not needed, but one may see *y* as function (1) in Chapter 5, made differentiable at t_0 and t_1 and with $p=\varepsilon=1$[3]. Furthermore it is assumed that the firm is obliged to meet this demand at any point of time:

$$Q(t) \geq y(t) \tag{1}$$

This modified model equals the model (5)-(12) in Chapter 5, with this constraint added and with S[Q,t] replaced by *y*(t). The Lagrangian (4.13) is

[2]The reason for this modification is that there are more jumps of the costates in this modified model.

[3]Unlike in chapter 5, the differentiability of the demand function is now crucial in the coupling procedure.

augmented with $\upsilon_3(K/k\text{-}y)$. With regard to the necessary conditions (4.14)-(4.24), (4.16), (4.20) and (4.22) are to be replaced by:

$$\dot{\lambda}_1 = -\frac{\partial \mathbb{L}}{\partial K} + i\lambda_1 = (i+a)\lambda_1 + \lambda_2(1\text{-}f)\{\frac{wl}{k} + a + r\} + \upsilon_2\text{-}\upsilon_1\text{-}\upsilon_3/k \tag{2}$$

$$\lambda_1(z) = -\gamma_2 + \gamma_1 + \gamma_3, \quad \lambda_2(z) = 1 + (1+b)\gamma_2 - \gamma_1 \tag{3}$$

If λ is discontinuous in τ, then:

$$\lambda_1(\tau^+) = \lambda_1(\tau^-) - \eta_1(\tau) + \eta_2(\tau) + \eta_3(\tau)/k \tag{4}$$

Furthermore, (4.19), (4.21) and (4.24) are to be supplemented with:

$$\upsilon_3(K/k\text{-}y) = 0, \ \upsilon_3 \geq 0 \tag{5}$$

$$\gamma_3\{K(z)/k\text{-}y(z)\} = 0, \ \gamma_3 \geq 0 \tag{6}$$

$$\eta_3(\tau)(K/k\text{-}y) = 0, \ \eta_3 \geq 0 \tag{7}$$

Only one optimal string will be studied. Suppose:

- $i < (1\text{-}f)r$ and $Y(0)=0$;
- $K(0)/k=y(0)$;
- during the slump the firm is not able to keep production equal to demand (i.e. the recession is severe). Due to the irreversibility of investments ($I \geq 0$), the capital goods stock does not diminish quickly enough: the firm suffers from excess capacity.
- during the slump the 'accounting cash-flow' becomes negative, forcing the firm to borrow money to meet its obligations (as in Chapter 5).

The optimal solution in this case is sketched in Figure 2. It can be compared with the optimal string 1-5-7-5-1 in Chapter 5. The firm tries to maintain $K/k=y$ as long as possible. At τ_1 however, the constraint $I \geq 0$ becomes active and the firm is forced to leave the boundary $K/k=y$. At τ_2 the 'accounting cash-flow' becomes negative and the firm is forced to borrow. If the recession is over and the 'accounting cash-flow' becomes positive again, the firm pays back its debt as quickly as possible. At τ_3 all debt is paid back. When the recession is over, y rises steadily and at τ_4 the period of excess capacity ends. From then on the firm maintains the equality between production and demand.

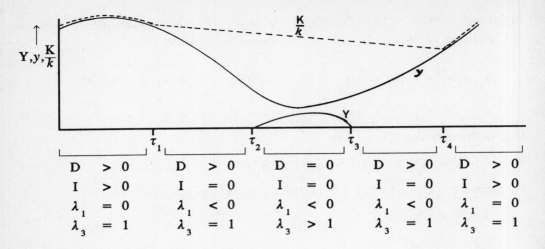

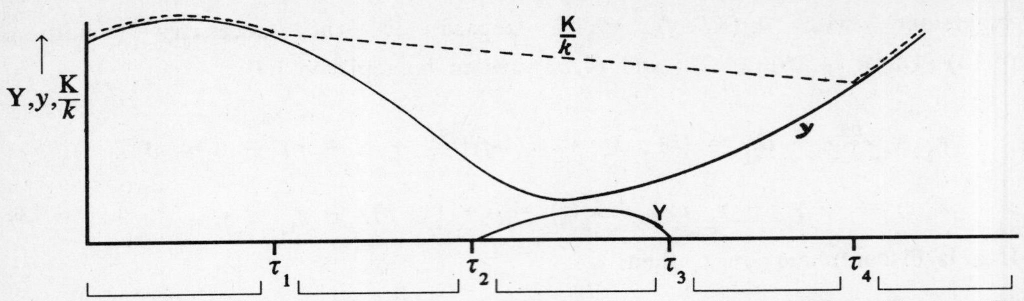

$D > 0$	$D > 0$	$D = 0$	$D > 0$	$D > 0$
$I > 0$	$I = 0$	$I = 0$	$I = 0$	$I > 0$
$\lambda_1 = 0$	$\lambda_1 < 0$	$\lambda_1 < 0$	$\lambda_1 < 0$	$\lambda_1 = 0$
$\lambda_3 = 1$	$\lambda_3 = 1$	$\lambda_3 > 1$	$\lambda_3 = 1$	$\lambda_3 = 1$

Figure 2: The optimal policy

Application of the coupling procedure reveals that λ_1 is discontinuous at τ_1 and τ_2 and λ_2 is discontinous at τ_2[4]. As said before (p.38), since the 'direct adjoining approach' is used to handle the pure state constraints, the costates can be interpreted as shadow prices of the state variables at timepoints where they are continuous (Feichtinger and Hartl [1986], p.176; a proof can be found in Maurer [1984]). So the value of a costate at time t equals the rate at which the objective function would grow, if we would inject the corresponding state variable with an extra unit at time t. With this in mind, the aim of this chapter is to explain the actual values of the costates and to interpret the jumps of the shadow prices.

Equations (2) and (4.17) can be written as (N.B. $\lambda_1(z)=0$, $\lambda_2(z)=1$, and $\upsilon_2=0$ everywhere):

$$\lambda_1(t) = \int_t^z e^{-(i+a)(\tau-t)} \left\{-\lambda_2(\tau)(1-f)\left(\frac{wl}{k}+a+r\right)+\upsilon_1+\upsilon_3/k\right\} d\tau + \text{'jumps'} \quad (8)$$

$$\lambda_2(t) = -\int_t^z e^{-\{i-(1-f)r\}(\tau-t)} \upsilon_1(\tau)\, d\tau + e^{-(i-(1-f)r)(z-t)} + \text{'jumps'} \quad (9)$$

Obviously, in order to use these equations to analyse λ_1 and λ_2, it is necessary to know <u>if</u> and <u>how</u> the multipliers of the pure state constraints υ_i can be interpreted. This is the subject of the next section.

---

[4]The jumps at τ_2 are similar to the jumps at $t_{1,5}$ in section 5.3.4.

6.3 A shadow price interpretation for υ

Like in linear programming, the shadow price of a constraint in a general static optimisation problem can be obtained by measuring the effect of 'perturbing' that constraint. By relaxing a constraint, one enlarges the number of 'feasible' points from which the optimal solution must be chosen, so the value of the objective function for the optimal solution will certainly not decrease. The rate at which the objective function increases is defined as the shadow price of the constraint, and in static optimisation this rate equals the value of the Lagrange multiplier belonging to that constraint. In a dynamic problem, the Lagrange multiplier is a function of time. Reasoning by analogy, one might expect that the value of this Lagrange multiplier function (υ_i) at time τ equals the effect of a momentary relaxation at time τ of the corresponding state constraint (h_i). This, in fact, is true, but it takes some hard mathematics to make it precise. What happens is, in short, the following:
Replace $h_i(x,t) \geq 0$ by $h_i(x,t) \geq \beta(t)$, where $\beta(t)$ is defined as[5]:

$$\begin{aligned} &\beta(t)=0 && \text{for } 0 \leq t \leq \tau, \\ &\beta(t)=\gamma/\in && \text{for } \tau \leq t \leq \tau+\in, \quad \gamma<0, \\ &\beta(t)=0 && \text{for } \tau+\in \leq t \leq z. \end{aligned} \tag{10}$$

Figure 3: The perturbation function

For $\in$ approaching zero, this perturbation resembles a momentary relaxation of the state constraint $h_i(x,t) \geq 0$. To measure the effect of such a perturbation, the 'optimal value function' $V(\alpha)$ is defined as the optimal value of the objective function if the constraint $h_i(x,t) \geq 0$ is replaced by $h_i(x,t) \geq \alpha(t)$. (N.B. in general, the optimal solution of a 'perturbed' problem will of course differ from the solution of the original

[5]This perturbation comes from Léonard [1987].

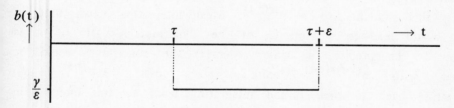

'unperturbed' problem). In Appendix 3 it is proved that: the directional derivative of the optimal value function $V(\alpha)$ in the direction of β (β defined as above) at $\alpha=0$ equals $\upsilon_i(\tau)$. So $\upsilon_i(\tau)$ can be seen as the rate at which the objective function would grow if the pure state constraint $h_i(x,t)\geq 0$ would be momentarily relaxed at time τ, and as the rate at which the objective function would decrease if the pure state constraint would be momentarily violated![6]

6.4 Interpretation of the costate variables

Using this interpretation of υ_i, the *integrals* in (8) and (9) can be interpreted as marginal contributions to the objective function of an injection of the state variable at time t (the values of the *jumps* I cannot explain, see section 5.3.4). To see this, one has to keep in mind that a shadow price is in fact the partial derivative of the optimal value function (as defined in the previous section) with regard to a state variable. Thus, when evaluating the effects of an extra unit of K (resp. X), X (resp. K) should be kept constant.

1) An extra unit of equity at time t, with K constant, would lead, as it were, to a negative debt. This can be viewed as lending: the firm puts this extra unit in the bank and thus it grows at a rate $(1\text{-}f)r$. At time z this amounts to $e^{(1-f)r(z-t)}$. Meanwhile, this extra unit of equity would lead to a violation of the constraint $K\text{-}X\geq 0$ (if it is active). To be precise, at time τ ($\tau\geq t$) the constraint would be violated with $e^{(1-f)r(\tau-t)}$ units. This 'costs' $e^{(1-f)r(\tau-t)}\upsilon_1(\tau)$. Discounting back to time t and integrating leads to the integral in (9).
2) An extra unit of capital at time t, which depreciates at a rate a, would lead, for X unchanged, to extra costs at time τ ($\tau\geq t$) of $e^{-a(\tau-t)}(1\text{-}f)(wl/k+a+r)$. Consequently retained earnings at time τ would decrease with this amount. So X would decrease at a rate $e^{-a(\tau-t)}(1\text{-}f)(wl/k+a+r)$ and in terms of the objective function this

[6]In the same way the interpretation of $\lambda_i(0)$ can be derived by perturbing the initial value of the corresponding state variable. Another example can be found in Maurer [1979,1984], who studies the effect of a "permanent" perturbation of $h_i(x,t)\geq 0$; he replaces $h_i(x,t)\geq 0$ by $h_i(x,t)\geq\beta$ for all t, with β a real number.

'costs' $\lambda_2(\tau)$ times that amount, since λ_2 is the shadow price of equity. Moreover, this extra unit of capital would lead, at time τ, to a relaxation of $K/k \geq y$ with $e^{-a(\tau-t)}/k$ units and a relaxation of $K-X \geq 0$ with $e^{-a(\tau-t)}$ units (if these constraints are active). This is worth $e^{-a(\tau-t)}\{(1/k)\upsilon_3(\tau)+\upsilon_1(\tau)\}$. Discounting these contributions back to time t and integrating leads to the integral in (8).

So it is clear that when interpreting the value of a costate, the effects on the constraints in which the corresponding state variable appears must be taken into account.[7] With regard to the jumps in (8) and (9) I can only say, as in section 5.3.4, that apparently they have to be added as separate contributions to the objective function.

But there is an other way to explain the actual values of λ_1 and λ_2. To understand this, it is useful (in spite of the danger of terminological confusion) to make the following distinction: <u>in principle</u> an extra unit of a state variable can be "invested" (i.e. be used to generate contributions to the objective function <u>in the future</u>) or "consumed" (i.e. be used to generate contributions to the objective function <u>now</u>). "In principle", since "consuming" an extra unit of equity means paying it out as dividends, and this is not possible if dividends are on their upper bound[8]. Likewise, "consuming" an extra unit of capital means lowering investments I by one unit, and this is not possible if investments are on their lower bound. Since the objective function is the discounted stream of dividends, "consuming" an extra unit of equity implies a contribution to the objective function equal to one, "consuming" an extra unit of capital implies a contribution to the objective function equal to zero. As can be seen from (8) and (9), the shadow prices λ_1 and λ_2 measure the effect of "investment" of the extra unit of the corresponding state variable. If "consumption" as well as "investment" are possible, their contributions to the objective

---

[7] Note again the resemblance to linear programming: if a decision variable in a linear programming problem appears in several constraints, the Lagrange multipliers of these constraints are interrelated.

[8] At this point it is important to be very careful with expressions like "an extra unit of equity". The costates measure the <u>marginal</u> contribution of a state variable to the objective function, so one should think in terms of an infinitesimal extra amount of the state variable instead of in terms of an extra unit. In other words, "an extra unit of equity" is in fact an extra unit of $\dot{X}$, measured in dollars per unit of time. From this and the differential equation for X ((5.7) or (4.3)) it is clear that "consuming" "an extra unit of equity" amounts to lowering D with one unit.

function must be equal along the optimal path (since otherwise the actual levels of I and D would not be optimal). Thus, in that case, λ_1, the shadow price of capital, must equal zero (being the value of "consuming" a capital good), and λ_2, the shadow price of equity, must equal one (being the value of "consuming" a unit of equity). Indeed, the necessary conditions show that λ_1 equals zero when the constraints on I are not active and that λ_2 equals one if the constraints on D are not active. If the firm does not invest (I=0), apparently "consuming" an extra unit of capital is more advantageous than "investing". Indeed, λ_1 is negative.[9] So it is clear that the flexibility with regard to the control variables determines whether "consumption" of a state variable is possible and together with the specification of the objective function this gives information about the value of the corresponding costate variable.[10]

6.5 Why and when does a costate jump?

In section 6.3 it was observed that λ_1 is discontinuous at τ_1 and τ_2 and λ_2 is discontinuous at τ_2 (see Figure 2). How are these jumps to be understood? Since the pure state constraints are of order one, the jump theorem of Appendix 1 can be applied, which for the model of this chapter amounts to:

> the costates can only jump if the control variables are continuous and the strong constraint qualification is not satisfied[11].

The matrix of the strong constraint qualification for the model in this chapter is:

---

[9]This explanation can easily be extended: for instance (see (4.15)), if $D=D_{max}$, $\lambda_2=1-\mu_4$. The firm pays out the maximal amount of dividends, so apparently "consuming" equity is more advantageous than "investing". This is in accordance with the fact that λ_2 is less than one.

[10]Note that the specification of the objective function plays an important role. If the objective function would have been the discounted value of future cash-flows $[(1-f)*(py-(wl/k)K)+faK-I]$, the value of "consuming" a capital good would equal one and the firm would only invest if the shadow price of capital would be larger than one.

[11]In the model of this chapter the situation that the control variables are discontinuous and the entry or exit is nevertheless tangential does not occur. See Appendix 1, p.152.

$$\begin{bmatrix} 1 & 0 & I & 0 & 0 & 0 & 0 & 0 & 0 \\ -1 & 0 & 0 & I_{max}-I & 0 & 0 & 0 & 0 & 0 \\ 0 & 1 & 0 & 0 & D & 0 & 0 & 0 & 0 \\ 0 & -1 & 0 & 0 & 0 & D_{max}-D & 0 & 0 & 0 \\ 1 & 1 & 0 & 0 & 0 & 0 & K-X & 0 & 0 \\ -1 & -(1+b) & 0 & 0 & 0 & 0 & 0 & (1+b)X-K & 0 \\ 1/k & 0 & 0 & 0 & 0 & 0 & 0 & 0 & K/k-y \end{bmatrix} \quad (18)$$

The costate variable λ_1 jumps in τ_1. Indeed, I and D are continuous in τ_1 and it is easy to verify that the strong constraint qualification is not satisfied in τ_1. But it is possible that I and D are also continuous in τ_4. Then the strong constraint qualification is not satisfied in τ_4 either. In that case the question is: why does λ_1 jump in τ_1 and not in τ_4? The jump theorem does not provide the answer. My suggestion for an answer is as follows:

> a costate variable, belonging to some state variable x, jumps if the entry or exit of a boundary of a constraint involving x could not be postponed: the restrictions on the control variables force the firm to leave or enter the boundary.[12]

At time τ_1, investments have reached their lower bound. Thus the firm has no choice there: to stay on the boundary $K/k=y$ would require a negative investment. It simply has to leave the boundary, forced by the restrictions on the control variables. At time τ_4, the firm could easily postpone entry: it would simply invest more to do so. Likewise, λ_1 and λ_2 jump at τ_2 because at that point the firm is forced to borrow money, that is, it is forced to leave the boundary of the constraint $K\text{-}X \geq 0$. Since this constraint involves both state variables, both costates jump. Note that I and D are continuous in τ_2 and that the strong constraint qualification is not satisfied. The entry of the constraint $K\text{-}X \geq 0$ in τ_3 could easily be postponed by borrowing some extra money. The strong constraint qualification is not satisfied at τ_3, but even if I and D are continuous in τ_3 (which is in principle possible), the costates will not jump. In the models of this thesis several jumps of costates occur, and all jumps occur at entry or exit points where the firm is forced to leave or enter the boundary, due to the restrictions on the control variables. In all other

[12] A boundary of a constraint is defined as an interval on which this constraint is active.

exit and entry points, where costates are continuous, the firm could avoid entry resp. exit (i.e. the restrictions on the control variables did not prevent them to postpone entry resp. exit).
In my view, it is intuitively plausible that such a forced entry or exit leads to a sudden change in the valuation of the state variables involved; or, in other words, to discontinuities in the corresponding costates.

It might seem strange that such a sudden change in the valuation of a state variable can occur in spite of the fact that the costate variable captures all future effects of a change in the state variable (to put it informally: at $t<\tau_1$ the firm 'knows' that the constraint $I \geq 0$ will become active; why is this knowledge not incorporated in the value of $\lambda(t)$?). However, this does not preclude that there can be discontinuities, in the course of time, in the effects of an extra unit of a state variable. For instance, if the firm would get an (undesired) extra capital good just before τ_1, it would simply "consume" it; extra capital goods which the firm gets after τ_1, however, cannot be "consumed". It is this discontinuity in the possibility of "consumption" that leads to the discontinuities in the costates. So again the flexibility with regard to the control variables is crucial. Before τ_1, there is flexibility with regard to I; after τ_1, there is no flexibility since the lower bound on I is active. One could say that if there is no flexibility (i.e. one or more bounds on a control variable are active), the firm is vulnerable to changes in the state variables in the neighbourhood of a jump: it can make an enormous difference if the firm gets an extra capital good just before time τ_1 or a fraction of time later.

6.6 Some general guidelines for the interpretation of costates

In discussions about the shadow price interpretation of the costates, one can often hear things like: "suppose at time t there is a tiny increment of the state variable. Then the corresponding costate measures the rate at which the objective function grows". If such a "tiny increment" occurs at time t , it seems to matter whether one has the opportunity to revise one's plans for the remaining part of the planning period or not. Bensoussan, Hurst and Näslund [1974] show that it does not matter. In the same spirit is the result of Léonard [1987], which states that it does not matter if the perturbation of the state variable was anticipated at time $t=0$ or not. Léonard explains these results, which run counter to economic intuition, as

follows (p.121): "We are dealing here with the rate at which gain could be made if we were to perturb the optimal path - which in the end we do not" (underlining added).
These two 'it does not matter'-results enable us to choose the most convenient formulation of the shadow price interpretation of the costates, most convenient in the sense of 'easiest to use in economic interpretations'. In this chapter shadow prices have been discussed on the basis of formulas (8) and (9), where the costates at time t are expressed as integrals over the time period from time t onwards. This implicitly assumes that the perturbation of the state was not expected and explicitly assumes that the plans are not changed at time t, since the 'old' values (i.e. the values from the solution of the unperturbed problem) of the state variables and the multipliers appearing in the integrands were used to interpret (8) and (9). Thus, I would recommend to interpret $\lambda(t)$ as the rate at which the objective function could increase as a result of an unexpected increment of the state variable at time t which does not lead to a change of plans on $[t,z]$. This also implies that an extra unit of a state variable at time t has no influence on the constraints in the sense that active constraints remain active. One has to keep, as it were, a separate account for this extra unit. Moreover, the effect of an extra unit of one state variable has to be evaluated while the other state variables do not change, since the costates are partial derivatives of the optimal value function.

6.7 Summary and conclusions

When interpreting the value of a costate variable in a model with pure state constraints, it is important to remember that an increment of the state variable at time t would not only have direct consequences (in economic terms: a change in revenues and costs) but also indirect consequences, namely the violation or relaxation of active state constraints. A violation leads to a negative contribution to the value of the costate, a relaxation to a positive one (section 6.4). The multipliers of the pure state constraints can be interpreted as shadow prices in the sense that they measure the effect of a momentary relaxation of these constraints (section 6.3).
An impression of the value of the costates, without actually computing them, can be obtained by comparing the effect of "investing" an extra unit

of a state variable (i.e. using it to generate contributions to the objective function in the future), which is measured by the costate, with the effect of "consuming" (i.e. using it to generate contributions to the objective function immediately). The constraints on the control variables determine whether "consumption" of a state variable is possible (section 6.4). These constraints on the control variables also play a crucial part in the interpretation and explanation of possible jumps of the costates: in the models of this thesis, a jump of a costate occurs when the constraints on the control variables force the firm to leave or enter a boundary (section 6.5).

It can be concluded that in the models of this thesis, which involve pure state constraints, the costate variables can still be interpreted as shadow prices. The actual values of the costates and the occurrence of jumps can be understood in terms of an interplay of the pure state constraints and the control constraints.

7

TECHNOLOGICAL PROGRESS IN VINTAGE MODELS OF THE FIRM: SCRAPPING CONDITION AND STEADY STATE

7.1 Introduction

In the previous chapters the environment of the firm changes in that its demand curve changes over time. In this chapter the environment changes on the supply side: due to an exogeneously given technological progress, the production function of the firm shifts over time[1]. The analysis will be restricted to a very specific type of technological progress, namely the 'embodied labour augmenting' type. The adjective 'embodied' means that the technological progress only applies to the latest capital goods: new investments are the vehicle of technological innovations. The adjective 'labour augmenting' means that these technological innovations lead to a higher productivity of the people working with these new investments[2]. So, although the capital productivity is not affected by this type of technological progress, the capital goods stock is no longer homogeneous.

In this context, the meaning of the constraint $I \geq 0$ changes. The assumption of zero scrap value is maintained, but the model is modified to allow for the scrapping of old capital goods. This implies that the firm regains some flexibility with regard to changing its size. The constraint $I \geq 0$ is maintained, since I(t) denotes the number of 'new' machines (i.e. machines incorporating the latest technological innovations). So $I \geq 0$ is now a logical restriction, while in previous chapters there was an economic assumption behind it.

There is a considerable amount of literature on the effects of technological progress on theories of economic growth (starting with articles by Johansen [1959] and Solow [1959]). Special attention is often given to questions of 'balanced growth' (see for instance Bliss [1968], Van

---

[1]Section 8.4 tries to combine *both* changes in one model.

[2]See Chapter 2 for the different types of technological progress.

den Goorbergh, De Groof and Peer [1979]). Especially in the Netherlands there have been a number of empirical applications of economic theories that incorporate technological progress, starting with Den Hartog and Tjan [1974], who use a vintage model, in which the technological progress is of the type described above, to explain the growing unemployment rate in the Netherlands. The central idea is that scrapping older vintages for economic reasons may lead to an increase of the unemployment rate, even though investments are taking place: the new capital goods require less labour than the same amount of old capital goods. This already indicates that the 'scrapping condition' (the rule which gives the optimal economic lifetime) plays an important part in vintage models. This scrapping condition will have an accordingly prominent place in this chapter. The 'balanced growth' theories and the empirical vintage models are macroeconomic. The need for micro-economic vintage models is expressed by Van den Goorbergh ([1978], p.7) : "Juist bij de jaargangentheorie, waarin het al dan niet handhaven van bestaande machines en arbeidsplaatsen micro-economisch gefundeerd wordt op het verschil van opbrengstprijs en (loon-)kosten per eenheid product -de zogenaamde afkapconditie-, is men geneigd te zoeken naar een micro-economisch geïnspireerde analyse van het investeringsgedrag, waardoor immers nieuwe machines en arbeidsplaatsen worden gecreëerd". Broer [1987] explicitly formulates a 'vintage theory of the firm'. His ultimate aim however is to perform empirical applications on an aggregated level.

This chapter will be of a more theoretical nature. In section 7.2 a vintage model is presented, based on the basic model of Chapter 4. The resulting model is more general than the usual vintage models in that it includes the financial decisions of the firm. The vintage structure asks for an adapted version of the Maximum Principle, which is used to derive the optimality conditions. In section 7.3 a general scrapping condition is presented and it is shown that it entails some well known, seemingly different, scrapping rules. Section 7.4 demonstrates that there exists a steady state solution for the model. Moreover, it is shown that the 'final path' *implies* this steady state. Section 7.5 gives a summary and conclusions. The optimal trajectories towards the steady state of the model in sections 7.2-7.4 are discussed in Chapter 8.

7.2 The model and the optimality conditions

7.2.1 The vintage structure and the role of taxes

The model to be presented is a so-called 'clay-clay' model in which the firm chooses its investment-, dividend-, and scrapping-policy to maximise the discounted stream of dividends. It is based on the basic model of Chapter 4. One of the differences concerns the production function. Broer ([1987], p.23) summarises the common ways to specify the production function in a vintage model: "The standard assumption made in the specification of this type of production function (i.e. a production function of a vintage model) is that strict separability obtains between capital goods of different ages, which results in a separate production function for each capital vintage. Here we must distinguish between specifications in which the firm can vary the labour intensity of capital goods equally before and after installation of the capital good ('putty-putty' production models) and specifications in which the firm lacks this freedom after installation ('putty-clay' specifications)". A third possibility, and the most simple one from a technical point of view, is that the firm cannot vary the labour intensity before and after installation ('clay-clay' specification). This chapter uses this last specification.

Concerning the scrapping and buying of capital goods, the following is assumed: a vintage is scrapped as a whole and the firm receives no scrap value for the scrapped capital goods. Moreover, the firm cannot buy second hand capital goods. Since newer capital goods are better than older ones, it will not happen that vintage $t+\tau$ will be scrapped while vintage t is still being used. Thus the vintages still in use at time t are given by an interval [N(t),t], where N(t) is the birth date of the oldest capital goods still in use at time t. For a clay-clay specification, this gives the following expressions for K, L and Q:

$$Q(t) = \frac{1}{k}\,K(t) = \frac{1}{k}\int_{N(t)}^{t} e^{-a(t-\tau)} I(\tau)\,d\tau,$$

$$L(t) = \int_{N(t)}^{t} e^{-a(t-\tau)} I(\tau)\frac{l(\tau)}{k}\,d\tau \qquad (1)$$

As before, k is the constant capital to output ratio and l(t) is the labour to output ratio at time t. The embodied labour augmenting technological progress is represented by the fact that l is a decreasing function of time.

Due to the vintage structure the capital goods stock not only decreases because of depreciation but also because of the scrapping of vintages. Until now, it has been assumed that fiscal depreciation equals technical depreciation. In practice capital goods are fiscally depreciated in a fixed number of years, which is in general less than the technical and economical lifetime. The Maximum Principle of Appendix 4, derived in order to handle constraints of type (1) (see section 7.2.4), also makes it possible to model fiscal depreciation in a more realistic way: from now on it will be assumed that capital goods depreciate technically at an exponential rate a (as before), and that a capital good is fiscally depreciated in a fixed number of years, which is shorter than the actual economic lifetime of the capital good. With this assumption, total depreciation at time t is:

$$A(t) = \int_{t-v}^{t} c(\tau)I(\tau)d(t-\tau)\, d\tau \tag{2}$$

where

A(t) : total depreciation at time t

c(t) : the price of a capital good at time t

d(t) : the rate of depreciation if a capital good is t years old

v : the number of years in which a capital good is fiscally depreciated.

The fact that a capital good is scrapped in v years according to the given depreciation scheme d is captured by the relation:

$$\int_{0}^{v} d(t)\, dt = 1 \tag{3}$$

The only further assumption on d is that it is a continuous function, which implies that very general depreciation schemes are included.

The fiscal book value of the capital goods stock is no longer equal to K. So if the balance sheet equation is used, it is necessary to make a distinction between the fiscal balance sheet and the commercial balance sheet[3]. In the following it is assumed that the upper bound on debt is in

---

[3]This also gives different values for equity. Therefore it is more straightforward to use a differential equation for debt instead of a differential equation for equity (as was done in the previous chapters). Moreover, if equity would be defined as K-Y, the right hand side of the differential equation of equity would contain the term

terms of the commercial value of the capital goods stock, that is: $Y \le \frac{b}{1+b} cK$. The differential equation for Y is:

$$\dot{Y}(t) = -(1-f)\{\, p(Q)Q(t) - w(t)L(t) - rY(t) \,\} + c(t)I(t) + D(t) - fA(t) \tag{4}$$

Note that the price of capital goods equals $c(t)$ instead of one. This is done in order to compare the results of the model with the results of other models.

7.2.2 The model

If the basic model of Chapter 4 is changed as explained in the previous subsection, the result is:

$$\max_{I,D,B} \int_0^\infty e^{-it} D(t)\, dt \tag{5}$$

$$K(t) = \int_{N(t)}^{t} e^{-a(t-\tau)} I(\tau)\, d\tau = \int_{V^{-1}(t)}^{t} e^{-a(t-\tau)} I(\tau)\, d\tau \tag{6}$$

$$Q(t) = K(t)/k \tag{7}$$

$$L(t) = \int_{N(t)}^{t} e^{-a(t-\tau)} I(\tau) l(\tau)/k\, d\tau = \int_{V^{-1}(t)}^{t} e^{-a(t-\tau)} I(\tau) l(\tau)/k\, d\tau \tag{8}$$

$$A(t) = \int_{t-v}^{t} c(\tau) I(\tau) d(t-\tau)\, d\tau \tag{9}$$

$$\dot{Y}(t) = -(1-f)\{\, p(Q)Q(t) - w(t)L(t) - rY(t) \,\} + c(t)I(t) + D(t) - fA(t) \tag{10}$$

$$\dot{V}(t) = B(t), \text{ for all } t \ge n_0, \text{ where } n_0 = N(0) \tag{11}$$

$$Y(t) \ge 0 \text{ for all } t \ge 0 \tag{12}$$

$$bc(t)K(t) - (1+b)Y(t) \ge 0 \text{ for all } t \ge 0 \tag{13}$$

$$0 \le I(t) \le I_{max}, \text{ for all } t \ge 0 \tag{14}$$

$$0 \le D(t) \le D_{max}, \text{ for all } t \ge 0 \tag{15}$$

$$e^{-a(t-N(t))} I(N(t)) \dot{N}(t),$$

since $\dot{X} = \dot{K} - \dot{Y}$ and $\dot{K}(t) = I(t) - aK(t) - e^{-a(t-N(t))} I(N(t)) \dot{N}(t)$ (see (1)).

It can easily be seen that the Maximum Principle in Appendix 4 cannot handle terms like $I(N(t))$.

$B_{min} \leq B(t) \leq B_{max}$, for all $t \geq n_0$ (16)

I(t) is given for $t \in [n_0, 0)$ (17)

Note that V equals N^{-1} (see (6) and (8)) and that B is the derivative of V (see (11)). The change from N to V^{-1} and the restrictions on B ((16)) will be discussed in the next subsection. The objective function (5) is the usual one. A infinite horizon is chosen for simplicity. Equations (6)-(8) have already been explained. The constraint $I \geq 0$ means that the firm can only buy a non-negative amount of new capital goods. Equation (17) replaces the usual "K(0) is given". Due to the vintage structure, K(0) no longer contains all relevant information from the past. Equation (17) gives the missing information, the number of capital goods of every vintage still in use at t=0.

7.2.3 Some properties of N(t)

At this point it is necessary to examine the function N(t) carefully. Define:

N(t): the birth date of the oldest capital goods still in use at time t.

V(t): the scrapping date of capital goods installed at time t.

Note that V(t) only makes sense if $I(t) > 0$. For the moment assume that indeed $I(t) > 0$ for all t.

The most obvious properties for N and V are:

$N(t) < t, \; V(t) > t$ (18)

Next assume that scrapping is irreversible. So if a capital good is scrapped at time t it cannot be used at a time $t' > t$. Assuming that N is continuous, this means that

$dN/dt \geq 0$ (19)

Moreover, it does not make sense to scrap newer capital goods earlier than older ones if there is technological progress. Assuming that V is continuous, this means that

$dV/dt \geq 0$ (20)

From the interpretation of N and V it is clear that

$V(N(t)) \geq t$ (21)

If it is also assumed that dN/dt and dV/dt are not equal to zero, then N and V have an inverse function. Then, if investments are positive

everywhere, N(t) equals $V^{-1}(t)$ (given the interpretation of N and V, $V(N(t)) > t$ leads to a contradiction. So (21) implies $N = V^{-1}$). Moreover, even if investments are not positive everywhere, replacing N by V^{-1} does not affect the model (see Appendix 5.4). In Appendix 4 it is made clear why this replacement is crucial from a technical point of view.
The existence of the inverse functions is based on the strict monotonicity of N and V. Strict monotonicity does not follow from (19) and (20). However, since the existence of the inverse function of N is indispensable from a technical point of view, B is bounded from below in (16) by an arbitrarily low but positive lower bound to ensure strict monotonicity of V and bounded from above by an arbitrarily high upper bound to ensure strict monotonicity of N (note that $\dot{N}(V(t)) = \dot{N}(N^{-1}(t)) = 1/B(t)$).[4] When interpreting particular optimal solutions, an active lower bound on B means that the firm would like to set B equal to zero, implying a constant V (which means that a number of vintages are scrapped at the same date), an active upper bound at t means that the firm would like to set B(t) equal to infinity, implying a constant N(V(t)) (which means that for some time no scrapping takes place). If $I > 0$, it will never be optimal to have $V(t) \leq t$, and thus there is no need to include the restriction $V(t) > t$ (see (18)) in the model.
It should be noted at this point that the assumptions concerning N and V (N and V are continuous, strictly increasing functions of time) are partly mathematically motivated: these assumptions are indispensable in Appendix 4.

7.2.4 The optimisation problem

As in the previous chapters I would like to apply Optimal Control Theory (in particular the Maximum Principle) to vintage models. In their survey article on Control Theory and the dynamics of the firm Lesourne & Leban [1982] suggest that this is very well possible. They state that "functions with generations of equipment (which) have not been used enough in microeconomic control theory models" (p.4). However, constraints of type (1) do not occur in standard optimal control problems. If the lower bounds of the integrals in (1) are given (finite or infinite), variations of the ordinary Maximum Principle exist that can handle constraints of type (1)

---

[4]In footnote 11 the assumption of strict monotonicity is relaxed.

(see Kamien and Schwartz [1981] and Hartl and Sethi [1984]). However, in the model of section 7.2.2., that lower bound is a state variable. Another possibility would be to apply the so-called 'Distributed Parameter Control', which Feichtinger and Hartl [1986] believe to be a suitable tool to handle vintage models (p.527). I did not succeed, however, in writing the model (5)-(17) as a 'distributed parameter control'-problem to which standard results could be applied. Broer [1987] states that a putty-clay or clay-clay vintage model "cannot easily be formulated as an optimal control problem in the absence of a suitable set of state variables (in principle the entire investment history is relevant, which makes the state vector infinite dimensional)" (p.119). He seems to be right, it cannot be done easily. However, if one reconciles oneself with this situation, one is forced to use more or less ad hoc methods to solve every 'vintage optimisation problem'. This is especially problematic if there are constraints involved in the model which do not contain control variables and if one wants to apply the path connecting procedure. Therefore I tried to derive a 'new' Maximum Principle for problems with constraints like (1). K, L, and A are not treated as state variables in the usual sense, but variables that are determined by the normal control and state variables <u>and</u> the equality constraints (6), (8), and (9). This 'Maximum Principle' is derived in Appendix 4 and will be used in the remainder of this chapter.

7.2.5 The optimality conditions

In correspondence with Appendix 4 the Hamiltonian and Lagrangian functions are defined as[5]:

$$\mathbb{H}_a = D + \lambda_3 B + \lambda_4\Big[-(1\text{-}f)\{\ p(K/k)K/k\text{-}wL\text{-}rY\ \} - fA + cI + D\Big] +$$

$$I(t)\int_t^{V(t)} e^{-(i+a)(\tau-t)}\{\ \lambda_1(\tau) + (l(t)/k)\lambda_2(\tau)\ \}\ d\tau +$$

$$I(t)c(t)\int_t^{t+v} e^{-i(\tau-t)}\lambda_5(\tau)d(\tau-t)\ d\tau \qquad (22)$$

$$\mathbb{H}_b = \lambda_3 B + I(t)\int_t^{V(t)} e^{-(i+a)(\tau-t)}\{\ \lambda_1(\tau) + (l(t)/k)\lambda_2(\tau)\ \}\ d\tau \qquad (23)$$

---

[5]In Appendix 4 the constraint (9) can be treated in the same way as the constraints (6) and (8). The derivation of the optimality conditions with constraint (9) added is straightforward.

$$\mathbb{L}_a = \mathbb{H}_a + \upsilon_1 Y + \upsilon_2\{bcK - (1+b)Y\} + \mu_1 I + \mu_2(I_{max}-I) +$$
$$\mu_3 D + \mu_4(D_{max}-D) + \mu_5(B-B_{min}) + \mu_6(B_{max}-B) \tag{24}$$
$$\mathbb{L}_b = \mathbb{H}_b + \mu_5(B-B_{min}) + \mu_6(B_{max}-B) \tag{25}$$

$\mathbb{H}_a$ and $\mathbb{L}_a$ are the usual Hamiltonian and Lagrangian; λ_1, λ_2 and λ_5 are the multipliers of the equality constraints (6), (8) and (9) for capital, labour and depreciation. Since the optimal B has to be determined on the interval $[n_0,\infty)$ instead of $[0,\infty)$, an additional Hamiltonian and Lagrangian ($\mathbb{H}_b$ and $\mathbb{L}_b$) are needed. $\mathbb{H}_b$ and $\mathbb{L}_b$ only contain the expressions in $\mathbb{H}_a$ and $\mathbb{L}_a$ that involve B. The optimality conditions (A4.47)-(A4.55) of Appendix 4 amount to:

$$\partial\mathbb{L}_a/\partial I=0 \Leftrightarrow \lambda_4 c + \int_t^{V(t)} e^{-(i+a)(\tau-t)}\{\lambda_1(\tau) + (l(t)/k)\lambda_2(\tau)\}\, d\tau$$
$$+ c(t)\int_t^{t+v} e^{-i(\tau-t)}\lambda_5(\tau)d(\tau-t)\, d\tau + \mu_1 - \mu_2 = 0,$$
$$\text{for all } t\geq 0 \tag{26}$$

$$\partial\mathbb{L}_a/\partial D=0 \Leftrightarrow 1 + \lambda_4 + \mu_3 - \mu_4 = 0, \text{ for all } t\geq 0 \tag{27}$$

$$\partial\mathbb{L}_b/\partial B=\partial\mathbb{L}_a/\partial B=0 \Leftrightarrow \lambda_3 + \mu_5 - \mu_6 = 0 \text{ for all } t\geq n_0 \tag{28}$$

$$\lambda_1(t) = \partial\mathbb{L}_a/\partial K = -(1-f)\lambda_4\{\partial S/\partial K\} + \upsilon_2 bc, \text{ for all } t\geq 0 \tag{29}$$

$$\lambda_2(t) = \partial\mathbb{L}_a/\partial L = \lambda_4(1-f)w, \text{ for all } t\geq 0 \tag{30}$$

$$\lambda_5(t) = \partial\mathbb{L}_a/\partial A = -\lambda_4 f \tag{31}$$

$$\dot\lambda_3(t) = i\lambda_3-\partial\mathbb{L}_a/\partial V = i\lambda_3-\partial\mathbb{L}_b/\partial V =$$
$$i\lambda_3(t) - I(t)e^{-(i+a)(V(t)-t)}\{\lambda_1(V(t)) + (l(t)/k)\lambda_2(V(t))\},$$
$$\text{for all } t\geq n_0 \tag{32}$$

$$\dot\lambda_4(t) = i\lambda_4-\partial\mathbb{L}_a/\partial Y = i\lambda_4(t) - \lambda_4(1-f)r - \upsilon_1 + (1+b)\upsilon_2 \tag{33}$$

$$\mu_1 I=0,\ \mu_2(I_{max}-I)=0,\ \mu_3 D=0,\ \mu_4(D_{max}-D)=0,\ \ \mu_i\geq 0, i=1,2,3,4,\ t\geq 0 \tag{34}$$

$$\mu_5(B-B_{min})=0,\ \mu_6(B_{max}-B)=0,\ \mu_5\geq 0,\ \mu_6\geq 0,\ t\geq n_0 \tag{35}$$

$$\upsilon_1 Y=0,\ \upsilon_2\{bcK-(1+b))Y\}=0,\ \upsilon_1\geq 0,\ \upsilon_2\geq 0 \tag{36}$$

$$\lambda_4(\tau^-) = \lambda_4(\tau^+) + \eta_1(\tau) - (1+b)\eta_2(\tau) \tag{37}$$

$$\eta_1(\tau)\geq 0,\ \eta_2(\tau)\geq 0,\ \eta_1(\tau)\mathrm{Y}(\tau)=0,\ \eta_2(\tau)\{bc(\tau)\mathrm{K}(\tau)\text{-}(1+c)\mathrm{Y}(\tau)=0 \tag{38}$$

Equations (26)-(28) state that the Hamitonians are maximised with regard to I, D, and B for all $t\geq 0$ and with regard to B also for $n_0\leq t<0$, subject to the constraints (14)-(16). Equations (29)-(31) give the values of the multipliers of the constraints (6), (8) and (9). Note that they are similar, but not identical, to the usual differential equations for the costate variables, (32) and (33). The differences between λ_3 and λ_4 on the one hand and λ_1, λ_2 and λ_5 on the other hand are explained in the next subsection. Equations (34)-(36) are the usual complementary slackness conditions. Equations (37) and (38) are the jump conditions, which are needed because of the presence of pure state constraints.
In Appendix 4 it is not *formally* proved that the conditions (26)-(38) are necessary for optimality. Instead, these conditions are supplemented with some concavity assumptions and it is proved in Appendix 4 that this augmented set of conditions is sufficient for optimality. Unfortunately, I am not able to prove the concavity of the maximised Hamiltonian in all cases, which is one of the concavity assumptions. So now the situation is somewhat unsatisfactory: on the one hand not all sufficiency conditions of Appendix 4 are satisfied, and on the other hand Appendix 4 only gives an heuristic derivation (instead of a formal proof) of the 'necessary' conditions (26)-(38). From now on I will treat (26)-(38) as necessary conditions.

7.3 The scrapping condition

7.3.1 A general scrapping condition

In the Netherlands there has been some discussion about the scrapping condition in clay-clay vintage models (see Den Butter [1976], Den Hartog, van de Klundert, Tjan [1976]). In the publications of the Central Planning Bureau, the scrapping condition is phrased as: a vintage is scrapped when the revenues of that vintage no longer cover the variable costs (i.e. labour costs). Malcomson [1975] phrases the scrapping condition as follows: "Equipment of a given vintage should be used only as long as the operating cost of producing a unit of output on equipment of that vintage is less than the the marginal cost of producing that output on the most recent vintage" (p.28). Den Butter [1976] asserted that these two formulations of the scrapping conditions are essentially different, but Den Hartog, Van de Klundert and Tjan [1976] have shown that the Malcomson-condition is exactly the same as the CPB-condition if one assumes perfect competition on the output market. In his article, Malcomson assumes a downward sloping demand curve. In the following a scrapping condition is derived for the model (5)-(17), which in its most general form is phrased in terms of a certain type of shadow prices of capital and labour. This scrapping condition is equivalent to:

Equipment of a given vintage should be used only as long as the marginal operating cost of producing on equipment of that vintage is less than **the marginal revenue** *of producing on equipment of that vintage.*

Note that this rule looks different from the Malcomson- and CPB-condition. However, it will be shown that both the Malcomson-condition and the CPB-condition are special cases of this condition. A careful examination of the content of the 'marginal revenue' will be the crucial issue.
Suppose that the constraints on B are not active. Then (28) implies $\lambda_3=0$. Combining $\lambda_3(t)=0$, $I(t)>0$ and (32) gives the scrapping condition:

$$\lambda_1(V(t)) + \{c_2(t)/k_1\}\lambda_2(V(t)) = 0 \quad [6] \tag{39}$$

To interpret this condition, it is necessary to know the interpretation of λ_1 and λ_2. Remember that λ_1 and λ_2 are the multipliers attached to the equality constraints (6) and (8) for capital and labour. In Appendix 3 it is shown that the multiplier of a constraint which involves state variables can be interpreted as the contribution to the objective function of a <u>momentary</u> perturbation of the constraint. Although (6) and (8) are different from the usual constraints, it is postulated that the multipliers $\lambda_1(t)$ and $\lambda_2(t)$ can likewise be interpreted as the contribution to the objective function of a momentary perturbation of the capital resp. labour stock at time t. It is important to note that this interpretation differs from the shadow price interpretation of costate variables: the costate variable measures the effect on the objective function of a <u>permanent</u>

---

[6] Broer [1987] derives a similar condition (p.153 for instance). His rule is even more general since his model incorporates utilisation grades.

addition to a state variable. For instance, suppose the capital good stock (denoted by K′) is a usual state variable and denote the corresponding costate by λ_1'. Then $\lambda_1'(t)$ measures the contribution to the objective function of an extra capital good which is added to K′ at time t and which the firm keeps from time t onwards. $\lambda_1(t)$, however, measures the contribution to the objective function of an extra capital good which the firm only has at its disposal during the instant t![7]

Now it is possible to interpret condition (39), which is the scrapping condition for capital goods installed at time t. $\lambda_1(V(t))$ measures the contribution to the objective function of an extra unit of capital at time V(t); $l(t)/k$ is the labour-to-capital ratio of vintage t; $\lambda_2(V(t))$ measures the contribution to the objective function of an extra unit of labour at time V(t). It is clear from the formulation of the model that capital yields a positive contribution to the objective function and labour a negative one. So $l(t)/k\lambda_2(V(t))$ is the (labour) 'cost' at time V(t) associated to an extra unit of capital of vintage t. So (39) means that capital goods of vintage t are scrapped when the 'marginal revenue' of this vintage equals the associated 'marginal labour cost'. This is the general scrapping rule as proposed in the beginning of this section. It is now clear that a careful examination of the marginal 'revenues' and 'costs' is crucial: the 'revenues' and 'costs' should be interpreted as contributions to the objective function and thus their interpretation strongly depends on the nature of the model.

Two final remarks conclude this section. In the first place note that λ_1 and λ_2 are more or less 'static' shadow prices: they measure the effects of some change which lasts only one instant of time and these effects are only different from zero at that instant. So it seems that the choice of the scrapping date is a 'static' problem. This is further discussed in section 7.3.4.

In the second place note that (39), the scrapping condition at time t, gives the date at which to scrap machines installed at time t. It may seem

---

[7]If one ,would define within this model the 'ordinary' shadow price of capital, λ_1, a natural definition would be:

$$\lambda_1'(t) = \int_t^{V(t)} e^{-(i+a)t(\tau-t)}\lambda_1(\tau)d\tau.$$

strange to determine the scrapping date of a machine when it is installed. It seems more appropriate to determine at time t which of the *old* machines should be scrapped. In a deterministic model however, there is no difference. If one substitutes N(t) for t in (39), then, since N is the inverse function of V, (39) becomes:

$$\lambda_1(t) + \{l(N(t))/k\}\lambda_2(t) = 0 \tag{40}$$

Now this rule gives N(t) and N(t) implicitly determines which old machines should be scrapped at time t.

7.3.2 Comparison with other scrapping rules

In the vintage models one finds in literature, the financial side of the decision making problem of the firm is ignored. To compare the model of this chapter with these models, set $Y(t)=\dot{Y}(t)=0$ for all t and f=0 in (5)-(17). Then D can be eliminated. The result is: maximise the discounted stream of cash-flows

$$\int_0^\infty e^{-it}\{\, p(Q(t)).Q(t) - w(t)L(t) - c(t)I(t)\,\}\, dt \tag{41}$$

with regard to I and B, subject to the constraints (6)-(8), (11), (14) and (16)-(17). In most vintage models, the constraint (15) on the cash-flows is ignored.

These simplifications lead to the following simplifications of the optimality conditions: set $\lambda_4(t)=-1$ and $\lambda_5(t)=\mu_3(t)=\mu_4(t)=\upsilon_1(t)=\upsilon_2(t)=0$ for all t in (22)-(38) and ignore (33), (37) and (38). Now (29) and (30) imply that $\lambda_1(t)=\partial S/\partial K(t)$ and $\lambda_2(t)=-w(t)$ (Note that this confirms the postulated interpretation for λ_1 and λ_2). Now the scrapping condition (39) is:

$$\partial S/\partial K(V(t)) - \{l(t)/k\}w(V(t)) = 0 \tag{42}$$

So a capital good of vintage t is scrapped when marginal revenue equals the wage costs of a unit of that vintage (only wage costs, no financing costs or depreciation costs!). It is now easy to see how this relates to the Malcomson-condition and the CPB-condition, as mentioned is section 7.3.1.

<u>The Malcomson condition</u>

Assume that the bounds on I are not active. Substituting $\mu_1=\mu_2=0$ and (29)-(30) in (26) and then differentiating (26) and using (39) gives:

$$\partial S/\partial K(t) = \frac{l(t)}{k} w(t) + ic(t) + ac(t) - \dot{c}(t) - \int_t^{V(t)} e^{-(i+a)(\tau-t)} \{ \frac{\dot{l}(t)}{k} \lambda_2(\tau) \} d\tau \qquad (43)$$

The right hand side of (43) can be interpreted as the marginal cost of producing on a machine installed at time t: the first four terms of the right hand side constitute the 'usual' marginal cost: wage cost plus capital costs (see, for instance, Nickell [1978b], p.10). But with the introduction of technological progress, the marginal cost is augmented by the last term in (43) (Note that $\dot{l}(t)$ is negative). This term accounts for the 'extra' wage cost the firm incurs due to forgone technological progress: if the firm would invest a moment later, the wage cost per unit of capital would be lower because newer capital goods require less labour. The higher the rate of technological progress (which means that the absolute value of $\dot{l}$ is large), the more expensive it is to invest now instead of a moment later.
So (43) implies that $\partial S/\partial K(V(t))$ equals the marginal cost of producing on machines of vintage V(t). So now the scrapping condition (42) can be rephrased: capital goods of vintage t are scrapped when the wage costs per capital good of vintage t equals the marginal cost of producing on a capital good of vintage V(t), i.e. on a *new* capital good. This is exactly the Malcomson-condition. Note that the Malcomson-condition is not valid when the upper bound on investments is active.

The CPB-condition

To arrive at the CPB-condition one additional assumption has to be made, namely: there is perfect competition on the output market. This implies that: $p=\partial S/\partial Q=k(\partial S/\partial K)$. Substituting this in (42) and multiplying (42) with the total output on capital goods of vintage t gives the CPB-condition.

7.3.3 Interpretation of the scrapping condition in the general model

In the general model, the values of λ_1 and λ_2 are more difficult to interpret. As stated before, λ_1 and λ_2 measure contributions to the objective function. An extra dollar cash-flow at time t means one unit *less* debt. The contribution to the objective function of a unit of debt equals λ_4 (since λ_4 is the shadow price of debt). So the contribution of an extra dollar cash-flow at time t to the objective function equals $-\lambda_4(t)$, which explains why λ_4 appears in the right hand sides of (29) and (30)[8].

If the bounds on D are not active, (27) gives $\lambda_4=-1$. In this case two situations have to be distinguished:

a) $\upsilon_2=0$, implying $Y \leq bX$.

In other words, the upper bound on debt is, in general, not active. Using $I>0$, $\lambda_3=0$ (see (28)) and $\lambda_4=-1$ and substituting (29) and (30) in (32) gives:

$$\partial S/\partial K(V(t)) - \{l(t)/k\}w(V(t)) = 0^{9} \tag{44}$$

This condition has the same interpretation as before: a vintage of capital goods is scrapped when the marginal revenue of producing with that vintage equals the marginal cost. As before the costs consist only of wages.

b) $\upsilon_2>0$, implying $Y=bX=bK/(1+b)$ and $\upsilon_1=0$.

---

[8]In the course of writing this thesis, many models were developed which were not good enough to be included. One of these models deserves to be mentioned in a lengthy note. This particular model is a vintage model in which: fiscal depreciation equals technical depreciation; the scrap value of capital goods is not zero but equals the book value; the firm faces adjustment costs. These assumptions forced me to use a differential equation of equity instead of debt. The scrapping rule in this model was:

$$\partial S/\partial K(V(t)) = w(V(t))l(t)/k + ac + ic$$

The remarkable difference with the scrapping rule in the main text is that the relevant costs are not the operating costs but the total costs, including depreciation and financing costs. In fact, the scrapping rule in the main text is phrased in terms of cash-inflows and cash-outflows, while the scrapping rule above is phrased in terms of revenues and costs. The reason is that the model in the main text is essentially based on cash-inflows and cash-outflows, which determine the differential equation for Y, while this alternative model is based on revenues and costs, which determine the differential equation for X. To evaluate the contribution to the objective function of one dollar, in the main text this dollar should be conceived as a cash-inflow which is then multiplied by the shadow price of debt, while in the alternative model this dollar should be conceived as a revenue which is then multiplied by the shadow price of equity.

[9]For a putty-clay model, this scrapping condition would have to be adjusted in the following way. The scrapping condition, which one can find in a similar way as for a clay-clay model, would be:

$$\partial S/\partial Q(V(t)) - \frac{L(t,t)e^{-a(V(t)-t)}w(V(t))}{Q(V(t),t)}=0,$$

where L(t,t), the amount of labour assigned to capital of vintage t, is an extra decision variable. The difference with the 'clay-clay' condition is that this condition is defined per unit of output instead of per unit of capital, since in a putty-clay model there is not such a simple relation between Q(t) and K(t). The interpretation of the condition is the same as in the clay-clay model.

Using λ_4=-1 in (33) gives $\upsilon_2(t)=\{i-(1-f)r\}/(1+b)$[10]. Substituting this in (29) and then substituting (29) and (30) in (32) gives:

$$\partial S/\partial K(V(t)) + \frac{bc\,(t)}{(1+b)} * \frac{i-(1-f)r}{(1-f)} - \{l(t)/k\}w(V(t)) = 0 \qquad (45)$$

In order to interpret (45), the second term on the left hand side has to be explained. Note that this term equals:

$$b\upsilon_2(V(t))c(V(t))/(1-f) \qquad (46)$$

According to the results in Appendix 3, $\upsilon_2(V(t))$ measures the contribution to the objective function of a momentary relaxation of the constraint

$$bc(V(t))K(V(t))-(1+b)Y(V(t)) \geq 0 \qquad (47)$$

at time V(t). An extra capital good at time V(t) would lead to a relaxation of the constraint with $bc(V(t))$ units. In terms of the objective function this is worth $bc(V(t))*\upsilon_2(V(t))$. This amount before taxes exactly equals (46). So the second term on the left hand side of (45) can be interpreted as part of the 'marginal revenue' at time V(t)! In general one can conclude that if a constraint involving the capital goods stock is active, marginal revenue includes the effects of the relaxation or violation of that constraint due to an extra capital good.

7.3.4 Another way to derive the scrapping condition?

Another interesting question concerning the scrapping condition is whether the scrapping decision at time t can be seen as the solution of a *static* optimisation problem at time t, independent of other (dynamic) decisions. As mentioned earlier (p.108), the scrapping condition has a somewhat static nature. Moreover, Broer [1987] derives his scrapping decision for time t through maximisation of total after tax cash-flows from operations at time t with regard to N and then uses this scrapping condition in the dynamic optimisation problem of maximising the stream of profits over an infinite horizon (leading to the optimal investment and optimal labour demand).
In the present model this approach amounts to maximising the 'accounting cash-flow' $(1-f)(S(K/k)-wL-rY)+fA$ (see (4.30)) with regard to N:

$$\frac{d}{dN}\,\{\, (1-f)(S(K/k) - wL - rY) + fA \,\} = 0 \qquad (48)$$

From (6) and (8):

---

[10]The combination of λ_4=-1 and $\upsilon_2>0$ only occurs if $i>(1-f)r$ (see (33)).

$$K(t) = \int_{N(t)}^{t} e^{-a(t-\tau)} I(\tau)\, d\tau, \qquad L(t) = \int_{N(t)}^{t} e^{-a(t-\tau)} I(\tau) l(\tau)/k\, d\tau.$$

So (48) is equivalent to:

$$(1-f)\left[-\frac{\partial S}{\partial K}(t) e^{-a(t-N(t))} I(N(t)) + w(t) e^{-a(t-N(t))} I(N(t)) l(N(t))/k \right] = 0 \qquad (49)$$

If $I(N(t)) > 0$, it is clear that (49) is equivalent to the scrapping condition for case a) ((44) for $t=N(t)$) .In this case the scrapping condition is indeed the solution of the static problem: maximise cash-flows at time t with regard to the birth date of the oldest capital goods still in use at time t[11]. The scrapping decision can be made *separate* from the investment and dividend decisions in this case.

For case b) however, it seems impossible to formulate a static maximisation problem that yields (45). So for case b) the scrapping condition can only be found by solving the complete dynamic optimisation problem (5)-(17). The separation of the scrapping decisions from the other decisions fails in this case. From a technical point of view it seems that this separation fails if and only if there are *active* constraints on K. In case a) only the restriction $Y \geq 0$, which does not involve K, is active. This is a plausible result: since the scrapping decision affects K, it is obvious that active constraints on K influence the scrapping decision.

7.4 A steady state solution

7.4.1 Existence of a steady state solution

For a model like the simplified model in section 7.3.2, Broer [1987] proves the existence of a steady state solution, if certain assumptions concerning the exogeneous variables are satisfied. This subsection investigates

---

[11]Now it is possible to relax the assumption that N and V are monotonic (see p.103). Equation (49) implies that capital goods of vintage t will be used at time τ if and only if $\partial S/\partial K(\tau) - w(\tau) l(t)/k \geq 0$. The equation $\partial S/\partial K(\tau) - w(\tau) l(t)/k = 0$ may have several solutions, implying that the set of years in which vintage t is used can be a union of disjunct intervals (cf. Broer [1987] p.122; Broer also examines the case (§4.4) where zero utilisation of capital goods is not costless).

whether there exists a steady state for the model (5)-(17), while making similar assumptions. Firstly the function l, which represents the technological progress, is specified as:

$$l(\mathrm{t}) = l(0)\mathrm{e}^{-h\mathrm{t}} \tag{50}$$

This means that the labour-to-output ratio is exponentially decreasing over time. Next it is assumed that there exist positive constants w^* and c^* such that:

$$\lim_{\mathrm{t}\to\infty} w(\mathrm{t})\mathrm{e}^{-h\mathrm{t}} = w^*$$
$$\lim_{\mathrm{t}\to\infty} c(\mathrm{t}) = c^* \tag{51}$$

The revenue function is assumed to have the following form (compare the price function (5.1) with $m=g=0$):

$$\mathrm{S(K)} = \left\{ \frac{\mathrm{K}}{k} \right\}^{1-1/e} \quad , \; e>1 \tag{52}$$

The assumption that the wage rate rises at a rate equal to the rate of technological progress implies that *labour* gets the benefits of the *labour* augmenting technological progress. In other words, the rise of the wage rate equals the rise of the labour productivity.
A steady state solution should have the following characteristics:

$$\lim_{\mathrm{t}\to\infty} \mathrm{K(t)} = \mathrm{K}^*$$
$$\lim_{\mathrm{t}\to\infty} \mathrm{I(t)} = \mathrm{I}^* \tag{53}$$
$$\lim_{\mathrm{t}\to\infty} \mathrm{V(t)-t} = \mathrm{T}^*$$

Equation (53) implies that the bounds on I and B are not active. Assume the bounds on D are also not active, and consider the case $i<(1\text{-}f)r$. This implies $\mu_i=0$, i=1..6, and $\upsilon_2=0$ in the steady state.
Given these assumptions, (44) is valid. Using $\mathrm{N(t)}=\mathrm{V}^{-1}(\mathrm{t})$, (44) implies:

$$\frac{\partial \mathrm{S}}{\partial \mathrm{K}}(\mathrm{t}) - \{l(\mathrm{N(t)})/k\}w(\mathrm{t}) = 0 \tag{54}$$

In the steady state:

$$(\partial \mathrm{S}/\partial \mathrm{K})^* = (1\text{-}1/e)(\mathrm{K}^*/k)^{-1/e}, \text{ a constant.}$$
$$\mathrm{N(t)} = \mathrm{t}-\mathrm{T}^* \tag{55}$$
$$w(\mathrm{t}) = w^*\mathrm{e}^{h\mathrm{t}}$$

Substituting this and the definition of l in (54) gives:

$$(1\text{-}1/e)(\mathrm{K}^*/k)^{-1/e} = l(0)/kw^*\mathrm{e}^{h\mathrm{T}^*} \tag{56}$$

The only unknowns in (56) are K^* and T^*.
The steady state solution must also satisfy (26). In Appendix 5.1.1 it is shown that substituting (50), the steady state values (51) and (53), the values for λ_1, λ_2, λ_4 and λ_5, and (54) in (26), and then differentiating (26) gives:

$$\frac{c^*}{1-f}\left\{ 1 - f \int_0^v e^{-i\tau} d(\tau)\, d\tau \right\} =$$

$$(l(0)w^*/k) \left\{ \frac{he^{-(i+a-h)T^*} + (i+a-h)e^{hT^*} - (i+a)}{(i+a-h)(i+a)} \right\} \qquad (57)$$

The left hand side of (57) is a positive constant (this can be derived from (3)). The right hand side is a function of T^*, $g(T^*)$. It is easily seen that:

$$g(0) = 0, \; g(\infty) = \infty \text{ and g is strictly increasing} \qquad (58)$$

This implies that (57) has an unique solution for T^*. Substituting this solution in (56) gives a unique value for K^*. In the steady state:

$$K^* = \int_{t-T^*}^{t} I^* e^{-a(t-\tau)} d\tau \qquad (59)$$

This gives for I^*:

$$I^* = aK^*/(1-e^{-aT^*}) \qquad (60)$$

So indeed there exists a steady state solution of the form proposed in (53).
Note that (53) implies that the optimal lifetime of capital goods approaches the constant T^*. From (57) the derivatives of T^* with regard to the parameters can be derived:

$$dT^*/dc^* > 0, \; dT^*/dk > 0, \; dT^*/dl(0) < 0, \; dT^*/dw^* < 0, \qquad (61)$$

The sign of dT^*/df depends on the value of f, the value of i and the depreciation scheme d. I did not succeed in determining analytically the signs of the derivatives of T^* with regard to a, i and h. One has to be very careful explaining the signs of these derivatives, since all parameters affect T^* and $(\partial S/\partial K)^*$ as well. A suggestive explanation of the results is as follows: there are two things to look at:
1) does the parameter affect the cost of a new capital good?
2) does the parameter affect the 'cost' of having 'old' capital goods?
ad 1) The before tax cost of a new capital good equals:

$$\frac{(i+a)c^*}{1-f}\left\{1 - f\int_0^v e^{-i\tau}\, d(\tau)\, d\tau\right\} \tag{62}$$

This cost consists of (technical) depreciation cost and financing cost, corrected for the present value of future tax savings due to fiscal depreciation of the capital good. The higher (62), the more expensive to buy new capital goods. If buying new capital goods is expensive, it is profitable to use the 'old' machines longer and thus a higher value of (62) leads to a larger T^*. This explains $dT^*/c^* > 0$ and dT^*/df: if the discount rate is low, and/or the depreciation scheme is such that a capital good is quickly depreciated in its first years, then a higher tax rate reduces the cost of a new capital good and thus it leads to a higher T^*. Finally, it can easily be seen that a higher a and a higher i lead to a higher cost (62) and consequently tend to increase T^*.

ad 2) the technological progress is embodied: it only affects newly installed machines. The corresponding rise of the wage rate, however, affects all workers, including the workers assigned to 'old' capital goods. Therefore it is more expensive for the firm to have 'old' capital goods, inducing the firm to lower T^* if the wage rate is high or if the number of workers per capital good is high. This explains dT^*/dw^*, dT^*/dk and $dT^*/dl(0)$.

The signs of the derivatives with regard to the parameters i and a cannot be determined analytically because these parameters have opposing effects with regard to questions 1) and 2). A higher discount rate i leads to a higher cost of new capital goods (inducing the firm to increase T^*), but a higher i increases the 'cost' of having 'old' capital goods (inducing the firm to decrease T^*). A higher technical depreciation rate a leads to a higher cost of new capital goods (inducing the firm to increase T^*), but a higher a leads to a higher average age of 'old' capital goods (inducing the firm to decrease T^*).

Finally, the rate of technological progress h has two opposing effects on T^* with regard to 2): a higher h leads to a higher wage rate (inducing the firm to decrease T^*), but a higher h also reduces the number of workers per unit of capital (inducing the firm to increase T^*).

The effect of the parameters on K^* and I^* can be derived using (see (59) and (60)):

$$dK^*/dT^* < 0, \; dI^*/dT^* < 0 \tag{63}$$

7.4.2 Is the steady state identical to the final path?

In the previous section a steady state solution was found, by *assuming* that there was such a solution and checking whether it fulfilled the optimality conditions. This is a very common way to treat an optimal control problem (as already discussed in Chapter 3), but in this thesis a different procedure was followed thusfar: so-called paths are derived and these paths are coupled to find the entire optimal solution. Since the steady state is a kind of a long run target, an obvious question from the viewpoint of this procedure is whether 'the' or 'a' final path is equivalent to the steady state. Assume that on the final path the bounds on the control variables are not active and that debt is zero ($i<(1-f)r$); that is , the final path is characterised by $\mu_i=0$, i=1..6 and $\upsilon_2=0$. It is easily checked that this path fulfils the transversality condition (A4.53). Now the question is: if one assumes (50) and (51) but nót (53), does this final path *imply* a steady state of the form (53).

Appendix 5.1.2 shows, more or less in the same way as in the previous subsection with the crucial difference that (48) is no longer assumed, that manipulation of (26) gives, after substitution of the limit values of c and w:

$$\varphi = \beta e^{h(t-N(t))} + h e^{-\beta((V(t)-t)}, \qquad (64)$$

where β and φ are constants, given by:

$$\beta = i+a-h \qquad (65)$$

$$\varphi = \left\{1 - f \int_0^v e^{-i\tau}\, d(\tau)\, d\tau\right\} \frac{i+a}{1-f}\,(i+a-h)\, \frac{c^* k}{w^* l(0)} + i+a \qquad (66)$$

Define:

M(t) := V(t)-t, the lifetime of capital goods installed at time t

T(t) := t-N(t), the lifetime of capital goods scrapped at time t.

Then (64) is equivalent to:

$$\varphi = \beta e^{hT(t)} + h e^{-\beta M(t)} \qquad (67)$$

It can easily be seen that <u>if</u> $M(t)=T(t)=T^*$, (67) is equivalent to (57). In other words, if the optimal lifetime on the final path approaches a constant T^*, this is exactly the same lifetime as the one found for the steady state solution in 7.4.1.

The question now is: is $M(t)=T(t)=T^*$ the only solution of (67), for $t\to\infty$? This is indeed the case, provided $\beta>0$!

$\beta>0$

Rewrite (67):

$$M(t) = -1/\beta \ln\{ (\varphi-\beta e^{hT(t)})/h \} \tag{68}$$

The argument of the logarithm has to be positive and M(t) also has to be positive. This implies:

$$\frac{1}{h} \ln\frac{\varphi-h}{\beta} < T(t) < \frac{1}{h} \ln\frac{\varphi}{\beta} \tag{69}$$

Note that $\varphi>0$ (using (3)) and that

$$\varphi-h = \beta(1+\delta) \text{ with } \delta>0 \tag{70}$$

(69) has to be satisfied for $t\to\infty$. From the definition of M and T and the fact that N is the inverse function of V, it is easily seen that:

$$M(t) = T(t+M(t)) \tag{71}$$

This implies that (69) has to be satified for $T(t+M(t))=M(t)$, $t\to\infty$. Thus:

$$\frac{1}{h} \ln\frac{\varphi-h}{\beta} < M(t) < \frac{1}{h} \ln\frac{\varphi}{\beta} \tag{72}$$

Again rewrite (67):

$$T(t) = 1/h \ln\{ (\varphi-he^{-\beta M(t)})/\beta \} \tag{73}$$

It is easily seen that T is an increasing function of M. Combining (72) and (73) gives new bounds on T(t), which are narrower than the bounds in (69). Using (71) these new bounds are also bounds for M(t), and this gives narrower bounds on T(t) using (73), and so forth. This way a sequence of lower and upper bounds on M(t) and T(t) is obtained, for $t\to\infty$.

The same phenomenon is observed by Malcomson [1975, 1979], who also finds a sequence of bounds on M(t) and T(t). However, even for special cases, Malcomson ([1975], p.33) was "unable to show analytically whether the upper and lower bounds converge to the same limit...." In Appendix 5.1.3 it is demonstrated that the lower and upper bounds do converge to the same limit and that this limit equals T^* (Using the method of Appendix 5.1.3 it can be shown that in Malcomson's articles the sequences of upper and lower bounds also converge to the same limit).

Remembering that (67) was derived from the optimality conditions after substitution of the limit values of $c(t)$ and $w(t)$ as defined in (51), it can now be concluded that on the final path the optimal lifetime of capital goods approaches T^* . Using (A5.7) this implies that $\partial S/\partial K$ approaches a constant $(\partial S/\partial K)^*$, and thus K approaches K^*, where K^* and $(\partial S/\partial K)^*$ are equal to the steady state values in section 7.4.1. Differentiating (6) with

$N(t)=t-T^*$ gives:

$$\frac{dK}{dt}(t) = I(t) - aK(t) - I(t-T^*)e^{-aT^*} \tag{74}$$

Substituting $K=K^*$ gives $I(t)=aK^*+I(t-T^*)e^{-aT^*}$ and thus:

$$I(t+nT^*) = aK^*(1+e^{-aT^*}+...+e^{-naT^*}) + I(t-T^*)e^{-(n+1)aT^*} \tag{75}$$

This shows that for $n\to\infty$, $I\to aK^*/(1-e^{-aT^*})$, which is exactly the steady state value in (60).

So, on the final path, characterised by $\mu_i=0$, $i=1..6$ and $\upsilon_2=0$, the optimal values of K, $\partial S/\partial K$, N, V, M, T and I approach their steady state values as $t\to\infty$. Using (7) it can be seen that

$$L(t) \to \frac{l(0)I^*}{k(a-h)}\{1-e^{(h-a)T^*}\}\, e^{-ht} \tag{76}$$

The right hand side of (76) is a decreasing function of time, so in the limit L is decreasing, as was to be expected. Using (10) (with $Y=0$), (9) and (3) this implies that dividends D approache a constant value D^*:

$$D^* = (1-f)\,[\,p(\frac{K^*}{k})\frac{K^*}{k} - w^*\frac{l(0)I^*}{k(a-h)}\{1-e^{(h-a)T^*}\}\,] + (f-1)c^*I^* \tag{77}$$

Note that the depreciation scheme has dropped out of (77).

$\beta<0$

Using the same procedure as for $\beta>0$, in case $\beta<0$ I only found a sequence of lower bounds for T and M, the same sequence as before. So it seems that it cannot be concluded now that the optimal solution on the final path approaches the steady state values. And since I have not been able to give a general solution of (67), it is impossible to say much about the behaviour of T and M on the final path and about the behaviour of the other relevant variables either. In fact I can only conclude that dT/dt, dM/dt and $d(\partial S/\partial K)/dt$ have the same sign and that in the limit $M(t)\geq T^*$ and $T(t)\geq T^*$. Note that $\beta<0$ means that $i+a<h$, which implies that the rate of technological progress is high. From now on it is assumed that $\beta>0$.

$(1-f)r<i$

If the cost of debt is lower than the cost of equity, the final path is most likely characterised by $\mu_i=0$, $i=1..6$ and $\upsilon_1=0$. It is easily seen that under these conditions (67) is still valid! This implies the same 'steady state' value for M and T. The steady state values for K,L,Y,D, and I are not the same as in the case $i<(1-f)r$, but they are easily derived from the optimality conditions and the steady state value T^*.

7.5 Summary and conclusions

This chapter studies the scrapping condition and the steady state solution in a vintage model of the firm. Section 7.2 shows that the Maximum Principle of Appendix 4, which is derived to handle the vintage structure, also makes it possible to model fiscal depreciation in a more realistic way: capital goods are fiscally depreciated in a fixed number of years. Section 7.3 derives the scrapping condition in terms of shadow prices and shows that various scrapping conditions in the literature are special cases of this condition. Section 7.4 shows that, with some additional conditions on the exogeneous variables, the optimal solution approaches, for $t \to \infty$, a unique steady state, characterised by a constant lifetime of capital goods.

As stated clearly in Chapter 3, not only the steady state solution of optimal control models are of interest. The optimal trajectories towards that steady state also deserve to be studied. This will be done in the next chapter.

8
OPTIMAL POLICIES IN MODELS WITH TECHNOLOGICAL PROGRESS, WITH AND WITHOUT A BUSINESS CYCLE

8.1 Introduction

In Chapter 7 the steady state of models with technological progress was studied, but nothing has been said about the optimal trajectory *towards* the steady state. This chapter discusses the optimal policies of the general and the simplified model of sections 7.2-7.3. Moreover, the business cycle of section 5.2 is introduced into these models.

8.2 The optimal solution for the simplified model of Chapter 7

8.2.1 Limitations of the coupling procedure

In the previous chapter it was shown that the optimal solution will approach the steady state solution, on the assumptions (7.50)-(7.51). As in all models thusfar, I would like to give the optimal solution for all $t \geq 0$, not only for $t \to \infty$. This requires more specific assumptions concerning the time paths of w and c. With (7.50)-(7.51) in mind, it seems a logical choice to assume:

$$w(t) = w^* e^{ht}, \; c(t) = c^*, \text{ for all } t \geq 0 \tag{1}$$

As before it is assumed that $l(t) = e^{-ht} l(0)$, so 'labour' gets the benefits of the labour augmenting technological progress. All other exogeneous variables are assumed to be constant. These assumptions are maintained throughout the rest of this chapter.

Since it appears to be very difficult to apply the coupling procedure to the general model (7.5)-(7.17) in Chapter 7, in this section an attempt is made to find the optimal solution for the simplified version of the model, as defined in section 7.3.2. To recall, this simplified model results from setting $Y = \dot{Y} = 0$ and $f = 0$ in (7.5)-(7.17). In section 7.3.2 the constraints on dividends D, which are now in fact constraints on the cash-flow $p(Q(t))Q(t) - w(t)L(t) - c(t)I(t)$, are ignored because they do not affect the scrapping condition or the steady state. However, if the entire optimal trajectory is studied, these constraints are relevant. An upper bound on the cash-flow is not necessary, since $p(Q(t))Q(t)$ cannot suddenly become infinite. The 'old' restriction $D \geq 0$ is now replaced by:

$$p(Q(t))Q(t) - w(t)L(t) - c(t)I(t) \geq 0 \tag{2}$$

Note that this imposes an upper bound on I, so that the restriction $I_{max} - I \geq 0$ can be dismissed. The resulting model is:

$$\max_{I,B} \int_0^\infty e^{-it} \{ p(Q(t))Q(t) - w(t)L(t) - c(t)I(t) \} \, dt \tag{3}$$

$$K(t) = \int_{N(t)}^{t} e^{-a(t-\tau)} I(\tau) \, d\tau = \int_{V^{-1}(t)}^{t} e^{-a(t-\tau)} I(\tau) \, d\tau \tag{4}$$

$$Q(t) = K(t)/k \tag{5}$$

$$L(t) = \int_{N(t)}^{t} e^{-a(t-\tau)} I(\tau) l(\tau)/k \, d\tau = \int_{V^{-1}(t)}^{t} e^{-a(t-\tau)} I(\tau) l(\tau)/k \, d\tau \tag{6}$$

$$\dot{V}(t) = B(t), \text{ for all } t \geq n_0, \text{ where } n_0 = N(0) \tag{7}$$

$$0 \leq I(t) \leq \frac{p(Q(t))Q(t) - w(t)L(t)}{c(t)}, \text{ for all } t \geq 0 \tag{8}$$

$$B_{min} \leq B(t) \leq B_{max}, \text{ for all } t \geq n_0 \tag{9}$$

$$I(t) \text{ is given for } t \in [n_0, 0) \tag{10}$$

The optimality conditions are not exactly the same as in section 7.3.2, because of the upper bound in (8). The meaning of all Greek symbols, except μ_2, remains the same as in Chapter 7: μ_2 is now the Lagrange multiplier of the constraint (2). It can easily be seen that the necessary conditions are:

$$-c + \int_t^{V(t)} e^{-(i+a)(\tau-t)} \{ \lambda_1(\tau) + \frac{l(t)}{k} \lambda_2(\tau) \} \, d\tau + \mu_1 - \mu_2 c = 0, \text{ for all } t \geq 0 \tag{11}$$

$$\lambda_3 + \mu_5 - \mu_6 = 0 \text{ for all } t \geq n_0 \tag{12}$$

$$\lambda_1(t) = \frac{\partial S}{\partial K}(t) \{ 1 + \mu_2(t) \}, \text{ for all } t \geq 0 \tag{13}$$

$$\lambda_2(t) = -w(t) \{ 1 + \mu_2(t) \}, \text{ for all } t \geq 0 \tag{14}$$

$$\dot{\lambda}_3(t) = i\lambda_3(t) -$$

$$\{ 1+\mu_2(V(t)) \}I(t)e^{-(i+a)(V(t)-t)}\{ \partial S/\partial K(V(t)) - \frac{l(t)}{k}w(V(t)) \},$$

$$\text{for all } t \geq n_0 \tag{15}$$

$$\mu_1 I=0,\ \mu_2\{p(Q(t))Q(t)-w(t)L(t)-c(t)I(t)\}=0,\ \mu_1(t)\geq 0,\ \mu_2(t)\geq 0,\ t\geq 0 \tag{16}$$

$$\mu_5(B-B_{min})=0,\ \mu_6(B_{max}-B)=0,\ \mu_5(t)\geq 0,\ \mu_6(t)\geq 0,\ t\geq n_0 \tag{17}$$

From (15) and the fact that $\mu_2 \geq 0$, it is clear that the scrapping condition in this model is the same as in Chapter 7[1]. Moreover, as in section 7.4, the final path (defined by $\mu_1=\mu_2=\mu_5=\mu_6=0$) implies the steady state solution of this model.

Now the limitations of the coupling procedure can be demonstrated. Suppose the final path starts at time Δ. Then[2]:

$$V(t)=t+T^* \text{ and } \partial S/\partial K(t)=(\partial S/\partial K)^* \text{ for all } t\geq \Delta$$

$$N(t)=t-T^* \text{ for all } t\geq V(\Delta)=\Delta+T^* \tag{18}$$

Assuming, as before, the revenue function $S(K)=\{K/k\}\{K/k\}^{-1/e}$ (see (7.52)), (18) also
determines $K(t)$ for $t\geq\Delta$. However, $I(t), t\geq\Delta$ is not determined by the optimality conditions for the final path! After all, for $t\geq\Delta$ $K(t)=K^*$, so $\dot{K}=0$. Differentiating (4) gives:

$$\dot{K}(t) = I(t) - aK(t) - e^{-a(t-N(t))}I(N(t))\dot{N}(t) \tag{19}$$

---

[1]Note that the scrapping condition is $\partial S/\partial K(V(t))-w(V(t))l(t)/k=0$, even if the constraint (2), which involves K, is active. This seems to contradict section 7.3.4, which states that the scrapping condition has to be adjusted if there are active constraints involving K. However, constraint (2) is a very special one, since it involves revenue S as well as labour costs wL, which are the determining factors of the scrapping decision. If such a constraint on K is active, the scrapping condition is not affected. In general, the statement in section 7.3.4 is true.

[2]Since (7.54) is used to derive (7.67) and (7.54) is in principle only valid for $t\geq V(\Delta)$, (7.67) is only valid for $t\geq V(\Delta)$. Now Appendix 5.1.3 can be used to conclude that $M(t)=T(t)=T^*$ for all $t\geq V(\Delta)$. This gives: $V(t)=t+T^*$ and $N(t)=t-T^*$ for all $t\geq V(\Delta)$. Since N and V are each others inverse, this implies $V(t)=t+T^*$ for all $t\geq\Delta$. Consequently, using (A5.6), $\partial S/\partial K(t)=\partial S/\partial K^*$ for all $t\geq\Delta$.

And thus I(t), for $t \geq \Delta$, depends on investments on the previous path and on B (and V) on the previous path (implicitly determining $N(t), t \geq \Delta$). In other words, the optimal control variables on the final path depend on the optimal control variables on the previous path, which depend in turn on the control variables of an earlier path, etcetera. This complicates the coupling procedure: for instance, if one wants to decide whether path x can preceed the final path, one has to check, among other things, if path x leads to an I on the final path which lies inside the control region; but one cannot check this unless one knows which path preceeds path x. It is clear that this in principle leads to a regress up to the first path, starting at $t=n_0$.

In general the conclusion is: in the earlier models the question "Can path y preceed path z" could simply be answered with yes or no. Now it may happen that one can only answer "yes (no), if path y is preceeded by path x and path x is preceeded by path w and path w ....". So the procedure looses its iterative character. The reason is that there is no state variable in the usual sense: in the previous models, I(t) for $t > \Delta$ only depends on $K(\Delta)$, nót on investments before Δ. All the relevant information from the past is summarised in the state variable K. In the present vintage model, however, $I(t \mid t \geq \Delta)$ not only depends on $K(\Delta)=K^*$, but also on investments before Δ. Again the quotation from Broer on page 104 seems appropriate: "the entire investment history is relevant, which makes the state vector infinite dimensional".

8.2.2 The optimal policy

With all this in mind, it seems sensible nót to try to find all feasible strings, but to 'guess' the optimal string for every set of initial conditions $\{V(n_0),\ I(t), n_0 \leq t < 0\}$, assuming that the 'steady state' path (defined by $\mu_i=0$) is the final path,

and to check afterwards whether this guess satisfies the optimality conditions.

To characterise the optimal string, it is convenient to translate the initial conditions into the pair $\{\partial S/\partial K(0),\ N(0)\}$. Note that N(0) equals $V(n_0)$ and that, given N(0), different investment histories can lead to the same $\partial S/\partial K(0)$. Remember that on the final path $\partial S/\partial K=(\partial S/\partial K)^*$ and that $\partial S/\partial K(t)=w(t)l(N(t))/k$ after some time on the final path. It seems logical that the optimal string depends on:

is $\partial S/\partial K(0)$ greater than, smaller than or equal to $(\partial S/\partial K)^*$? (20)
is $\partial S/\partial K(0)$ greater than, smaller than or equal to $w(0)l(N(0))/k$?

This gives nine possible combinations. The process of finding the optimal policy for each combination did not have the solid, iterative character as in the previous chapters, but a more 'trial and error' character. The result is as follows. If the initial volume of the capital goods stock is small, the optimal policy can be summarised as follows:

use $I(t)$ to close the gap between $\partial S/\partial K(t)$ and $(\partial S/\partial K)^*$ as quickly as possible (21a)
use $B(N(t))$ to close the gap between $\partial S/\partial K(t)$ and $w(t)l(N(t))/k$ as quickly as possible (21b)

In appendix 5.2 this rule is closely examined for two initial situations and it is shown what are the difficulties if the initial volume of the capital goods stock is not small (in short the difficulty is: if one of the gaps in (21) is closed, it is not always possible to keep it closed and to close the remaining gap at the same time! In such cases the optimal policy is not clear to me).

Note that (21) suggests that the decisions concerning I and B are taken separately. This corresponds to the alternative way of deriving the scrapping rule in this model (see p.112), where N is chosen independently of I.

Before illustrating (21), it is useful to reflect on the meaning of N and V, or of $\dot{N}$ and $\dot{V}=B$. As said before, if a machine is installed at time t, it seems a bit awkward to decide right away when it will be scrapped (in technical terms: decide what $V(t)$ is). It is more realistic to say: at time t a decision is made about the level of investment ($I(t)$), and a decision is made about the scrapping of old vintages ($N(t)$). In a deterministic model there is no difference between these two approaches. However, when discussing the model in economic terms, it is far more convenient to think in terms of $I(t)$ and $N(t)$, than in terms of $I(t)$ and $V(t)$. For instance, for the development of $\partial S/\partial K(t)$ and $K(t)$ over time, one is interested in $I(t)$ and $N(t)$, and nót in $V(t)$ (see (19)). Technically, however, the model is built in terms of I, V and B. The 'first' decision to be made at $t=0$ is about $I(0)$ and $B(n_0)$. This seems to be nonsense: the decision $B(n_0)$ was taken at time n_0, not at time 0! But $B(n_0)$ equals $1/\dot{N}(0)$ (because $\dot{N}(t)=1/B(N(t))$). So at $t=0$ in fact $I(0)$ and $\dot{N}(0)$ are chosen. The moral is: when discussing the model in economic terms, it is most convenient to think in terms of I and $\dot{N}$; for technical purposes (checking the necessary conditions), one must translate I(t) and $\dot{N}(t)$ into I(t) and B(N(t)), using $\dot{N}(t)=1/B(N(t))$.

Now the 'decision rule' given above in (21) can be illustrated.
Suppose: $\partial S/\partial K(0) > (\partial S/\partial K)^*$ and $\partial S/\partial K(0) > w(0)l(N(0))/k$.
Given a concave revenue function S, the first inequality implies that the capital goods stock K is smaller than K^*. The second inequality implies that the oldest vintage at t=0, is still profitable, since marginal revenue is larger than marginal cost on machines of vintage N(0). Therefore it seems optimal to scrap as little as possible and to invest as much as possible. Scrapping as little as possible means prolonging the lives of the old vintages as much as possible[3]. In technical terms: $B(t)=B_{max}$ for $t \geq n_0$, or $\dot{N}(t)=1/B_{max}$ for $t \geq 0$. As a consequence $\partial S/\partial K$ will decrease and $w(t)l(N(t))/k$ will increase[4]. Thus the two aims in the 'decision rule' (21) are not conflicting. At a certain point of time, one of the two aims will be fullfilled. Which one is fulfilled first, depends on the parameters and the initial conditions. If $\partial S/\partial K=(\partial S/\partial K)^*$ is fulfilled first, the optimal policy is: maintain $\partial S/\partial K=(\partial S/\partial K)^*$ and continue $B=B_{max}$ until $w(t)l(N(t))/k$ reaches $(\partial S/\partial K)^*$. If $\partial S/\partial K=w(t)l(N(t))/k$ is fulfilled first, the optimal policy is: maintain $\partial S/\partial K=w(t)l(N(t))/k$ and continue to invest at the maximal rate until $\partial S/\partial K$ reaches $(\partial S/\partial K)^*$[5].
The next illustration is a bit more difficult.
Suppose: $\partial S/\partial K(0) > (\partial S/\partial K)^*$ and $\partial S/\partial K(0) < w(0)l(N(0))/k$.
The first inequality implies that K(0) is smaller than K^*, the second inequality implies that the oldest vintage at t=0 is not profitable. Now the two aims in (21) are conflicting. On the one hand ((21a)) the firm wants to grow as quickly as possible, which suggests investing as much as possible and prolonging the lives of existing vintages. On the other hand ((21b)) the firm wants to scrap the oldest vintages as quickly as possible,

---

[3]If there was no positive lower bound on $\dot{N}$, we would have found: $\dot{N}(t)=0$ for $t \geq 0$, implying no scrapping at all (see the discussion on page 103).

[4]Given the assumptions for l and w: $w(t)(l(N(t))/k)=\{(l(0)w^*)/k\}e^{\alpha T(t)}$, where $T(t)=t-N(t)$. Note that $\dot{T}(t)=1-1/B_{max}$, so that T increases if the artificial boundary B_{max} is high enough. This implies that $(l(N(t))/k)w(t)$ increases.

[5]In Appendix 5.2 it is shown that I and B or I and $\dot{N}$ cannot always be chosen separately, as suggested on p.125.

since they are not profitable. In appendix 5.2 it is shown that it is optimal to adhere to (21), even though the two aims in (21) are conflicting. Disregarding (21b) and scrapping as little as possible in order to grow as quickly as possible is *not* optimal. The optimal policy for this situation is depicted in Figure 1.

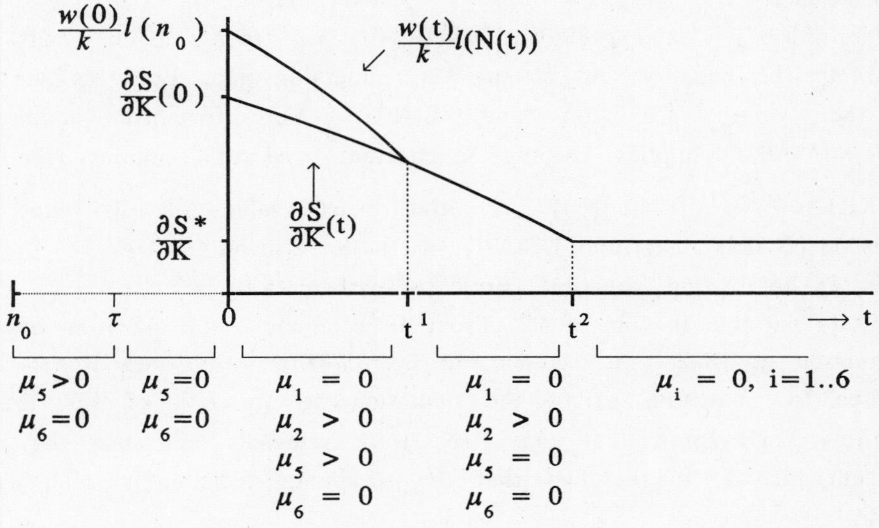

Figure 1: An optimal trajectory

The firm starts scrapping at the maximal rate ($\dot{N}(t)=1/B_{min}$) and investing at a maximal rate ($I(t)=\{S(K(t))-wL(t)\}/c$). At $t=t^1$, all unprofitable vintages are scrapped and from t^1 onwards the firm employs the scrapping condition and continues to invest as much as possible. At $t=t^2$ marginal revenue reaches its steady state value and the final path starts. The optimal lifetime of capital goods installed at time t, M(t), decreases for $t<t^1$, and $M(t)=T^*$ for $t>t^2$. It is not possible to make general statements concerning M(t) for $t\in(t^1,t^2)$. For $t<t^1$ the capital goods stock increases relatively slowly due to the maximal scrapping of old vintages. For $t\in(t^1,t^2)$ the capital goods stock increases more rapidly.

8.2.3 A decision rule?

The 'decision rule' (21) looks like the feedback decision rule of Chapter 4. A feedback decision rule gives the values of the control variables at time t, given the values of the state variables at time t. In the present case, there are no normal state variables. Instead the situation at time t is summarised in $\partial S/\partial K(t)$ and $N(t)$, which are not state variables in the usual sense. This leads to two differences between (21) and a normal feedback decision rule. The first difference is that $\partial S/\partial K(t)$ and $N(t)$ do not determine $I(t)$ and $B(t)$, but $I(t)$ and $B(N(t))$. The second difference is as follows. If $\partial S/\partial K(t) \neq (\partial S/\partial K)^*$ and $\partial S/\partial K(t) = w(t)l(N(t))/k$, or $\partial S/\partial K(t) = (\partial S/\partial K)^*$ and $\partial S/\partial K(t) \neq w(t)l(N(t))/k$, then (21) calls for maintaining the equality and closing the remaining gap. But this does not give the values for $I(t)$ and $B(N(t))$! For instance, maintaining $\partial S/\partial K(t) = (\partial S/\partial K)^*$ implies keeping K constant, and this implies (see (19)) $I(t) = aK(t) + e^{-a(t-N(t))}I(N(t))\dot{N}(t)$. So the exact value of $I(t)$ not only depends on $\partial S/\partial K(t)$, $N(t)$ and $1/B(N(t)) = \dot{N}(t)$, but also on $I(N(t))$.

This is an interesting situation. From a mathematical point of view, there is no state variable in this model. From an economic point of view however, the situation at time t is summarised by $\partial S/\partial K(t)$, $N(t)$ and $I(N(t))$. This relativises to a certain extent the quotation at the end of the previous subsection. The reason that only $I(N(t))$ is relevant, and not the entire investment history, is the fact that the scrapping decision is a 'marginal' decision.

The impossibility of a deriving a 'real' feedback decision rule can be illustrated in yet another way. In previous chapters, the decision rule was phrased in terms of the marginal return on investment and the marginal return on equity. An analogue for the present model would be to find an expression for marginal return on investment. The level of investment would then have to follow from a comparison of this marginal return on investment and the discount rate i. Define:

$$R(t) = \left\{\partial S/\partial K(t) - w(t)l(t)/k - ac^* - \int_t^{V(t)} e^{-(i+a)(\tau-t)}\, w(\tau)\dot{l}(t)/k\}d\tau\right\}/c^* \qquad (22)$$

This seems to be a reasonable candidate for the marginal return on investment (see the discussion of the Malcomson scrapping condition in section 7.3.2). Indeed, if $\mu_1 = \mu_2 = 0$, and the scrapping rule $\partial S/\partial K(V(t)) = w(V(t))l(t)/k$ is valid, differentiation of (11) gives (after substitution of (13) and (14)) $R(t) = i$. In particular this equality is valid on the final path. So this seems to suggest the following decision rule: if $R(t) > i$, then invest as much as possible; if $R(t) < i$, then $I=0$; and if $R(t) = i$, choose I to maintain this. However, this is nót a feedback decision rule, because $R(t)$ cannot be computed at time t using only data from the

past: R(t) depends on V(t), V(t) depends (according to the scrapping rule) on $\partial S/\partial K(V(t))$, and $\partial S/\partial K(V(t))$ depends on I(t) for all $t \in [t, V(t))$. Trying to find these I(t) using the just developed 'decision rule' leads to an infinite regress. The reason is that (22) 'looks forward' (involves V(t)), while the decision rule (21) 'looks backward' (involves only N(t)). The optimal policy *does* obey the decision rule in terms of R(t), but this rule cannot be used to *find* the optimal policy.
The conclusion is: although there is no feedback decision rule in the usual sense for this model, (21) is an economically plausible and workable rule[6].

8.3 The optimal solution for the general model

The general model of Chapter 7 can be seen as the simplified model with the financial decisions added or as the basic model of Chapter 4 with the vintage structure added. The optimal solutions for the basic model and for the simplified model are available. Still, 'merging' these two optimal solutions does not work. To be more precise: it is the *combination* of, on the one hand, the fact that the objective function consists of dividends instead of cash-flows (as in the basic model), and, on the other hand, the fact that there are constraints of type (7.6), (7.8) and (7.9) (as in the simplified model of the previous subsection), that prohibits the merging of the two solutions. The reason is that concepts like the marginal return on investment or the marginal return on equity can only be defined in terms of the shadow price of equity. This is best illustrated by means of a special case.
Suppose the initial conditions are the same as in the first example in section 8.2.2:
$\partial S/\partial K(0) > (\partial S/\partial K)^*$ and $\partial S/\partial K(0) > w(0)l(N(0))/k$.
Moreover, assume that $i < (1-f)r$. Just as in the simplified model, the final path implies a steady state with a constant $\partial S/\partial K = (\partial S/\partial K)^*$ (with of course a different value than in the simplified model!), with $N(t) = t - T^*$, and with $\partial S/\partial K(t) = w(t)l(N(t))/k$. The initial conditions are such that the capital goods stock is smaller than its steady state value and that the oldest vintage is still profitable. So it seems that the best policy is to scrap as little as possible and to invest at the maximal rate in order to grow as

---

[6]It should be noted, however, that this rule only applies to 'growth situations' (see the beginning of section 8.2.2 and Appendix 5.2).

quickly as possible. But, remember the optimal solution of the basic model: growing as quickly as possible also implies attracting debt if the marginal return on investment exceeds the cost of debt, and paying back the debt if the marginal return on investment equals the cost of debt ($R(K)=(1-f)r$, while keeping K constant (see p.44 and Figure 4.2)).

The easiest way to see if this policy is also valid in the present model is to find out whether there is a consolidation path (the path with $R(K)=(1-f)r$ and Y decreasing; path 4 in Chapter 4). In the basic model, the technical characteristics of path 4 are: $\mu_1=\mu_2=\upsilon_2=\upsilon_3=0$. This implies (see (4.14) and (4.16)):

$$\lambda_1=0 \Rightarrow \lambda_2(t)(1-f)\{\partial S/\partial K(t)-wl/k-a-r\}=0 \Rightarrow \partial S/\partial K(t)=wl/k+a+r,$$

which is equivalent to: the marginal return on investment equals $(1-f)r$. The crucial fact to note here is that the shadow price of equity, λ_2, drops out! The corresponding path in the general vintage model of Chapter 7 is a path with $\mu_1=\mu_2=\mu_5=\mu_6=\upsilon_1=\upsilon_2=0$. Substituting this in the optimality conditions (7.26)-(7.38) and differentiating (7.26), using (7.32) and $\lambda_3=0$, gives:

$$-\lambda_4(t)(1-f)\{\frac{\partial S}{\partial K}-w(t)\frac{l(t)}{k}\}-ac^*\left\{-\lambda_4-f\int_t^{t+v} e^{-i(\tau-t)}(-\lambda_4(\tau))d(\tau-t)\ d\tau\right\}$$

$$+\quad(1-f)\quad\int_t^{V(t)} e^{-(i+a)(\tau-t)}w(\tau)\frac{\dot{l}(t)}{k}(-\lambda_4(\tau))\quad d\tau$$

$$=(1-f)rc^*\left\{-\lambda_4(t)-f\int_t^{t+v} e^{-i(\tau-t)}(-\lambda_4(\tau))d(\tau-t)\ d\tau\right\} \tag{23}$$

Note that

$$\Pi(t):=c^*\left\{-\lambda_4(t)-f\int_t^{t+v} e^{-i(\tau-t)}(-\lambda_4(\tau))d(\tau-t)\ d\tau\right\} \tag{24}$$

is the purchasing cost of a capital good: the price c^* multiplied by $-\lambda_4$ minus the discounted value of tax savings, where each tax saving is also multiplied by $-\lambda_4$. Remember (see section 7.3.3) that the contribution to the objective function of one dollar equals $-\lambda_4$. Dividing both sides of (23) by $\Pi(t)$ gives:

$$\Big\{-\lambda_4(t)(1-f)\{\partial S/\partial K-w(t)l(t)/k\}-a\Pi(t)\quad +$$

$$(1-f)\int_t^{V(t)} e^{-(i+a)(\tau-t)}w(\tau)\dot{l}(t)/k(-\lambda_4(\tau))d\tau\Big\}\ /\ \Pi(t)\ =\ (1-f)r \tag{25}$$

Comparing this with the definition of marginal return on investment in (22) (keeping in mind the meaning of Π), it is clear that (25) is quite similar to "$R(t)=(1-f)r$". However, the shadow price of debt, λ_4, does nót drop out, because of the two integrals in (23). If there is no technological progress ($\dot{l}(t)=0$) and fiscal depreciation is treated as in earlier chapters, the integrals in (23) disappear and λ_4 drops out of (25).

Summarising: if the objective function consists of dividends, every dollar has to be multiplied with the shadow price of debt (λ_4) to know its contribution to the objective function. If moreover the model involves technological progress, this shadow price is inextricably bounded up with the optimality conditions (as is clear from the example above). This makes it very difficult to find the optimal policy for a model which involves dividends-maximisation ánd technological progress, as illustrated in a special case.

Another example of the same phenomenon concerns the scrapping decision. In the simplified model the optimal policy was: try to reach $\partial S/\partial K(t)=w(t)l(N(t))/k$ as quickly as possible and maintain it. This was based on (15): $\mu_5=\mu_6=0$ leads to $\partial S/\partial K(V(t))=w(V(t))l(t)/k$. In the general model (see (7.44)) "$\mu_5=\mu_6=0$ leads to $\partial S/\partial K(V(t))=w(V(t))l(t)/k$" as long as $\upsilon_2=0$. But if $\upsilon_2>0$ during some time the scrapping rule is:

$$\partial S/\partial K(V(t))+b\upsilon_2(V(t))c(V(t))/(1-f)=w(V(t))l(t)/k$$

(see (7.45-7.46)). In other words, the optimal scrapping rule is nót "reach and maintain $\partial S/\partial K(V(t))=w(V(t))l(t)/k$", but "reach and maintain $\lambda_1(V(t))=-\lambda_2(V(t))l(t)/k$" (this follows implicitly from (7.32); see also Appendix 5.2).

The conclusion seems inevitable: the optimal policy for the general model can only be characterised in terms of shadow prices. Define:

$$F(t)=\int_t^{V(t)} e^{-(i+a)(\tau-t)}\{\lambda_1(\tau)+\{l(t)/k\}\lambda_2(\tau)\}\,d\tau \qquad (26)$$

The optimal policy can be characterised as follows:

1) The scrapping decision (see (7.32))

IF $\lambda_1(V(t)) < -\{l(t)/k\}\lambda_2(V(t))$ THEN $B(t)=B_{min}$

IF $\lambda_1(V(t)) > -\{l(t)/k\}\lambda_2(V(t))$ THEN $B(t)=B_{max}$

IF $\lambda_1(V(t)) = -\{l(t)/k\}\lambda_2(V(t))$ THEN $B_{min}<B(t)<B_{max}$ to maintain the equality.

2) The investment decision (see (7.26))

IF $F(t) > \Pi(t)$ THEN I(t) maximal

IF $F(t) < \Pi(t)$ THEN $I(t)=0$

IF $F(t) = \Pi(t)$ THEN $0 < I(t) < \{S(Q)-wL\}/c^*$ to maintain the equality.

3) The dividend decision (see (7.27))

IF $-\lambda_4(t) < 1$ THEN $D(t)=D_{max}$

IF $-\lambda_4(t) > 1$ THEN $D(t)=0$

IF $-\lambda_4(t) = 1$ THEN $0 < D(t) < D_{max}$ to maintain the equality.

Using the interpretation of the shadow prices it is easy to interpret this 'rule':

Part 1) is simply the scrapping rule which is interpreted in section 7.3.3.

Part 2) can be explained as follows: F(t) can be interpreted as the marginal contribution to the objective function of one unit of investment at time t: note that one capital good at time t depriciates at a rate a. So at time $\tau > t$, there is $e^{-a(\tau-t)}$ left of this capital good. The marginal revenue in terms of the objective function at $t=\tau$ of this capital good equals $e^{-a(\tau-t)}\lambda_1(\tau)$, the marginal cost in terms of the objective function at $t=\tau$ equals $e^{-a(\tau-t)}(l(t)/k)\lambda_2(\tau)$ (using the shadow price interpretations for λ_1 and λ_2, as in section 7.3). Discounting these revenues and costs back to time t and summing up all revenues and costs during the entire life of the capital good gives the contribution to the objective function of an extra unit of capital, installed at time t. The costs in terms of the objective function of acquiring a capital good at time t is $\Pi(t)$. Now part 2) of the 'rule' is evident.

Part 3) of the 'rule' simply compares, from the point of view of the shareholder, the value of a dollar inside the firm ($-\lambda_4$) with the value of a dollar in his or her hands (1).

Note that the 'rule' has nothing to do with a decision rule. It does not tell the firm what to do. It gives the optimal actions on the basis of the values of the shadow prices. But these values are only known if the entire optimal solution is known, in which case no rule is needed. In fact, the 'rule' is nothing more than a different way to write down the optimality conditions.

8.4 Technological progress and a business cycle in one model

8.4.1 Introduction

If it is assumed that the revenue function in the models of Chapter 7 is the same as in Chapter 5, then these models incorporate technological progress as well as a business cycle. For such a model the derivation of the steady state is still valid, until it is concluded that K is constant because $\partial S/\partial K$ is constant. This is no longer true, as is clear from Chapter 5. Moreover, I is no longer a constant in the steady state. Remembering the analysis in Chapter 5, one might expect that $I \geq 0$ may be violated when the recession is severe. How severe the recession must be to bring about a violation of $I \geq 0$ will be studied in the next subsection. Remember that in the models of Chapter 7 the restriction $I \geq 0$ is a logical restriction, whereas in Chapter 5 the assumption of irreversibility of investments is behind it.

In the previous subsection the optimal solution has been characterised for the general model with technological progress. In fact the specification of the revenue function did not play any role at all in that subsection. Thus the characterisation of the optimal policy derived there is equally valid for the model including technological progress and a business cycle. However since this characterisation (the 'rule') is not 'operational', it is clear that it does not give insight into the consequences of a fluctuating demand for a firm with an age-structured capital goods stock. A more modest approach is to study the incorporation of a business cycle in the simplified model of this chapter. This is done in section 8.4.3.

8.4.2 When does the steady state solution violate $I \geq 0$?

As said before, the optimality conditions and the derivation of the steady state $\{(\partial S/\partial K)^*, T^*\}$ do not depend on the specification of S. From now on it is assumed that S is specified as in Chapter 5 (see (5.1)). The values of $(\partial S/\partial K)^*$ and T^* are given by (7.67), (7.56) and (7.55).

In Chapter 5 it was assumed that on $t=0$ the firm is in its *desired situation* (the 'final path', implying a constant marginal revenue) and then the optimal policy 'over the cycle' was derived for different values of *m* (remember that *m-g* measures the steepness of the slump). The first step was to find out for which values of *m* the business cycle had no influence, that is: for which values of *m* can the firm maintain the desired position it has at t=0. The conclusion was that for $m \leq a+g$ the optimal policy is to stay on the final path with constant marginal revenue. For values of *m* larger than $a+g$, keeping marginal revenue constant leads to a negative investment, which is not allowed in the model.

The same procedure is followed now for the general vintage model of Chapter 7: if $\partial S/\partial K(0)=(\partial S/\partial K)^*$ and $M(0)=T(0)=T^*$, for which values of *m* is the firm able to maintain $\partial S/\partial K(t)=(\partial S/\partial K)^*$ and $M(t)=T(t)=T^*$, without violating $I \geq 0$?

From the assumption that $\partial S/\partial K(t)=(\partial S/\partial K)^*$ for all t, the fact that $\partial S/\partial K=(1-1/e)p(K,t)$, and the definition of the price function (5.1), K(t) can be derived for all t. Next,

$$K(t) = \int_{t-T^*}^{t} I(\tau)e^{-a(t-\tau)}\, d\tau \tag{27}$$

can be used to find I(t) for all $t \geq 0$. This is done in Appendix 5.3. From that it should be possible to conclude for which values of *m* the constraint $I \geq 0$ is not violated. The optimal I (see Appendix 5.3) looks as follows (with the assumption that I(t),t<0 has the 'steady state' value):

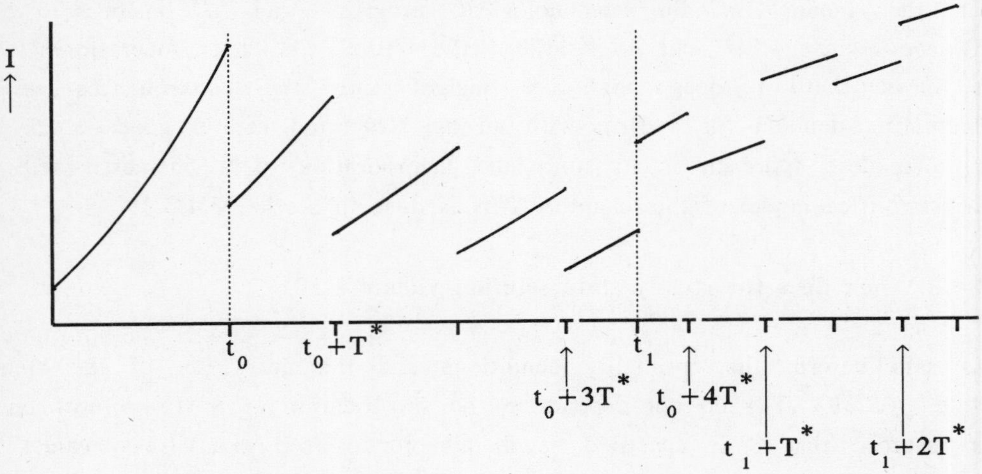

Figure 2: The optimal investment pattern

To keep $\partial S/\partial K$ at a constant level, investments have to grow steadily before t_0, as in the business cycle model without technological progress. At $t=t_0$ the recession starts and K will have to decrease to keep $\partial S/\partial K$ constant. In the model without technological progress the capital goods stock only decreases due to depreciation. Now the capital goods stock also decreases as a consequence of the scrapping of the vintage installed T^* years ago. In fact (see (19)):

$$\dot{K}(t) = I(t) - aK(t) - e^{-aT^*} I(t-T^*) \tag{28}$$

At t_0 investments will drop downward because now K has to decrease instead of increase (cf. Figure 5.2). After t_0 investments will rise (even though K decreases) because the amount of capital scrapped ($I(t-T^*)e^{-aT^*}$) grows. At $t=t_0+T^*$ the amount of scrapped capital jumps downward, as a consequence of the jump of I at t_0. Since K must decrease in such a way to keep $\partial S/\partial K$ constant, this downward jump in the amount of scrapped capital goods is accompanied by a downward jump of investments. So the original jump at t_0 repeats itself T^* years later. Likewise, the jump of I which occurs at t_1 as a consequence of the upturn of the price function, repeats itself at t_1+T^*, t_1+2T^*, etc. These jumps do die down, because of (technical) depreciation: the jump in investments at, for instance, t_0+T^* is e^{-aT^*} times the jump in investment in t_0.

In Appendix 5.3 it is shown that $I\left\{\left[t_0+(n+1)T^*\right]^+\right\}$ (to be precise: the limit of I(t) for $t{\downarrow}t_0+(n+1)T^*$) is smaller than $I\left\{\left[t_0+nT^*\right]^+\right\}$, as long as $t_0+(n+1)T^* < t_1$. I have not been able to proof whether (see Figure 2) $I\left\{\left[t_0+4T^*\right]^+\right\}$ is larger or smaller than $I\left\{\left[t_0+3T^*\right]^+\right\}$. So the conclusion is that, if m grows, the point of time where I will become negative for the first time is t_0+NT^* or $t_0+(N+1)T^*$, where N is such that $t_0+NT^* < t_1 < t_0+(N+1)T^*$.

If it is assumed, as does Nickell [1975], that the recession is shorter than the optimal lifetime of capital goods ($t_1-t_0 < T^*$, which implies N=1), then it is possible to prove that $I(t_0^+)$ is smaller than $I(t_0+T^{*+})$. So the crucial point is: when does $I(t_0^+)$ become negative. In Appendix 5.3 it is derived that this is the case if

$$m > (a+g)/\{1-e^{-(a+g)T^*}\} \tag{29}$$

If m is smaller than or equal to the right hand side of (29), then the policy to keep T and $\partial S/\partial K$ constant is feasible. Note that in the model without technological progress we found that it is only feasible to keep $\partial S/\partial K$ constant at its desired level if $m \leq g+a$. The right hand side of (29) is larger than $g+a$. So in the presence of technological progress it is possible to stay in the desired situation for larger values of m than in the model of Chapter 5. This is because the bottleneck in Chapter 5 is the constraint $I \geq 0$, which prevents a rapid decrease of K. In the model with technological progress the capacity to let K decrease is larger due to the scrapping of old vintages.

8.4.3 The business cycle in the simplified model

Equation (29) in the last subsection is of course also valid for the simplified model, although T^* will have a different value than in the general model. Maintaining the assumption that $t_1 - t_0 < T^*$, the next step is to find the optimal policy of $m > (a+g)/\{1-e^{-(a+g)T^*}\}$. A logical suggestion for the optimal policy is: there will be a zero investment period during the recession; in the second expansion phase, the firm will return to the 'final' (steady state) path.

In Appendix 5.4 the problems that arise when there is a 'zero investment'-period are discussed. The conclusion is that it is not clear whether the length of the 'zero investment'-period and the values of V during that period are determined by the optimality conditions. This contradicts Nickell, who states (p.58): "It is clear that the necessary conditions will determine a scrapping date V(t) for *all* t, even if no capital is in fact purchased at t".

An analysis of the optimal policy becomes very complicated (if not impossible), if V(t) is not determined during a 'zero investment'-period. Note that the problem disappears if the lower bound for I would be positive instead of zero. In that case it is indeed clear that the scrapping condition $\partial S/\partial K(V(t)=w(V(t))l(t)/k$ is valid for $t \in (\alpha,\beta)$ (see (15)), where (α,β) is the period during which the lower bound on investment is active. For that reason, it will be assumed from now on that the scrapping condition is valid even if $I=0$. Now an optimal policy which involves a 'zero investment'-period can be investigated.

Suppose that there is a 'zero investment'-period (α,β) and that for $t \leq \alpha$ and $t \geq \beta$ the firm is on the 'final path' (characterised by $\mu_i=0$). This implies for instance: $\partial S/\partial K(\alpha)=\partial S/\partial K(\beta)=(\partial S/\partial K)^*$. Equivalently:

$$\int_\alpha^\beta \frac{d}{dt}\frac{\partial S}{\partial K}(t)\, dt = 0 \tag{30}$$

Define:

$$s_1(t) = \int_t^{V(t)} e^{-(i+a)(\tau-t)} \{\frac{\partial S}{\partial K}(\tau)-w(\tau)l(t)/k\}\, d\tau - c^* \tag{31}$$

Then: $s_1(\alpha)=s_1(\beta)=0$ (use (11)). Define $s_2(t)=e^{-(i+a)t}s_1(t)$. Then $s_2(\alpha)=s_2(\beta)=0 \Rightarrow \int_\alpha^\beta \dot{s}_2(t)\, dt = 0$. Differentiating (11) and using the scrapping condition shows that this is equivalent to (for a similar 'tric', see Appendix 5.4):

$$\int_\alpha^\beta e^{-(i+a)t} \left\{\frac{\partial S}{\partial K}(t)-w(t)l(t)/k-ac^*-ic^* + \int_t^{V(t)} e^{-(i+a)(\tau-t)}\, w(\tau)\dot{l}(t)/k\}d\tau\right\} = 0 \tag{32}$$

Note that the two equations (30) and (32) contain two unknowns, α and β. In fact, $s_2(\alpha)=0$ and $s_2(t)<0$ for $t\in(\alpha,\beta)$ are equivalent to:

$$\int_\alpha^z e^{-(i+a)(t-\alpha)} \left\{\frac{\partial S}{\partial K}(t)-w(t)l(t)/k-ac^*-ic^* + \int_t^{V(t)} e^{-(i+a)(\tau-t)}\, w(\tau)\dot{l}(t)/k\}d\tau\right\} dt = 0 \tag{33}$$

$$\int_t^z e^{-(i+a)(u-t)} \left\{\frac{\partial S}{\partial K}(u)-w(u)l(u)/k-ac^*-ic^* + \int_u^{V(u)} e^{-(i+a)(\tau-u)}\, w(\tau)\dot{l}(t)/k\}d\tau\right\} du < 0,\ t\in(\alpha,\beta) \tag{34}$$

Equations (33) and (34) are the analogues of (5.21) and (5.22) of the business cycle model, with exactly the same interpretation. The only difference is that marginal cost in the present model includes 'missed technological progress' (see section 7.3.2).

Nickell [1975] also studies the effect of demand variations on the optimal policy of the firm. His business cycle is different, but similar. He assumes that there is no technological progress, but still there is a vintage structure since the maintenance costs of a capital good depend on its age. I will now analyse the zero investment period in the same way as Nickell and compare the results.

It has been assumed that the scrapping condition is always valid. So for $t\in(\alpha,\beta)$, $\partial S/\partial K(V(t))=w(V(t))l(t)/k$. Moreover, since: 1) $V(\alpha)>\beta$ (otherwise the capital good stock would be zero at $t=\beta$); 2) V is an increasing function; and 3) $\partial S/\partial K(t)=(\partial S/\partial K)^*$ for $t>\beta$, it is clear that: $\partial S/\partial K(V(t))=(\partial S/\partial K)^*$ for $t\in(\alpha,\beta)$, and thus the scrapping condition implies: $V(t)=t+T^*$ for $t\in(\alpha,\beta)$.

This implies that (32) is equivalent to:

$$\int_\alpha^\beta e^{-(i+a)t} \left\{\frac{\partial S}{\partial K}(t) - C\right\} dt = 0 \tag{35}$$

where C is a constant.

Moreover, $s_2(t)<0$ for $t\in(\alpha,\beta)$ and thus $\int_\alpha^t \dot{s}_2(\tau)d\tau<0$ for $t\in(\alpha,\beta)$. This implies:

$$\int_\alpha^t e^{-(i+a)\tau} \left\{\frac{\partial S}{\partial K}(\tau) - C\right\} d\tau > 0, \text{ for all } t\in(\alpha,\beta) \tag{36}$$

From (35) and (36) it is clear that during the 'zero-investment'-period $\partial S/\partial K$ must first rise above $\partial S/\partial K^*$ (note that $(\partial S/\partial K)^*=C$) and then fall below $(\partial S/\partial K)^*$. See Figure 3a:

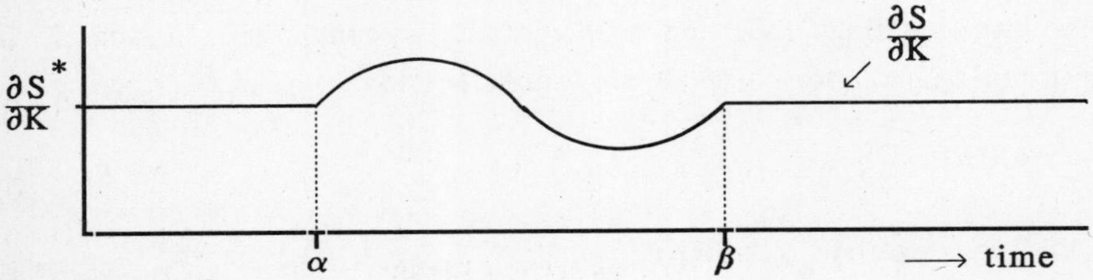

Figure 3a

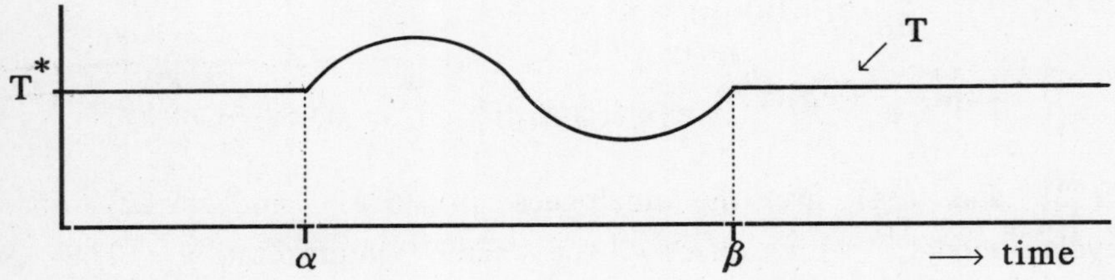

Figure 3b

Figure 3: Marginal revenue and lifetime of capital goods during a 'zero investment'-period

Until now there has been no difference with the analysis of Nickell. However, Nickell finds that there are backward echo effects of these fluctuations of marginal revenue: he finds the same cyclical fluctuations in the intervals $(\alpha-T^*,\beta-T^*)$, $(\alpha-2T^*,\beta-2T^*)$, etcetera. The reason for these echo effects are the age-dependent maintenance costs. In the present model,

however, $\partial S/\partial K(t)$ equals $(\partial S/\partial K)^*$ for all $t \leq \alpha$. Thus the *age*-dependent maintenance costs dó produce backward echo effects, while the *time*-dependent labour productivity does not. The labour productivity of a capital good only depends on the date of purchase, Nickell's maintenance costs of a capital good depend on the date of purchase ánd the age of the capital good. Nickell remarks that in the presence of these backward echo-effects in the optimal policy, the firm has to predict demand variations long in advance. In the present model that is not necessary.
In principle, (30) and (32) can be solved to give α and β. This would require integrating $\partial S/\partial K$ and $(d/dt)\partial S/\partial K$. This was possible in Chapter 5 (because $K(t)=e^{-a(t-t_{15})}K(t_{15})$, where t_{15} is the starting point of the 'zero investment'-period). In the present model, however, I cannot solve the differential equation for $\partial S/\partial K$, due to the vintage structure of K (see Appendix 5.4). Thus it is impossible to compute the starting and ending point of the zero-investment interval. Moreover, it is impossible to check whether B(t) lies in the interior of the control region for all t. Note that differentiation of the scrapping condition gives $(d/dt)\partial S/\partial K=\{w^* l(0)/k\}e^{h(t-N(t))}h(1-\dot{N}(t))$. This implies that $\dot{T}(t)$ $(=1-\dot{N}(t))$ has the same sign as $(d/dt)\partial S/\partial K(t)$. Since $\partial S/\partial K$ first rises above $(\partial S/\partial K)^*$ and then falls below $(\partial S/\partial K)^*$, T(t) (the age of the machines that are scrapped at time t) first rises above T^* and then falls below T^* (see Figure 3b).
Conclusion: if the recession is not very hard, the firm will maintain the steady state values for $\partial S/\partial K$ and T. At $t=t_0$ and $t=t_1$ investments will jump and due to the vintage structure there will be an echo of these jumps every T^* years. If the recession gets harder, there will be a zero-investment interval, during which $\partial S/\partial K$ and T make a one-period cyclical movement. The analysis of this 'zero investment'-period depends crucially on the assumption that the scrapping condition is always valid. It is impossible to compute the length and the position of the 'zero investment'-period, so that comparisons with Chapter 5 cannot be made. For even harder recessions, it may happen that B hits the boundary of the control region. In that case it is not clear what the optimal policy will be.

8.5 Summary and conclusions

Section 8.2 and 8.3 discuss the optimal trajectories of the models of Chapter 7. As the models get more difficult, the characterisation I can give of the optimal policy is more modest. For the basic model in Chapter 4 a feedback decision rule was found. For the simplified model of Chapter 7, such a decision rule has not been found, but it was possible to characterise the optimal policy in 'real' terms, that is, without the use of auxiliary variables like shadow prices. Although usual state variables are not available, the 'economic state variables' $\partial S/\partial K(t)$, $N(t)$ and $I(N(t))$ contain all information needed to determine the optimal policy (section 8.2). For the general model in Chapter 7, only a characterisation of the optimal policy in terms of shadow prices has been found (section 8.3). Section 8.4 introduces the business cycle of Chapter 5 into the models of Chapter 7. Under the assumption that the recession is shorter than the steady state lifetime of capital goods, it is derived for which values of the severeness of the recession the firm is not affected, and the pattern of investments is given. If the "$I \geq 0$"-constraint becomes active during the recession, only very limited statements can be made concerning the optimal policy, based on the *assumption* that the scrapping condition is valid during 'zero investment'-periods. For the simplified model of Chapter 7, augmented with the business cycle, it is shown that marginal revenue and the lifetime of capital goods make a one-period cyclical movement, *without* backward or forward echo-effects. More detailed statements are impossible to obtain because of the complexity of the (differential) equations.

9
SUMMARY AND CONCLUSIONS

The goal of this thesis is to find the optimal investment, financing and dividend policies of a firm facing technological progress and a fluctuating demand curve. This requires a stretching of the limits of the application of dynamic optimisation to economics. Chapter 3 argues that this thesis (and much related work) is still in the phase of working on the 'tool box', which is a 'preliminary to the main attack' (i.e. empirical applications). Chapter 3 derives three guidelines for this working on the tool box, which are followed in the remainder of the thesis:

1) make clear the motivation of the assumptions of the mathematical models.
2) pay attention to the economic interpretation of (aspects of) the mathematical tools
3) consider not only the 'steady state solution' of a model, but also the path *towards* this steady state, even though this is often difficult and time consuming.

Chapter 4 treats the basic model of this thesis. The environment of the firm is stationary and this makes it possible to derive a feedback decision rule, which prescribes the optimal policy for almost every initial condition. Guideline 1) plays an important role in this chapter.

In Chapter 5 guideline 3) asks for a stretching of the limits of the application of the path connecting procedure. In this chapter the firm is confronted with a fluctuating demand curve. The resulting model is non-autonomous and this complicates, but does not make impracticable, the path connecting procedure. The role of debt during the business cycle and the interrelationships between investment decisions and financing decisions are crucial in this chapter. If the recession is 'moderate', the firm stops investment before the start of the recession and resumes investments some time after the recession is over. During 'heavy' recessions the firm has to abandon its desired level of debt in order to cope with liquidity problems. If these liquidity problems are severe, the length of the 'zero-investment'-period is affected. For certain parameter configurations the recession causes bankruptcy. The conditions determining the length and position of the 'zero investment'-period can be interpreted economically. In the presence of a business cycle, the decision rule of Chapter 4 is no longer applicable.

Chapter 6 puts into practice guideline 2). In Chapters 4 and 5, the costate variables, which can usually be interpreted as shadow prices of the state variables, occasionally jump. This complicates the shadow price interpretation. Chapter 6 extends the shadow price interpretation of the costate variables, using a newly developed (Appendix 3) shadow price interpretation of the multipliers of the pure state constraints, and it explains the jumps from an economic viewpoint: jumps occur if the firm is forced by the constraints on the control variables to leave or enter a boundary. Chapter 6 also explains the values of the costate variable by comparing the immediate and the future contributions to the objective function of an extra unit of a state variable. Unfortunately, no explanation has been found for the *size* of jumps.

Chapter 7 treats a vintage model of the firm. This chapter makes perfectly clear that the mathematical tools strongly restrict the freedom of the economic model builder. In the first place, an extension of the Maximum Principle has to be derived (Appendix 4) to be able to deal with vintage models at all. In the second place, although this extension gives the economic model builder many new opportunities, it also functions as a straitjacket: the vintage models have to be moulded to a certain extent to meet the requirements of the extended Maximum Principle. This implies that some assumptions are clearly mathematically motivated (guideline 1!). Nevertheless, some interesting results are derived in Chapter 7. A scrapping rule is derived which includes some earlier scrapping rules as special cases and which is phrased in terms of shadow prices: equipment of a given vintage should be used as long as the marginal *contribution to the objective function* of producing on that equipment is positive. This contribution to the objective function is measured by several auxilliary variables which can be interpreted as shadow prices. Moreover, Chapter 7 describes how the scrapping decision is affected if there are active constraints on the capital goods stock. Finally Chapter 7 shows the existence of a steady state solution (implying a constant lifetime of capital goods and a constant marginal revenue) and proves that the optimal solution will indeed converge to this steady state.

Chapter 8 brings into practice guideline 3) with regard to the model of Chapter 7 and a combination of the models of Chapters 5 and 7. Whereas for the basic model in Chapter 4 a feedback decision rule has been derived (*pre*scribing the choice of the control variables), for the model of Chapter 7 only a *des*cription of the optimal policy can be given. For a simplified model of Chapter 7 it is possible to characterise the optimal policy in 'real terms' (that is, without the use of shadow prices). For the general model of Chapter 7 only a characterisation of the optimal policy in terms of shadow prices can be given, which is in fact nothing more than a reformulation of the optimality conditions. With regard to the model incorporating technological progress as well as the business cycle, Chapter 8 shows that the firm is more flexible than in Chapter 5, due to the vintage structure. Moreover, if the optimal policy involves a 'zero investment-period', the cyclical movement of price and marginal revenue, which is similar to the movement in Chapter 5, is accompanied by a cyclical movement of the optimal lifetime of capital goods.

Only the future can tell to what extent this thesis can contribute to "framing theories with empirical content" (see p.20). Pointing out directions for future research thus is a precarious undertaking.
With regard to the application of deterministic dynamic optimisation models to firm behaviour, the models in this thesis indicate two directions of research: in the first place it seems worthwhile to give a more detailed description of the firm itself (cf. the vintage structure of the capital goods stock in Chapter 7 instead of a homogeneous capital goods stock). The second direction of research is to pay more attention to modelling the markets in which the firm is involved (cf. the business cycle in Chapter 5). With regard to modelling the *interaction* of the firm with 'the market' or with specific competitors, a cooperation with game theoretic models might be useful.
It seems obvious that the application of stochastic dynamic optimisation to economics is a fruitful area of research, which has many advantages over deterministic optimisation. A really user-friendly presentation of the mathematical theory of stochastic optimisation seems desirable.
Finally, the path connecting procedure, possibly combined with numerical solution methods (which might help to 'guess' the optimal string, cf. Chapter 8) strengthens the probably biggest advantages of deterministic

optimisation over stochastic optimisation, namely the capability to deal with 'many' aspects in one model and the possibility to derive analytical results which can be interpreted economically.

APPENDICES

APPENDIX 1
OPTIMALITY CONDITIONS FOR THE BASIC MODEL OF CHAPTER 4

A1.1 Necessary and sufficient conditions

After elimination of Y, Q and L, the model (4.1)-(4.10) is:

<u>Model I</u>:

$$\max_{I,D} \int_0^z e^{-it} D(t)\, dt + e^{-iz} X(z) \tag{A1.1}$$

$$\dot{K}(t) = I(t) - aK(t), \; K(0)=K_0 \tag{A1.2}$$

$$\dot{X}(t) = (1-f) \left\{ S[\frac{K(t)}{k}] - \frac{wl}{k} K(t) - aK(t) - r\{K(t)-X(t)\} \right\} - D(t),$$

$$X(0)=X_0 \tag{A1.3}$$

$$K(t) - X(t) \geq 0 \tag{A1.4}$$

$$(b+1)X(t) - K(t) \geq 0 \tag{A1.5}$$

$$0 \leq I(t) \leq I_{max} \tag{A1.6}$$

$$0 \leq D(t) \leq D_{max} \tag{A1.7}$$

In this appendix the necessary and sufficient conditions are stated in a more precise manner than in Chapter 4, using section 6.2 of Feichtinger & Hartl [1986]. All expressions appearing in the objective function, the differential equations and the control constraints need to be continuously differentiable as functions of (K,X,I,D,t). For model I, which is 'almost' linear in (K,X,I,D), this simply means that S has to be continuously differentiable with regard to K. Moreover, the left hand sides of the two pure state constraints (A1.4-A1.5) (i.e. constraints that do not explicitly contain one or more control variables) have to be twicely continuously differentiable with regard to (K,X,t). It is obvious that this is satisfied. Note that the pure state constraints are both of order one, which means that the first total time derivative of those constraints depends explicitly on at least one control variable. In this appendix two constraint qualifications are needed, a weak one and a strong one. From now

on the control constraints are written as $g(u,t) \geq 0$[1], with g s-dimensional and the pure state constraints as $h(x,t) \geq 0$, with h q-dimensional.
The *weak constraint qualification* is satified if the following matrix has maximal row rank:

$$\begin{bmatrix} \partial g_1/\partial u & g_1 & \cdots & 0 \\ \vdots & \vdots & \ddots & \vdots \\ \partial g_s/\partial u & 0 & \cdots & g_s \end{bmatrix} \tag{A1.8}$$

For model I, this matrix takes the following form ($g_1 = I$, $g_2 = I_{max} - I$, $g_3 = D$, $g_4 = D_{max} - D$):

$$\begin{bmatrix} 1 & 0 & I & 0 & 0 & 0 \\ -1 & 0 & 0 & I_{max}-I & 0 & 0 \\ 0 & 1 & 0 & 0 & D & 0 \\ 0 & -1 & 0 & 0 & 0 & D_{max}-D \end{bmatrix} \tag{A1.9}$$

The *strong constraint qualification* is satisfied if the following matrix has maximal row rank:

$$\begin{bmatrix} \partial g_1/\partial u & g_1 & \cdots & 0 & 0 & \cdots & 0 \\ \vdots & \vdots & \ddots & \vdots & \vdots & & \vdots \\ \partial g_s/\partial u & 0 & \cdots & g_s & 0 & \cdots & 0 \\ \frac{\partial}{\partial u} dh_1/dt & 0 & \cdots & 0 & h_1 & \cdots & 0 \\ \vdots & \vdots & & \vdots & \vdots & \ddots & \vdots \\ \frac{\partial}{\partial u} dh_q/dt & 0 & \cdots & 0 & 0 & \cdots & h_q \end{bmatrix} \tag{A1.10}$$

For model I this matrix takes the following form ($h_1 = K - X$, $h_2 = (1+b)X - K$):

---

[1]u will always stand for the vector of control variables and x for the vector of state variables

$$\begin{bmatrix} 1 & 0 & I & 0 & 0 & 0 & 0 & 0 \\ -1 & 0 & 0 & I_{max}-I & 0 & 0 & 0 & 0 \\ 0 & 1 & 0 & 0 & D & 0 & 0 & 0 \\ 0 & -1 & 0 & 0 & 0 & D_{max}-D & 0 & 0 \\ 1 & 1 & 0 & 0 & 0 & 0 & K-X & 0 \\ -1 & -(1+b) & 0 & 0 & 0 & 0 & 0 & (1+b)X-K \end{bmatrix} \qquad (A1.11)$$

Necessary conditions

It is easily seen that the weak constraint qualification is always satisfied in model I, since $I_{max} \neq 0$ and $D_{max} \neq 0$. Thus Theorem 6.2 of Feichtinger & Hartl can be applied, which uses the so-called 'direct adjoining approach' to handle the pure state constraints (A1.4) and (A1.5). The Hamiltonian and the Lagrangian are defined as follows:

$$\mathbb{H}(x,u,\lambda,t) = \lambda_0 D + \lambda_1(I-aK) + \lambda_2\{(1-f)(S-wL-aK-rY)-D\} \qquad (A1.12)$$

$$\mathbb{L}(x,u,\lambda,\mu,\upsilon,t) = \mathbb{H} + \mu_1 I + \mu_2(I_{max}-I) + \mu_3 D + \mu_4(D_{max}-D)$$
$$+ \upsilon_1(K-X) + \upsilon_2((1+b)X-K) \qquad (A1.13)$$

Now the Maximum Principle states that for an optimal (I,D,K,X) there exist a constant λ_0, piecewise continuously differentiable functions $\lambda_i(t)$, piecewise continuous functions $\mu_i(t)$ and $\upsilon_i(t)$[2], constants γ_i, and for each timepoint τ where λ is discontinuous a vector $\eta(\tau)$, such that for all timepoints t where (I,D) and λ are continuous:

---

[2]Feichtinger and Hartl note (p.178) that in general some extra conditions are required to assure that a piecewise continuous function υ exists. These conditions can be found in Appendix 3, p.183-184.

$$\frac{\partial \mathbb{L}}{\partial I} = 0 \iff \lambda_1 + \mu_1 - \mu_2 = 0 \tag{A1.14}$$

$$\frac{\partial \mathbb{L}}{\partial D} = 0 \iff \lambda_0 - \lambda_2 + \mu_3 - \mu_4 = 0 \tag{A1.15}$$

$$\dot{\lambda}_1 = -\frac{\partial \mathbb{L}}{\partial K} + i\lambda_1 = (i+a)\lambda_1 + \lambda_2(1-f)\{\frac{wl}{k} + a + r - \frac{dS}{dK}\} - \upsilon_1 + \upsilon_2 \tag{A1.16}$$

$$\dot{\lambda}_2 = -\frac{\partial \mathbb{L}}{\partial X} + i\lambda_2 = \{i-(1-f)r\}\lambda_2 + \upsilon_1 - (1-b)\upsilon_2 \tag{A1.17}$$

$$\mu_1 I=0,\ \mu_2(I_{max}-I)=0,\ \mu_3 D=0,\ \mu_4(D_{max}-D)=0,\ \ \mu_i \geq 0,\ i=1,2,3,4 \tag{A1.18}$$

$$\upsilon_1(K-X)=0,\ \upsilon_2\{(1+b)X-K\}=0,\ \upsilon_1 \geq 0,\ \upsilon_2 \geq 0 \tag{A1.19}$$

$$\lambda_1(z) = \gamma_1 - \gamma_2\ ,\ \ \lambda_2(z) = \lambda_0 e^{-iz} - \gamma_1 + (1+b)\gamma_2 \tag{A1.20}$$

$$\gamma_1\{K(z)-X(z)\}=0,\ \gamma_2\{(1+b)X(z)-K(z)\}=0,\ \gamma_1 \geq 0,\ \gamma_2 \geq 0 \tag{A1.21}$$

If λ is discontinuous in τ, then:

$$\lambda_1(\tau^+) = \lambda_1(\tau^-) - \eta_1(\tau) + \eta_2(\tau) \tag{A1.22}$$

$$\lambda_2(\tau^+) = \lambda_2(\tau^-) + \eta_1(\tau) - (1+b)\eta_2(\tau) \tag{A1.23}$$

$$\eta_1(\tau)\{(\tau)-X(\tau)\} = 0,\ \eta_2(\tau)\{(1+b)X(\tau)-K(\tau)\} = 0,\ \eta_1(\tau) \geq 0,\ \eta_2(\tau) \geq 0 \tag{A1.24}$$

On page 155 it is derived that for the final paths considered in this thesis, γ_1 and γ_2 equal zero. This makes it possible to use 'Remark 6.7' of Feichtinger & Hartl (p.167), which leads to the conclusion that $\lambda_0=1$ (see also Exercise 6.1 of Feichtinger & Hartl (p.177)).

Sufficiency

Regarding sufficiency, theorem 7.1 of Feichtinger & Hartl, together with their remark 7.1, can be applied. This theorem states that if the salvage value term is concave in x, g(u,t) is quasi-concave in u, h(x,t) is quasi-concave in x, and, last but not least, $\mathbb{H}(x,u,\lambda,t)$ is concave in (x,u), a solution (x^*,u^*) of the necessary conditions is an optimal solution.

In problem I the salvage value term, g and h are linear and thus quasi-concave in (x,u,t). The Hamiltonian is linear with regard to I, D and X and concave with regard to K since the revenue function S is by assumption concave. Therefore the necessary conditions are also sufficient for problem I.

Uniqueness

Regarding uniqueness, Theorem 7.3 of Feichtinger & Hartl states that if there is a solution which satisfies the sufficient conditions and for which $\mathbb{H}^{o}(x,\lambda,t) = \max_{u}\{\mathbb{H}(x,u,\lambda,t) \mid g(u,t) \geq 0\}$ is strictly concave in x for every (λ,t), then every optimal control u leads to the same state trajectory x. Feichtinger & Hartl show that the concavity of $\mathbb{H}^{o}$ is implied by the stronger condition that $\mathbb{H}$ is strictly concave in (x,u). In problem I however, $\mathbb{H}$ is linear in X. So it seems impossible to establish uniqueness a priori.

A theorem on jumps

In all models in this thesis, the pure state constraints are of order one, and the control variables appear linearly. Therefore a very useful theorem of Feichtinger & Hartl (Corollary 6.3) can be applied. Define a boundary of the constraint h_i as an interval on which h_i equals zero. Suppose (α,β) is such an interval, then α is called the entry point and β is called the exit point. The Corollary of Feichtinger & Hartl states:

(a) If the control variables are continuous in an entry or exit point of one or more boundaries h_i and the strong constraint qualification is satisfied, then the corresponding jump parameters η_i equal zero and thus λ is continuous.

(b) If the entry to or exit from one or more boundaries h_i occurs in a non-tangential way, then the corresponding jump parameter η_i equal zero and thus λ is continuous.

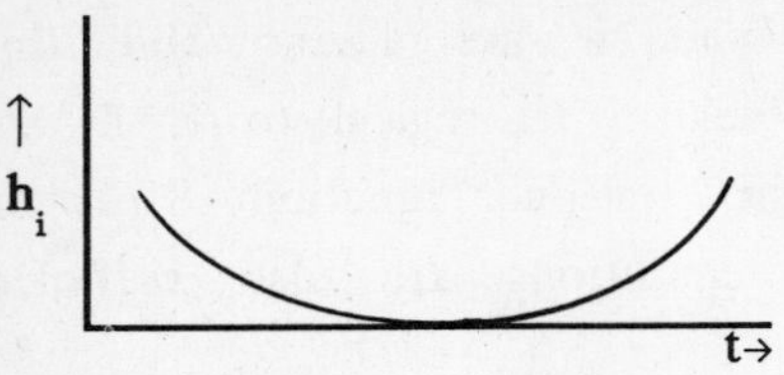

Tangential entry and exit

Figure 1a

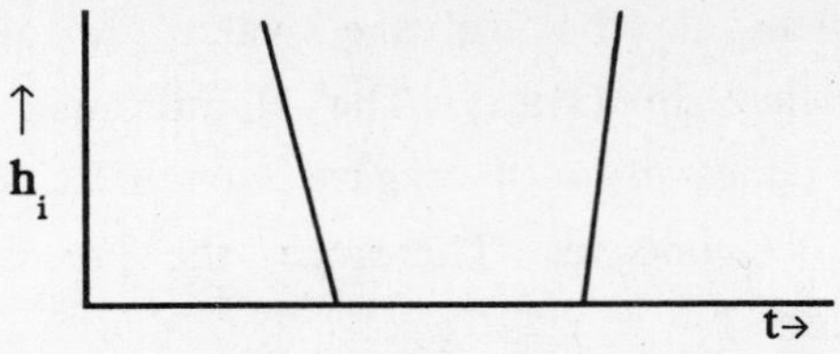

Non-tangential entry and exit

Figure 1b

Let τ be an exit or entry point of h_i. The entry or exit of this boundary occurs non-tangential if and only if dh_i/dt is discontinuous in τ.

$$\frac{dh_i}{dt} = \frac{\partial h_i}{\partial t}\frac{dx}{dt} + \frac{\partial h_i}{\partial t}$$

For model I this amounts to:

$$\frac{d(K\text{-}X)}{dt} = I + D - aK - (1\text{-}f)\left\{S[\frac{K(t)}{k}] - \frac{wl}{k}K(t) - aK(t) - r\{K(t)-X(t)\}\right\}$$

$$\frac{d\{(b+1)X\text{-}K\}}{dt} = -(b+1)D - I + aK + (b+1)(1\text{-}f)\left\{S[\frac{K(t)}{k}] - \frac{wl}{k}K(t) - aK(t) - r\{K(t)-X(t)\}\right\}$$

Note that K and X are continuous and that S is a continuous function of K. Now it can be immediately concluded that the entry or exit of the constraints (A1.4-A1.5) is non-tangential if only one of the control variables is discontinuous. Moreover, the entry or exit is tangential if both control variables are continuous. Finally, if both control variables are discontinuous, the entry or exit will in general be non-tangential; however, it *is* possible that dh_i/dt is continuous if both control variables are discontinuous.

This result will play an important part further on in the coupling procedure of Van Loon.

A1.2 The coupling procedure

A1.2.1 The paths

A *path* is defined as an interval of time on which the set of active constraints does not change. A path is thus determined by the values of the six multipliers (μ_i, i=1..4, υ_i, i=1,2). If a multiplier is zero, the corresponding constraint is in general not active; if the multiplier is positive, the constraint is active (see (A1.18) and (A1.19)). Since model I contains six constraints, there are in principle $2^6=64$ different paths. Fortunately, many paths can be excluded (are not feasible), for instance because of the simple fact that the upper and lower bound on the control variables D and I and on Y cannot be active at the same time.

Furthermore, in Chapter 4 it has been asserted that the upper bounds on the control variables are artificial. They serve to prevent infinite values for the control variables. If a pure state constraint is active, the controls are partly determined by the fact that they have to keep the state variables on the boundary. For instance, if on an interval K=X, then also dK/dt=dX/dt on that interval. Thus (use (A1.2) and (A1.3)):

$$I - aK = (1-f)\{ S(K/k)-(wl/k)K-aK-r(K-X) \} - D.$$

Equivalently:

$$I + D = aK + (1-f)\{ S(K/k)-(wl/k)K-aK-r(K-X) \}.$$

Since K and X have finite values, the control variables are bounded from above by this equation. It is assumed that the artificial upper bounds are never reached if at least one of the pure state constraints is active. This again excludes a number of paths.

Finally it can easily be shown that some paths imply $i=(1-f)r$, which is excluded (see p.41). Careful elimination leads to the exclusion of fifty paths. The remaining fourteen are summarised in table 1:

path	μ_1	μ_2	μ_3	μ_4	υ_1	υ_2
1	0	0	0	0	+	0
2	0	0	0	0	0	+
3	0	0	+	0	+	0
4	0	0	+	0	0	0
5	+	0	0	0	+	0
6	+	0	0	0	0	+
7	+	0	+	0	0	0
8	0	0	0	+	0	0
9	0	+	0	+	0	0
10	0	+	+	0	0	0
11	+	0	0	+	0	0
12	0	0	+	0	0	+
13	+	0	+	0	0	+
14	+	0	+	0	+	0

Table 1: The definitions of the feasible paths

Paths 13 and 14 will be excluded since they are borderline cases. For instance, consider path 13: on path 13 I=D=0 and K=X. K=X on an interval implies dK/dt=dX/dt, so $-aK=(1-f)\{S(K/k)-(wl/k)K-aK\}$. And thus,
$(1-f)S(K/k)= \{(1-f)(wl/k+a)-a\}K$.

The left hand side is a concave function of K, the right hand side is a linear function of K. Moreover, both sides equal zero for K=0. So the equality has at most one solution ($\neq 0$) for K. Since K is decreasing on path 13, this means that path 13 is only feasible during one instant of time. The same is true for path 14. Paths lasting only an instant of time can be ignored.

It can easily be seen (using $\mu_3=\mu_4=0 \Rightarrow \lambda_2=1$, (A1.17), and the fact that $\upsilon_1 \geq 0$ and $\upsilon_2 \geq 0$) that paths 1 and 5 are only feasible if $i<(1-f)r$ and that paths 2 and 6 are only feasible if $i>(1-f)r$.

From Table 1 the properties of the remaining twelve paths can be derived, leading to Table 1 in Chapter 4. For a more elaborate description of the translation of a table like the one above into a table like Table 1 in Chapter 4, see Van Loon [1983] or Kort [1989]. Van Loon and Kort also give a detailed description of the coupling procedure.[3] In Chapter 4 the idea of the coupling procedure is explained. The essential technical elements of the coupling procedure are that the state variables are required to be continuous at coupling points (which, for instance, excludes the coupling of a path with $\upsilon_1>0$ (Y=0) and a path with $\upsilon_2>0$ (Y=bX)), and that in many coupling points the multipliers μ_i must be continuous. Suppose path x is to be coupled before path y at time τ. If, for instance, $\mu_3=0$ on path y and μ_3 must be continuous in τ, then the coupling of path x before path is only feasible if $d\mu_3/dt(\tau^-)$ is negative (because μ_3 must be non-negative everywhere). In this way many possible couplings can be excluded, and many couplings are only feasible under specific conditions.

In the models of Van Loon [1983], Van Schijndel [1988] and Kort [1989] continuity of μ_i is a consequence of the continuity of λ_i. However, in the models of Chapters 5 and 6 λ_i is not always continuous, so it can never be *assumed* that λ_i will be continuous at a certain coupling point. Instead, the theorem on jumps of the costates will be used to see if λ_i is continuous at a coupling point or not.

A1.2.2 Derivation of the final paths

A final path of an optimal string has to satisfy the transversality conditions (A1.20) and (A1.21). These transversality conditions are a bit ambiguous, since λ_i may jump at time z. After all, theoretically z can be an entry- or exit point. The transversality condition (A1.20) should be read as follows:

$$\lambda_1(z^+)=0,\ \lambda_1(z^-)=\gamma_1-\gamma_2 \qquad \text{(A1.25)}$$

$$\lambda_2(z^+)=1,\ \lambda_2(z^-)=1-\gamma_1+(1+b)\gamma_2 \qquad \text{(A1.26)}$$

Using (A1.14) and (A1.15) this leads to:

$$\mu_2(z^-)-\mu_1(z^-) = \gamma_1-\gamma_2 \qquad \text{(A1.27)}$$

$$\mu_3(z^-)-\mu_4(z^-) = 1-\gamma_1+(1+b)\gamma_2 \qquad \text{(A1.28)}$$

From (A1.21) it is clear that γ_2 and γ_1 cannot both be positive, so there are three possibilities:

---

[3]Van Loon uses the socalled 'Russak-method' to handle pure state constraints, which is different from the method used in this appendix; see Feichtinger & Hartl, ch.6.

$$1)\quad \gamma_1=\gamma_2=0 \Rightarrow \begin{cases} \mu_2(z^-)=\mu_1(z^-) \Rightarrow \mu_2(z^-)=\mu_1(z^-)=0 \\ \mu_3(z^-)=\mu_4(z^-) \Rightarrow \mu_3(z^-)=\mu_4(z^-)=0 \end{cases} \tag{A1.29}$$

The only paths with these properties are 1 and 2

$$2)\quad \gamma_2>0,\ \gamma_1=0 \Rightarrow \begin{cases} Y(z) = bX(z) \\ \mu_2(z^-)-\mu_1(z^-) = -\gamma_2 & \Rightarrow \mu_1(z^-)>0 \\ \mu_3(z^-)-\mu_4(z^-) = (1+b)\gamma_2 & \Rightarrow \mu_3(z^-)>0 \end{cases} \tag{A1.30}$$

The only path with these properties is 7

$$3)\quad \gamma_2=0,\ \gamma_1>0 \Rightarrow \begin{cases} Y(z)=0 \\ \mu_2(z^-)-\mu_1(z^-) = \gamma_1 & \Rightarrow \mu_2(z^-)>0 \\ \mu_3(z^-)-\mu_4(z^-) = -\gamma_1 & \Rightarrow \mu_4(z^-)>0 \end{cases} \tag{A1.31}$$

There are no paths with these properties

So the only feasible *final* paths are 1, 2 and 7. Path 7 is a peculiar final path: the transversality conditions imply that $Y(z)=bX(z)$. Moreover, I and D are zero on path 7. Thus on path 7 the capital goods stock decreases, debt rises and reaches its upper bound precisely at time z, and X decreases. So in fact the firm is bankrupt at time z, since the 'accounting cash-flow' (see (4.30)) is negative (this is implied by $I=D=0$ and Y increasing) and debt is on its upper bound. In other words, on path 7 the firm comes to a crash halt at time z. On economic grounds path 7 is excluded as a final path. In Chapter 4 only path 1 and path 2, on which dS/dK is constant, are considered as final paths.

A1.2.3 The coupling procedure

In this subsection the coupling procedure for model I is illustrated by finding the predecessors of path 1.

The first thing to realise is that path 1 is only feasible if $i<(1\text{-}f)r$. Since i,f and r are constants, $i<(1\text{-}f)r$ must also hold on predecessors of path 1. This excludes path 2 and path 6.

The next important fact is that the state variables have to be continuous. Therefore it is impossible that on predecessors of path 1 $Y=bX$, since $K=X$ $(Y=0)$ on path 1 and $b>0$. This excludes path 12.

Since the upper bounds on I and D are artificial (they only have to prevent I and D from becoming infinite), D_{max} and I_{max} are set arbitrarily high, so that that the firm can only finance $I=I_{max}$ and/or $D=D_{max}$ by 'heavy' borrowing : paths with $D=D_{max}$ or $I=I_{max}$ are 'short' adjustment paths. This implies that at the end of paths 8,9,10 and 11 debt is positive. Since Y has to be continuous in coupling points (Y=K-X and K and X are continuous), these paths cannot be predecessors of path 1.

Now paths 3,4,5 and 7 are left as possible predecessors of path 1.

* can path 3 precede path 1?

  λ_1 equals zero on path 1 and path 3. Thus λ_1 is continuous in the coupling point and this implies $\eta_2=\eta_1$ (see (A1.22)). Moreover, K=X on path 3 and path 1, so η_2 must be zero at the coupling point (see (A1.24)). Thus we have $\eta_2=\eta_1=0$, which means that λ_1, λ_2 and μ_3 are continuous at the coupling point. If the coupling point is τ, then this implies $\dot{\mu}_3(\tau^-)\leq 0$. The properties of path 3 reveal that $\dot{\mu}_3(\tau^-)\leq 0$ if $dS/dK(\tau)\geq wl/k+a+i/(1\text{-}f)$. This does not exclude the coupling of path 3 before path 1, since on path 1 $dS/dK(\tau)=wl/k+a+i/(1\text{-}f)$.

* can path 4 precede path 1?

  on path 1 dS/dK equals $wl/k+a+i/(1\text{-}f)$ and on path 4 dS/dK equals $wl/k+a+r$. Thus coupling path 1 and path 4 would imply a jump of dS/dK. Since dS/dK is a continuous function of K, K would also have to jump, which is prohibited. So path 4 cannot preceed path 1.

* can path 5 precede path 1?

  Again, just as in the case of path 3, $\eta_1=\eta_2=0$, so that λ_1, λ_2 and μ_1 are continuous in the coupling point. If the coupling point is τ, the properties of path 5 imply that $\dot{\mu}_1(\tau^-)\leq 0$ if $dS/dK\leq wl/k+a+i/(1\text{-}f)$. This does not exclude the coupling of path 5 before path 1.

* can path 7 precede path 1?

  If so, the coupling point is the entry point of the restriction $K\text{-}X\geq 0$. Since K and X are continuous, this implies that $K\neq(1+b)X$ at the coupling point, so $\eta_2=0$ (see (A1.24)). Thus (A1.22) reduces to $\lambda_1(\tau^+)=\lambda_1(\tau^-)\text{-}\eta_1$. This implies that if λ_1 jumps at the coupling point τ, it jumps downward. But $\lambda_1=0$ on path 1 and $\lambda_1=\text{-}\mu_1<0$ on path 7. This leads to a contradiction, thus λ_1 must be continuous in the coupling point. This implies $\eta_1=0$ and consequently λ_2, μ_1 and μ_3 are continuous in the coupling point. The properties of path 7 reveal that $\dot{\mu}_1(\tau^-)\leq 0$ if $dS/dK\leq wl/k+a+r$ and that $\dot{\mu}_3(\tau^-)\leq 0$ if $i<(1\text{-}f)r$. This does not exclude the coupling of path 7 before path 1.

So the possible predecessors of path 1 are the paths 3, 5 and 7. The next step of the coupling procedure would be to find the predecessors of the strings 3-1, 5-1 and 7-1. Careful reasoning along the same lines as above leads to the desired results. In Appendix 2 a full representation of all strings of the model in Chapter 5, which is an extension of the model in this appendix, will be given.

For future reference the possible coupling 5-7 is examined here. The coupling point between 5 and 7 is an exit point of the restriction $K\text{-}X\geq 0$. Therefore it can be concluded immediately that $\eta_2=0$ in that coupling point (see (A1.24)). Moreover, $I=0$ on path 5 and path 7, so I is continuous at the coupling point. *If* D is discontinuous, then the jump theorem states that λ will not jump. In that case, μ_3 is also continuous (see (A1.15)). The properties of path 7 reveal that $\dot{\mu}_3(\tau^+)\geq 0$ implies $i>(1\text{-}f)r$ which contradicts the properties of path 5. Thus path 5 can only precede path 7 if D is continuous and λ jumps[4]! This implies (from the definition of D on path 5; use (A1.3) and the fact that $\dot{X}=\dot{K}=aK$ on path 5) that $S(K/k)$ equals $\{wl/k\text{-}fa/(1\text{-}f)\}K$ in the coupling point. This in fact means that the 'accounting cash-flow' becomes zero on path 5 and the firm is forced to borrow money.

Finally, also for future reference, is the string 5-7-5-1 possible? It is easily seen that the coupling 7-5 is feasible and that λ is continuous in the coupling point. Moreover, as just derived, in $t_{5,7}$ (which is the point of time at which the firm switches from path 5 to path 7) the 'accounting cash-flow' equals zero. This implies that $K(t_{5,7})=\tilde{K}$ (see Figure 7 of Chapter 4). On path 7 $I=0$, so K decreases for $t>t_{5,7}$ and the 'accounting cash-flow' *except* interest expenses becomes positive. Thus, since $I=D=0$ on path 7, the firm has money to pay back debt (see (4.30)). But Y equals zero at $t_{5,7}$. The conclusion is that the coupling of path 5 before path 7 would lead to a violation of the constraint $Y\geq 0$ for $t\geq t_{5,7}$. Thus the string 5-7-5-1 is not feasible for model I.

---

[4]Note that at the coupling point the strong constraint qualification is not satisfied, so that there is no contradiction with part (a) of the jump theorem.

APPENDIX 2
THE MATHEMATICAL DETAILS OF CHAPTER 5

This appendix contains the details concerning the optimality conditions for the model of Chapter 5. Section A2.1 gives some general remarks. Section A2.2 corresponds to section 5.3.3. Section A2.3 corresponds to section 5.3.4 and also contains the analysis of strings beginning with path 5. Section A2.4 corresponds to section 5.3.5. Section A2.5 discusses the uniqueness of the solution. The numerical exercises for the case $i<(1\text{-}f)r$ can be found in section A2.6. Section A2.7 corresponds to section 5.4.

A2.1 General remarks

Since the model of Chapter 5 is, except for the formulation of the revenue function, identical to the basic model, much of what has been said in Appendix 1 is still valid. To be precise, the matrices of the weak and the strong constraint qualification are the same as for the basic model; the necessary conditions are identical (with $\partial S/\partial K$ instead of dS/dK); the statements on sufficiency and uniqueness are still valid, since S is again a concave function of K for each t; the same argumentation concerning the exclusions of paths can be applied so that there are again twelve feasible paths; and the characteristics of these paths are the same. Only the coupling procedure yields different results. The final paths are the same as before, but the set of possible strings is considerably larger, due to the fact that $\partial S/\partial K$ is a cyclical function of time for a given value of K. In particular, it is now possible that *cycles* occur, that is, it is possible that a certain path x appears more than once in an optimal string. For instance, at the end of Appendix 1 it was shown that the string 5-7-5-1 was not feasible. In the business cycle model, however, that string is feasible! In Appendix 1 the reasoning was as follows: suppose the string 5-7-5-1 is feasible; then the 'accounting cash-flow' is zero in $t_{5,7}$ (this is still true); moreover, on path 7 K decreases (this is also still true), *and thus, K is smaller than* $\tilde{K}$ (see Figure 7 of Chapter 4) *and 'the accounting cash-flow' before interest becomes positive immediately after*

$t_{5,7}$! This is no longer true: $\tilde{K}$ is now a function of time. Thus, although immediately after $t_{5,7}$ K falls below $\tilde{K}(t_{5,7})$, it is nót clear whether $K(t) < \tilde{K}(t)$ for $t > t_{5,7}$. In other words, it is not clear whether the 'accounting cash-flow' *before* interest expenses becomes positive after $t_{5,7}$. In fact, it is easily derived from the definition of $p(Q,t)$ (cf. equation 5.1) that p decreases on path 7 if the recession is 'moderate' (m-$g > a$). Moreover, it can easily be derived that on path 7:

$$dY/dt(t) = -(1-f)\left\{\frac{p}{k} - \frac{wl}{k} + \frac{fa}{1-f}\right\} K(t) + (1-f)rY(t), \tag{A2.1}$$

and this equals minus the 'accounting cash-flow'. Note that in $t_{5,7}$ $Y=0$ and the 'accounting cash-flow' equals zero, which implies $p/k = wl/k - fa/(1-f)$. The right hand side of this equation is a constant and p decreases on path 7. Thus (A2.1) implies that dY/dt will increase on path 7 during the recession. So the string 5-7-5-1 cannot be excluded on the same grounds as in Appendix 1. Moreover, it can be shown that there are no grounds at all to exclude 5-7-5-1. This illustrates that a path may occur more than once in a string.

A conscientious application of the coupling procedure yields the following schedule of all possible strings ending with path 1. For reasons just explained, this schedule takes the form of a recursive tree:

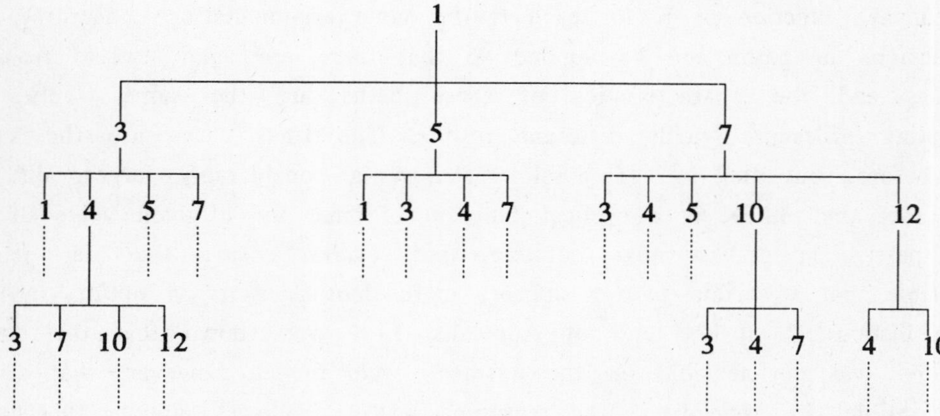

One final remark has to be made concerning the coupling procedure. In Chapter 5 it has been stated that the price function is not continuously differentiable, but that this does not matter. What I did in fact, was to 'smoothen' p in the neighbourhood of t_0 and t_1 so that it becomes a continuously differentiable function; next I applied the coupling procedure to find all strings. For all these strings, the differentiability of the price function is not essential, so I can from now on use the 'old' function p. In other words, the discontinuities were temporarily removed to make sure that all possible strings are found. Note that for the given specification of p, p itself and $\partial S/\partial K$ are continuous.

A2.2 The details of section 5.3.3

1-5-1

Equation (5.18) of section 5.3.3 is:

$$\int_{t_{1,5}}^{t_{5,1}} \frac{d}{dt}\frac{\partial S}{\partial K}(\tau)\, d\tau=0 \tag{A2.2}$$

On path 5 I=0, so (see (5.3) and (5.4)):

$$\frac{d}{dt}\frac{\partial S}{\partial K} = (1/k)(1-1/e)p(Q,t) * \{ (x+a)/e \}, \tag{A2.3}$$

where x equals g during expansions and g-m during a recession. Furthermore, on path 5:

$$K(t) = e^{-a(t-t_{1,5})} K(t_{1,5}). \tag{A2.4}$$

Using $t_{1,5} \le t_0$ and $t_{5,1} \ge t_1$, and formula (5.1) for p, (A2.2) can be rewritten as:

$$\frac{1-1/e}{k}\left[K(t_{1,5})\exp(-at_{1,5})/k\right]^{-1/e} \left\{ \int_{t_{1,5}}^{t_0} (g+a)e^{(g+a)\tau/e}\, d\tau \right.$$

$$+ e^{(m/e)t_0} \int_{t_0}^{t_1} (g-m+a)e^{(g-m+a)\tau/e}\, d\tau +$$

$$\left. e^{-(m/e)(t_1-t_0)} \int_{t_1}^{t_{5,1}} (g-m+a)e^{(g-m+a)\tau/e}\, d\tau \right\} =0. \tag{A2.5}$$

It is easy to show that this leads to (5.19).

The other condition for 1-5-1 is (5.20): $\lambda_1(t_{1,5})=\lambda_1(t_{5,1})=0$ and $\lambda_1(t)<0$ for $t\in(t_{1,5},t_{5,1})$. This condition is derived from the fact that $\lambda_1=0$ on path 1 and λ_1 is continuous in $t_{1,5}$ and $t_{5,1}$, and from the fact that $\lambda_2(t)=-\mu_1(t)<0$ on path 5.

On path 5 $\mu_2=\mu_3=\mu_4=\upsilon_2=0$, so the optimality conditions (4.14)-(4.17) lead to: $\lambda_2=1$, $\upsilon_1=(1\text{-}f)r\text{-i}$, and thus:

$$\dot{\lambda}_1 = (i+a)\lambda_1 + (1\text{-}f)\left\{\frac{wl}{k} + a + \frac{i}{1\text{-}f} - \frac{\partial S}{\partial K}\right\}, \tag{A2.6}$$

or equivalently:

$$\dot{\lambda}_1 - (i+a)\lambda_1 = (1\text{-}f)\left\{\frac{wl}{k} + a + \frac{i}{1\text{-}f} - \frac{\partial S}{\partial K}\right\} \tag{A2.7}$$

Multiplying both sides with $e^{-(i+a)t}$ gives:

$$e^{-(i+a)t}\dot{\lambda}_1(t) - e^{-(i+a)t}(i+a)\lambda_1(t) =$$

$$e^{-(i+a)t}(1\text{-}f)\left\{\frac{wl}{k} + a + \frac{i}{1\text{-}f} - \frac{\partial S}{\partial K}\right\} \tag{A2.8}$$

The left hand side of this expression equals the total time derivative of $e^{-(i+a)t}\lambda_1(t)$. Therefore:

$$e^{-(i+a)t_{5,1}}\lambda_1(t_{5,1}) - e^{-(i+a)t}\lambda_1(t) =$$

$$\int_t^{t_{5,1}} e^{-(i+a)\tau}\ (1\text{-}f)\{wl/k+a+i/(1\text{-}f) - \frac{\partial S}{\partial K}\}\ d\tau \tag{A2.9}$$

Substituting $\lambda_1(t_{5,1})=0$ in (A2.9) and noting that on path 1 $\partial S/\partial K = wl/k+a+i/(1\text{-}f)$ leads to (5.21) and (5.22).

To perform the sensitivity analysis with regard to $t_{1,5}$ and $t_{5,1}$, the integral in (5.21) can be calculated in the same way as above to give (after substitution of (5.19)):

$$e^{-\{g+a-e(i+a)\}t_{1,5}/e} = \pi, \tag{A2.10}$$

with:

$$\pi = -(\delta_2/\delta_4)\ \frac{g+a}{e(\ i\ +a)} \tag{A2.11}$$

$$\delta_2 = \exp\{-m(i+a)(t_1\text{-}t_0)/(g+a)\} - 1, \tag{A2.12}$$

$$\delta_4 = \Big\{m/\{g\text{-}m+a\text{-}e(i+a)\}\Big\}\ \Big\{\exp\{\ (g+a\text{-}e(i+a))t_0/e\ \}\Big\}$$

$$\Big\{\{\ \exp\{(g\text{-}m+a\text{-}e(i+a))(t_1\text{-}t_0)/e\}\ -\ 1\ \}\Big\} \tag{A2.13}$$

To derive this, one has to use that $K(t_{1,5})=\exp(gt_{1,5})K(0)$ and:

$$\frac{\partial S}{\partial K}(0) = \frac{wl}{k}+a+\frac{i}{1-f} \Rightarrow K(0) = \left\{ k\{\frac{wl}{k}+a+\frac{i}{1-f}\}/(1-1/e) \right\}^{-e}. \qquad (A2.14)$$

It can be shown that $g+a-e(i+a)=0$ implies $\pi=1$ and then (A2.10) contains no information. This borderline case is excluded. It is easily seen that if $m=g+a$, (A2.10) yields $t_{1,5}=t_0$ as expected. For $m>g+a$, (A2.10) yields $t_{1,5}<t_0$. For (A2.10) to have a non-negative solution for $t_{1,5}$, π must be <1 if $g+a-e(i+a)>0$, and π must be >1 if $g+a-e(i+a)<0$. Equation (A2.10) can now be used to perform the analytical and numerical sensitivity analysis.

To perform the sensitivity analysis with regard to t^*, an expression for t^* is needed. Note that on path 5 the firm uses all the 'accounting cash-flow' to pay out dividends (use (5.6), (5.7), $\dot{Y}=\dot{K}-\dot{X}$ and the fact that I=0 on path 5):

$$D = \{ (1-f)(p/k-wl/k-a) + a \} K \quad \text{on path 5} \qquad (A2.15)$$

(A2.15) equals zero if:

$$p = wl-fak/(1-f) \qquad (A2.16)$$

Definition (5.1) and (A2.14) can now be used to find:

$$t^* = \frac{e}{g+a-m} \{ \frac{a+g}{e} t_{1,5} - \frac{m}{e} t_0 + \ln\Phi \}, \qquad (A2.17)$$

$$\text{where } \Phi=(1-1/e) \frac{wl/k - f a /(1-f)}{wl/k+a+i/(1-f)} \qquad (A2.18)$$

The value m^* can be found by setting $t^*=t_1$ in (A2.17).

A2.3 The details of section 5.3.4

<u>1-5-7-5-1</u>

For this string (5.18) and (5.19) are again valid. Although $t_{1,5}$ and $t_{5,1}$ may differ, the derivation is the same, since I=0 on path 7 as well.

Condition (5.26) can be rephrased as: $t_{5,7}=t^*$, with t^* as in (A2.17). The second condition (5.27) can be worked out as follows. On path 7 (using (5.6), (5.7), $\dot{Y}=\dot{K}-\dot{X}$, and the fact that I=D=0 on path 7):

$$\begin{aligned} dY/dt &= -aK -(1-f)\{ (p/k-wl/k-a)K-rY \} \\ &= + (1-f)rY - (1-f)\{p/k-wl/k+fa/(1-f)\}K \qquad (A2.19) \end{aligned}$$

$$\Rightarrow dY/dt - (1-f)rY = - (1-f)\{p/k-wl/k+fa/(1-f)\}K \qquad (A2.20)$$

$$\Rightarrow \frac{d}{dt} e^{-(1-f)rt} Y(t) = - e^{-(1-f)rt} (1-f)\{p/k-wl/k+fa/(1-f)\}K(t) \tag{A2.21}$$

The procedure is now: integrate both sides of (A2.21) over the interval $[t_{5,7},t_{7,5}]$; substitute $K(t)=e^{-a(t-t_{1,5})}K(t_{1,5})= e^{-at+(a+g)t_{1,5}}K(0)$ and $K(0)$ (see (A2.14)) into (A2.21) twice: for $K(t)$ itself and in the formula for p; integrate the resulting expression; use (A2.17) with $t_{5,7}=t^*$ to eliminate $t_{1,5}$; The result is an expression only containing $t_{5,7}$ and $t_{7,5}$:

$$\frac{1}{r(1-f)+a}\{ e^{-(r(1-f)+a)t_{7,5}+ (g-m+a)t_{5,7}/e} - e^{(\beta+m-a)t_{5,7}/e} \}$$

$$- \frac{e}{\beta-a} e^{-mt_1/e} e^{-(\beta-a)t_{7,5}/e} + \frac{e}{\beta+m} e^{-(\beta+m)t_{5,7}/e} =$$

$$= - \frac{me}{(\beta-a)(\beta+m-a)} e^{-(\beta+m-a)t_1/e}, \tag{A2.22}$$

where $\beta=e\{r(1-f)+a\}-g$.

This expression is non-linear and it is impossible to reformulate it to get an expression like $t_{7,5}=F(t_{5,7})$.

The last condition is (5.30), together with (5.31). To derive (5.31), note that from equation (4.23):

$$\eta_1(t_{5,7}) = \lambda_2(\tau^+_{5,7})-\lambda_2(t^-_{5,7}) = \lambda_2(\tau^+_{5,7})-1. \tag{A2.23}$$

Moreover, $\lambda_2(t^+_{7,5})=1$ and on path 7:

$$\frac{d}{dt}\lambda_2 = (i-(1-f)r)\lambda_2 \tag{A2.24}$$

This gives:

$$\lambda_2(t^+_{7,5}) = - \int_{t_{5,7}}^{t_{7,5}} \frac{d}{dt}\lambda_2(\tau)\, d\tau + 1 = - \int_{t_{5,7}}^{t_{7,5}}\{i-(1-f)r\}\lambda_2(\tau)\, d\tau + 1 \tag{A2.25}$$

Together (A2.23) and (A2.25) yield (5.31).

Now (5.30) can be obtained in the same way as (5.21). Calculating (5.30) gives a non-linear expression with four unknowns: $t_{1,5}$,$t_{5,7}$,$t_{7,5}$ and $t_{5,1}$:

$$\frac{-1}{1-f}\,e^{((1-f)r-i)t_{7,5}\,-\,((1-f)r+a)t_{5,7}} + \frac{1}{1-f}\,e^{-(i+a)t_{5,7}} =$$

$$= \frac{wl/k+a+i/(1-f)}{(i+a)}\left\{e^{-(i+a)t_{5,1}} - e^{-(i+a)t_{1,5}} + e^{-(i+a)t_{5,7}}\right\} -$$

$$- \frac{\{wl/k-fa/(1-f)\}\,\{(1-f)r-i\}}{(i+a)(a+(1-f)r)}\,e^{-(i+a)t_{7,5}}$$

$$- \frac{wl/k+a+r}{(1-f)\,r+a}\left\{e^{((1-f)r-i)t_{7,5}-((1-f)r+a)t_{5,7}}\right\} +$$

$$+ e(wl/k+a+i/(1-f))e^{-(a+g)t_{1,5}/e}\left[\frac{-m}{\delta(\delta-m)}\,e^{\delta t_0/e} + \right.$$

$$+ e^{mt_0/e}\,e^{(\delta-m)t_{5,7}/e}\left\{\frac{1}{\delta-m} - \frac{1}{g-m+a-e((1-f)r+a)}\,e^{((1-f)r-i)(t_{7,5}-t_{5,7})}\right\}$$

$$+ \frac{m}{(-\beta+a-m)(-\beta+a)}\,e^{-m(t_1-t_0)/e}\,e^{(-\beta+a)t_1/e}\,e^{((1-f)r-i)t_{7,5}} +$$

$$\left. + \frac{e((1-f)r-i)}{(-\beta+a)\delta}\,e^{\delta t_{7,5}/e} + \frac{1}{\delta}\left\{e^{-m(t_1-t_0)/e}\,e^{\delta t_{5,1}/e} - e^{\delta t_{1,5}/e}\right\}\right],$$

(A2.26)

where $\delta=g+a-e(i+a)$ and β is as before.
The set of conditions (5.19), (A2.17) with $t^*=t_{5,7}$, (A2.22) and (A2.26) is a set of four (partly) nonlinear equations in four unknowns, from which I have not been able to derive beautiful analytical results. For the numerical exercises in section A2.6 this set of equations was solved on a computer, using procedure C05NBF of the NAG-library.

Before discussing the remaining strings beginning with path 1, the more simple strings beginning with path 5 are exemplified.

<u>5-1</u>

As with 1-5-1 (5.18) and (5.19) are valid, with $t_{1,5}=0$. Moreover $\lambda_1(0)=-\mu_1(0)\leq 0$ (using 4.14). Now substituting $\lambda_1(t_{5,1})=0$ in (A2.9) and imposing $\lambda_1(0)\leq 0$ leads to the condition: $\pi<1$ if $g+a-e(i+a)<0$ and $\pi>1$ if $g+a-e(i+a)>0$.

5-7-5-1

For this string (5.19) and (A2.17) are valid with 0 substituted for $t_{1,5}$ and $t_{5,7}$ for t^*, and (A2.22) is valid.

5-7-3-1

For strings containing path 3 there is an additional difficulty. On path 5 and path 7 I=0 and on path 1 I=(a+*g*)K. This gives a nice expression for *p*, ∂S/∂K and d/dt(∂S/∂K) on these paths. But on path 3:

$$I = \{(1-f)(p/k-wl/k-a)+a\}K. \tag{A2.27}$$

Substituting this in the formula for d/dt(∂S/∂K) (see (5.3) and (5.4)) gives a first order ordinary differential equation for ∂S/∂K:

$$\frac{d}{dt}\,\partial S/\partial K = \Lambda(\partial S/\partial K)^2 + \Pi(\partial S/\partial K), \tag{A2.28}$$

where

$$\Lambda = e(1-f)/(1-1/e), \tag{A2.29}$$

$$\Pi = (g+(1-f)(wl/k+a))/e. \tag{A2.30}$$

Rewriting (A2.28):

$$\frac{d\ \partial S/\partial K}{\Lambda(\partial S/\partial K)^2+\Pi(\partial S/\partial K)} = dt.$$

Integrating both sides (using that the primitive of $1/(ax^2+bx)$ equals $(1/b)\ln(\frac{x}{x+b/a})$) gives:

$$\partial S/\partial K(t) = \frac{C(\Pi/\Lambda)e^{\Pi t}}{1-Ce^{\Pi t}}, \text{ where C is a constant.} \tag{A2.31}$$

Now the conditions for the switching points of 5-7-3-1 can be derived. Three conditions are needed. The first is of course (A2.17) with $t_{1,5}=0$ and $t^*=t_{5,7}$. The second is (5.27) or (A2.22) with $t_{7,3}$ instead of $t_{7,5}$. Knowing $t_{7,3}$ implies knowing $\partial S/\partial K(t_{7,3})$. Substituting this in (A2.31) gives the constant C. Then (A2.31) also gives $\partial S/\partial K(t_{3,1})$. Equating $\partial S/\partial K(t_{3,1})$ with $wl/k+a+i/(1-f)$ gives the third condition.

5-7-4-3-1

Four conditions are needed for this string. The first is similar to (5.18): from $\partial S/\partial K(t_{7,4})=wl/k+a+r$ (see Table 1 in Chapter 4) and $\partial S/\partial K(0)=wl/k+a+i/(1-f)$ it can be derived that:

$$t_{7,4} = \frac{m}{g+a}(t_1-t_0) + \frac{e}{g+a}\ln\left[\frac{wl/k+a+r}{wl/k+a+i/(1-f)}\right] \quad \text{(A2.32)}$$

Note that since the second term of the right hand side is positive, the 'zero investment'-period is now longer than in strings 1-5-1, 1-5-7-5-1, 5-1, and 5-7-5-1.

The second condition is (A2.17) with $t_{1,5}=0$ and $t^*=t_{5,7}$.

The third condition is given by: $Y(t_{4,3})=0$. Solving the differential equation for Y on path 7 and substituting the values for $t_{5,7}$ and $t_{7,4}$ gives $Y(t_{7,4})$. Next the differential equation for Y on path 4 can be solved and finally $Y(t_{4,3})=0$ is imposed.

The fourth condition is given by: $\partial S/\partial K(t_{4,3})=wl/k+a+r$ and $\partial S/\partial K(t_{3,1})=wl/k+a+i/(1-f)$. Equation (A2.31) can be used to work this out.

1-5-7-3-1

Four conditions are needed. The first is (A2.17) with $t^*=t_{5,7}$. Like in the case of 5-7-5-3-1 $t_{7,3}$ and $t_{3,1}$ can be computed, but now as a function of $t_{1,5}$. Finally: $\lambda_1(t_{1,5})=\lambda_1(t_{7,3})=0$. Working out these last two conditions requires solving the differential equation for λ_1 on path 5 and path 7, which was done before (see A2.6-A2.9). Moreover, the magnitude of the jump has to be computed, which is now very difficult. It requires determining $\eta_1(t_{5,7})=\lambda_2(t^+_{5,7})-\lambda_2(t^-_{5,7}) = \lambda_2(t^+_{5,7})-1$ (see (A2.23)). To compute $\lambda_2(t^+_{5,7})$ the differential equation for λ_2 on path 7 and path 3 must be integrated, using $\lambda_2(t_{3,1})=1$. However, on path 3:

$$\frac{d}{dt}\lambda_2 = \{\, wl/k+a+i/(1-f)-\partial S/\partial K \,\}\,(1-f)\,\lambda_2 \quad \text{(A2.33)}$$

This, combined with the rather difficult expression for $\partial S/\partial K$ on path 3 (see (A2.31)), seems to be an unsolvable differential equation. So a full set of conditions for the switching points of the string 1-5-7-3-1 cannot be obtained.

1-5-7-4-3-1

Five conditions are needed. It is relatively easy to get four of these five conditions (see the strings 5-7-4-3-1 and 1-5-7-3-1), but again it is impossible to work out $\lambda_1(t_{1,5})=\lambda_1(t_{4,3})=0$. Similar to the case 5-7-4-3-1:

$$t_{7,4} = t_{1,5} + \frac{m}{g+a}(t_1-t_0) + \frac{e}{g+a}\ln\left(\frac{wl/k+a+r}{wl/k+a+i/(1-f)}\right), \quad \text{(A2.34)}$$

which implies that the 'zero investment'-period (i.e. the interval $(t_{1,5}, t_{7,4})$) is longer in this string than in the strings 1-5-1 and 1-5-7-5-1.

A2.4 The details of section 5.3.5

At some time during the expansion p/k becomes equal to $wl/k\text{-}fa/(1\text{-}f)$ ('accounting cash-flow' before interest expenses becomes zero). Let this timepoint be τ. This τ can be calculated as a function of $t_{5,7}$ using the differential equation for p on path 7. The differential equation for Y on path 7 can be solved for $t > \tau$:

$$\mathrm{Y(t)} = \left\{ \frac{1}{k} \frac{\Delta}{(g+a)/e\text{-}a\text{-}r(1\text{-}f)} \right\} \mathrm{e}^{\{(g+a)/e\text{-}a\}(\mathrm{t}\text{-}\tau)}$$

$$+ \Gamma\, \mathrm{e}^{(1\text{-}f)r(\mathrm{t}\text{-}\tau)} - \frac{\Delta}{r(1\text{-}f)+a} \mathrm{e}^{-a(\mathrm{t}\text{-}\tau)}, \qquad \text{(A2.35)}$$

where

$$\Delta = -(1\text{-}f)\mathrm{K}(\tau)\{wl/k\text{-}fa/(1\text{-}f)\}$$

$$\Gamma = \mathrm{Y}(\tau) - \frac{1}{k} \frac{\Delta}{(g+a)/e\text{-}a\text{-}r(1\text{-}f)} + \frac{\Delta}{r(1\text{-}f)+a}$$

With regard to the question whether Y explodes, the third term in (A2.35) can be ignored, since that term will fade out quickly. It can easily be seen that Δ is negative. The sign of Γ depends on $\mathrm{Y}(\tau)$. The second term in (A2.35) explodes if $\Gamma > 0$.

If $(g+a)/e\text{-}a\text{-}r(1\text{-}f) < 0$, the sign of Γ depends on the value of $\mathrm{Y}(\tau)$; if $\mathrm{Y}(\tau)$ is large, then Γ will be positive, thus Y as a whole explodes. If $\mathrm{Y}(\tau)$ is small and Γ is negative, then Y will tend to zero, even if $(g+a)/e > 0$. In the latter case the decrease of the second term in (A2.35) dominates the increase of the first term.

If $(g+a)/e\text{-}a\text{-}r(1\text{-}f) > 0$, $\mathrm{e}^{\{(g+a)/e\text{-}a\}\mathrm{t}}$ explodes, but $\frac{\Delta}{(g+a)/e\text{-}a\text{-}r(1\text{-}f)} < 0$. so the first term of Y in (A2.35) decreases rapidly. Γ is now positive, but since $(g+a)/e\text{-}a > (1\text{-}f)r$, Y as a whole will decrease: the decrease of the first term dominates the increase of the second term.

The borderline case where the firm is at one moment on the brink of bankruptcy but does not go bankrupt is characterised by the fact that the firm starts with 5-7 and on path 7 Y/X just reaches its maximum at b. The moment at which this happens is given by:

$$d/dt\ (Y/X)(t) = 0 \text{ and } Y(t) = bX(t) \qquad (A2.36)$$

Since the differential equations for K an Y on path 5 and path 7 are easy to solve, and $t_{5,7}$ equals t^* in (A2.17) with $t_{1,5}=0$, (A2.36) leads to a system of two non-linear equations with two variables, m and t. This implicitly gives m^{**}.

A2.5 Uniqueness of the solution

As was mentioned in Appendix 1, uniqueness is not guaranteed. So one might wonder whether it is possible that several strings are optimal for the same initial conditions. In particular, is it possible that strings beginning with path 5 are also optimal in cases where we proposed strings beginning with path 1 as optimal solution. Or, is it possible that 1-5-1 and 1-5-7-5-1 are optimal for the same set of parameter values?

Concerning the first question: the answer seems to be no. In any case, 5-1 and 1-5-1 cannot be optimal for the same set of parameter values. This can be seen from the conditions on π which were derived above for 1-5-1 and 5-1 (see p.162 and p.165).

It would be nice to make this result more general: 1-5-x and 5-y cannot be optimal for the same set of parameter values for arbitrary feasible strings x and y. However, since the equations that determine the 'switching times' of strings beginning with 1-5-7-.. are so difficult, this generalisation can only be conjectured for reasons of analogy, using numerical examples to corroborate it.

The second question posed was: can 1-5-1 and 1-5-7-5-1 be optimal for the same set of parameter values? It seems not impossible: on 1-5-7-5-1 the firm would stop investing later at the cost of having to borrow some time later on. The benefits of the growth during the first expansion phase would have to offset the cost of borrowing. Again, it is difficult to give a complete analytical answer. However, it is possible to narrow down the set of values of m for which 1-5-1 and 1-5-7-5-1 could be optimal for the same set of parameter values.

In the first place, 1-5-1 cannot be optimal if $m > m_b$ (where m_b can be found by setting $t^* = t_1$ and $t_{1,5} = 0$ in (A2.17) and rewriting it), since in that case the firm will get into liquidity problems even if it stops investing at $t=0$.

In the second place, $t_{5,7}$ must be smaller than t_1. $t_{5,7}$ equals t^* in (A2.17) and from (A2.17) it can be seen that $t_{5,7}$ becomes larger if $t_{1,5}$ becomes larger. This insight leads to the following observation: if for $t_{1,5}$ equal to t_0, $t_{5,7}$ is larger than t_1, then $t_{5,7}$ will certainly be larger than t_1 for every possible value of $t_{1,5} \in (0,t_0)$ and thus 1-5-7-5-1 is not possible in that case. This leads to the condition that a necessary condition for 1-5-7-5-1 to be optimal is that $t_{5,7}$ must be smaller than t_1 if $t_{1,5} = t_0$. Substituting t_0 for $t_{1,5}$ in (A2.17) gives:

$$\frac{1}{g+a-m}\left\{ (g+a)t_0 - mt_0 + e\ln \frac{(1-1/e)\,(wl/k-fa/(1-f))}{wl/k+a+i/(1-f)} \right\} < t_1 \qquad \text{(A2.37)}$$

This is equivalent to:

$$m > m_a, \text{ with } m_a = g+a - \frac{e}{t_1-t_0} \ln \frac{(1-1/e)\,(wl/k-fa/(1-f))}{wl/k+a+i/(1-f)} \qquad \text{(A2.38)}$$

Summarising: 1-5-1 cannot be optimal if $m > m_b$ and 1-5-7-5-1 cannot be optimal if $m < m_a$. Since $m_b > m_a$, 1-5-1 and 1-5-7-5-1 can only be optimal for the same set of parameter values if $m_a < m < m_b$. For this region of m it seems not possible to derive analytically whether 1-5-1 and 1-5-7-5-1 can indeed be optimal for the same set of parameter values or not. Numerical exercises show that 1-5-1 and 1-5-7-5-1 are never optimal for the same set of parameter values.

A2.6 Numerical illustrations

For a start the following parameter values are used:

$a=0.04$	$f=0.4$	$g=0.04$	$i=0.05$	$t_0=10$	$t_1=50$
$r=0.09$	$k=6$	$l=1$	$w=1/3$	$e=2$ or 3	

If $m \leq g+a = 0.08$, the optimal policy is simply path 1. For m larger than 0.08, 1-5-1 will be optimal. For instance:

If $m=0.1$ and $e=2$, then 1-5-1 is optimal with $t_{1,5} \approx 7.8$ and $t_{5,1} \approx 57.8$

If $m=0.1$ and $e=3$, then 1-5-1 is optimal with $t_{1,5} \approx 7.7$ and $t_{5,1} \approx 57.7$

Leban & Lesourne and Nickell claim that for small values of m,g and a, the 'zero investment'-period is symmetrical with regard to t_1-t_0, that is,

t_0-$t_{1,5} \approx t_{5,1}$-t_1. Apparently, the values in this example are already 'large', since this symmetry is not found.
Letting *m* grow further:

If $m=0.2$ and $e=2$, then 1-5-1 optimal with $t_{1,5} \approx 1.9$ and $t_{5,1} \approx 101.9$
If $m=0.2$ and $e=3$, then 1-5-1 optimal with $t_{1,5} \approx 1.4$ and $t_{5,1} \approx 101.4$

Letting *m* grow with steps of 0.01, the outcomes differ for $e=2$ and $e=3$ from $m=0.23$ onwards. For $e=2$, t^* gets smaller than t_1 for $m=0.23$, while $t_{1,5}$ is still positive.

If $m=0.23$ and $e=2$, then 1-5-7-5-1 is optimal with $t_{1,5} \approx 1.0$; $t_{5,7} \approx 48.3$; $t_{7,5} \approx 57.9$; $t_{1,5} \approx 116.0$
If $m=0.24$ and $e=2$, then 1-5-7-5-1 is optimal with $t_{1,5} \approx 0.8$; $t_{5,7} \approx 46.0$; $t_{7,5} \approx 77.6$; $t_{1,5} \approx 120.7$

Note that $t_{7,5}$ increases very rapidly, that is, the time it takes the firm to pay back the debt increases rapidly. The reason is that in this case we have $(g+a)/e-a-(1-f)r<0$, which means (see (5.35)) that if the firm accumulates too much debt during the recession, this debt will explode. The critical value of *m* in this respect is approximately 0.24, since debt already explodes for $m=0.25$.
For $e=3$, a different pattern of optimal solutions appears: for $m=0.25$ $t_{1,5}$ becomes negative while t^* is still larger than t_1. Therefore:

If $m=0.23$ or 0.24 and $e=3$, then 1-5-1 is optimal.
If $m=0.25$ and $e=3$, 5-1 is optimal with $t_{5,1}=125$.

$m_b \approx 26.7$, so for $m>26.7$, 5-1 is no longer possible.

If $m=0.27$ and $e=3$, 5-7-5-1 is optimal with $t_{5,7} \approx 49.4$; $t_{7,5} \approx 53.3$; and $t_{5,1}=135$.

Of course Y will explode again for larger *m*. Note that for $e=3$ 1-5-1 is optimal for higher values of *m* than for $e=2$ and that for $e=3$ the firm survives for higher values of *m* than for $e=2$.

The chosen values for the parameters may not be realistic. In particular, the values of *m* for which 1-5-1 is no longer optimal are large. For instance, $m=0.25$ means that the demand function is decreasing at a rate of 21% (note that $g=0.04$). However, these values were chosen only to demonstrate that strings beginning with 1-5 as well as strings beginning with 5 can be optimal, but never for the same set of parameter values. For $e=2$, $k=2$, $l=3$ and $w=2/3$ and the same values for the other parameters, 1-5-1 is no longer optimal if $m=0.14$. But this set of parameter values has another 'unrealistic' characteristic, namely that in order to be sure that Y does not explode, g must be such that $(g+a)/e-a-(1-f)r>0$ (see (5.34)) and this means $g>0.148$, which implies that the economy grows at approximately 15% during the expansion. However, for: $e=1.1$, $g=0.07$, $k=2$, $l=3$, $w=2/3$, and the same values as before for the other parameters, Y will not explode. The optimal policy is (letting m grow with steps of 0.1):

If $m\leq 0.11$ path 1 is optimal;

If $0.12\leq m\leq 0.19$ string 1-5-1 is optimal

If $0.20\leq m\leq 0.22$ string 1-5-7-5-1 is optimal.

For instance, for $m=0.22$:

$t_{1,5}\approx 4.6$; $t_{5,7}\approx 40.8$; $t_{7,5}\approx 82.9$; $t_{5,1}\approx 81.2$

For $m=0.23$ debt is still positive if $\partial S/\partial K$ becomes equal to $wl/k+a+r$ during the second expansion. So the optimal policy is 1-5-7-4-3-1. For $m=0.22$ $\partial S/\partial K$ is smaller than $wl/k+a+i/(1-f)$ when Y reaches zero. For the chosen parameter values $wl/k+a+i/(1-f)=1.1233333..$ and $wl/k+a+r\approx 1.13$. These values do not differ much, thus the case that Y is still positive if $\partial S/\partial K=wl/k+a+i/(1-f)$ and already zero if $\partial S/\partial K=wl/k+a+r$ will hardly ever occur. In fact already for $m=0.221$ the optimal policy is 1-5-7-4-3-1. For $m=0.2205$, the just mentioned situation occurs and thus 1-5-7-3-1 is optimal in this case.

A2.7 The details of section 5.4

2-6-2

Again (A2.2)-(A2.5) are valid with $t_{2,6}$ and $t_{6,2}$ instead of $t_{1,5}$ and $t_{5,1}$. This leads to (5.39).

The other condition for this string is: $\lambda_1(t_{2,6})=\lambda_1(t_{6,2})=0$ and $\lambda_1(t)<0$ for $t\in(t_{2,6},t_{6,2})$. For path 6 we have: $\mu_2=\mu_3=\mu_4=\upsilon_1=0$, so the optimality conditions (A4.14)-(A4.17) lead to: $\lambda_2=1$, $\upsilon_2=(i-(1-f)r)/(1+b)$, and thus:

$$\dot{\lambda}_1 = (i+a)\lambda_1 + (1-f)\left\{\frac{wl}{k} + a + \frac{i}{(1-f)(1+b)} + \frac{b\,r}{1+b} - \frac{\partial S}{\partial K}\right\} \qquad \text{(A2.39)}$$

Proceeding in the same way as for 1-5-1 (see (A2.6)-(A2.9)) gives (5.41) and (5.42).

To perform the sensitivity analysis for $t_{2,6}$ and $t_{6,2}$, an expression for $t_{2,6}$ is needed. Substituting (5.39) in (5.41), using $\partial S/\partial K(0)=wl/k+a+br/(1+b)+i/\{(1-f)(1+b)\}$, and then calculating (5.41) gives:

$$e^{-\{g+a-e(i+a)\}/et_{2,6}} = \pi.$$

This can be used to perform the analytical and numerical sensitivity analysis (see (A2.11) for π).

To perform the sensitivity analysis for $\hat{t}$, an expression for $\hat{t}$ is derived in the same way as the expression for t^*. The result is:

$$\hat{t} = \frac{e}{g+a-m} \left\{ \frac{a+g}{e} t_{2,6} - \frac{m}{e} t_0 + \ln \Psi \right\}, \qquad \text{(A2.40)}$$

where $\Psi=(1-1/e) * \dfrac{wl/k+a+br/(1+b) - a/\{(1-f)(1+b)\}}{wl/k+a+br/(1+b)+i/\{(1-f)(1+b)\}}$.

This can be used to perform the analytical and numerical sensitivity analysis.

The value of $\hat{m}$ can be found by setting $\hat{t}=t_1$ in (A2.40).

<u>2-7-6-7-2</u>

The four equations for the switching times of this string are (5.39), (5.44), (5.45) and the analogue of (5.29).

Equation (5.44) is equivalent to (this can easily be derived from the properties of path 6):

$$(1-f)\{p(t_{7,6})/k-wl/k-a-rb/(1+b)\} = -a/(1+b). \qquad \text{(A2.41)}$$

This leads to:

$$t_{7,6}-t_{2,6} = \frac{m}{g+a}(t_1-t_0) +$$

$$\frac{e}{g+a} \ln \frac{(1-1/e)\{wl/k+a+rb/(1+b)-a/((1-f)(1+b))\}}{wl/k+a+br/(1+b)+i/\{(1-f)(1+b)\}}. \qquad \text{(A2.42)}$$

It can easily be seen that the logarithm is negative so that (5.39) and (A2.42) automatically imply that $t_{7,6}<t_{6,2}$. Note that $t_{7,6}-t_{2,6}$ is larger if m is larger.

Since I=0 on path 6 and on path 7, (5.45) is equivalent to:

$$Y(t_{6,7})=\frac{b}{1+b}\, e^{-a(t_{6,7}-t_{2,6})}\, e^{gt_{2,6}}\, K(0) \tag{A2.43a}$$

$$Y(t_{7,6})=\frac{b}{1+b}\, e^{-a(t_{7,6}-t_{2,6})}\, e^{gt_{2,6}}\, K(0) \tag{A2.43b}$$

Moreover, from the differential equation of Y on path 7 it can be derived that:

$$e^{-(1-f)rt_{7,6}}\, Y(t_{7,6}) - e^{-(1-f)rt_{6,7}}\, Y(t_{6,7}) =$$

$$= - \int_{t_{6,7}}^{t_{7,6}} (1-f)e^{-(1-f)r\tau} \left\{\frac{p(\tau)}{k} - \frac{wl}{k} + \frac{fa}{1-f}\right\} K(\tau)\, d\tau \tag{A2.44}$$

In (A2.44) $p(\tau)$, $Y(t_{6,7})$, $Y(t_{7,6})$ and $K(\tau)=e^{-a(\tau-t_{2,6})}e^{gt_{2,6}}K(0)$ are known. Moreover, the value of K(0) is known (because $\partial S/\partial K(0)=wl/k+a+br/(1+b)+i/\{(1-f)(1+b))\}$. However, it is not known whether $t_{6,7}$ is larger or smaller than t_0. This is important to know, since p has to be integrated over the interval $[t_{6,7}, t_{7,6}]$. Therefore a distinction must be made between the two cases, $t_{6,7}<t_0$ and $t_{6,7}\geq t_0$. For each case the right hand side of (A2.44) can easily be calculated. After rearranging, for $t_{6,7}\geq t_0$ (A2.44) amounts to:

$$\left\{ e^{-(a+(1-f)r)t_{7,6}} - e^{-(a+(1-f)r)t_{6,7}} \right\} \frac{1-1/e}{r(1-f)+a}\, e^{-mt_0/e}\, e^{(g+a)t_{2,6}/e}$$

$$* \;\frac{-wl/k+fa/(1-f)-br/(1+b)-ba/((1-f)(1+b))}{wl/k+a+br/(1+b)+i/((1-f)(1+b))} =$$

$$= -\frac{1}{\beta}\left\{ e^{-\beta t_1} - e^{-\beta t_{6,7}}\right\} - e^{-mt_1/e}\left\{ e^{-\alpha t_{7,6}} - e^{-\alpha t_1}\right\}\frac{1}{\alpha}, \tag{A2.45}$$

where $\beta=\dfrac{g+a-m-e(a+(1-f)r)}{e}$ and $\alpha=\beta+m/e$.

For $t_{6,7}<t_0$:

$$\text{"left hand side of (A2.44)"} = -e^{-mt_0/e}\left\{ e^{-\beta t_0} - e^{-\beta t_{6,7}}\right\}\frac{1}{\beta} -$$

$$-\left\{ e^{-\beta t_1} - e^{-\beta t_0}\right\}\frac{1}{\beta} - e^{-mt_1/e}\left\{ e^{-\alpha t_{7,6}} - e^{-\alpha t_1}\right\}\frac{1}{\alpha} \tag{A2.46}$$

Before the analogue of (5.29) is given, it is shown that λ_1 and λ_2 jump at $t_{7,6}$. Suppose path 7 preceeds path 6. From (4.23) and (4.24) and the fact that $Y=bX$ in the coupling point (note that the state variables K and X must be continuous, which implies that Y must be continuous), it follows that $\eta_1=0$. If η_2 is also zero, then λ_1 and λ_2 are continuous. But if this is the case, then also μ_3 is continuous and this implies that path 7 cannot preceed path 6 if $r(1\text{-}f)<i$ (see the reasoning in Appendix 1, section A1.2.3). So, *if* path 7 is to proceed path 6, η_2 must be positive and λ_1 and λ_2 are discontinuous. Now the second part of the 'jump theorem' in Appendix 1 states that the entry in the constraint $(b+1)X\text{-}K\geq 0$ must be tangential. Since I is continuous in the coupling point of path 7 and path 6, the entry can only be tangential if D is also continuous in the coupling point. This means:

$$D(t^{+}_{7,6}) \;=\; (1\text{-}f)\;\{\;S[\tfrac{K}{k}]\text{-}\;\tfrac{wl}{k}\;K\text{-}aK\text{-}r(K\text{-}X)\;+\;\tfrac{aK}{1+b}\;\}\;=\;0 \qquad \text{(A2.47)}$$

But the first part of the 'jump theorem' shows that if the control variables are continuous and the strong constraint qualification is satisfied, the costate variables are continuous. Since it was just concluded that the coupling of path 7 before path 6 is only possible if λ_1 and λ_2 *and* the control variables are continuous, the strong constraint qualification must be violated if path 7 is to proceed path 6. And indeed, since $I=D=0$ in the coupling point, the last matrix on p.149 of Appendix 1 shows that the strong constraint qualification is violated. Now the conclusion finally is: provided the control variables are continuous at the coupling point and the costate variables are discontinuous, path 7 can be a predecessor of path 6.

The analogue of (5.29), which can be derived in the same way as (5.29), is:

$$\int_{t_{2,6}}^{t_{6,7}} e^{-(i+a)(\tau-t_{2,6})} (1\text{-}f)\left[\frac{\partial S}{\partial K} - \left\{\frac{wl}{k}+a+(\frac{b}{1+b}\ r)+\frac{1}{1+b}\ \frac{i}{1\text{-}f}\right\}\ \right] d\tau$$

$$+ \quad \int_{t_{6,7}}^{t_{7,6}} e^{-(i+a)(\tau-t_{2,6})} (1\text{-}f)\lambda_2(\tau)\left[\frac{\partial S}{\partial K} - \left\{\frac{wl}{k}+a+r\right\}\right) d\tau\ \Big] +$$

$$\int_{t_{7,6}}^{t_{6,2}} e^{-(i+a)(\tau-t_{2,6})} (1\text{-}f)\left[\frac{\partial S}{\partial K} - \left\{\frac{wl}{k}+a+(\frac{b}{1+b}\ r)+\frac{1}{1+b}\ \frac{i}{1\text{-}f}\right\}\ \right] d\tau$$

$$- e^{-(i+a)(t_{7,6}-t_{2,6})} * \eta_2 = 0 \tag{A2.48}$$

where

$$\eta_2 = \frac{1}{1+b} \int_{t_{6,7}}^{t_{7,6}} \{i\text{-}(1\text{-}f)r\}\ \lambda_2(\tau)\ d\tau \tag{A2.49}$$

Calculating (A2.48) gives the analogue of (A2.26). Together with (5.39), (A2.44) and (A2.45) resp. (A2.46) this forms a set of four, partly non-linear equations, which were again solved numerically using procedure C05NBF of the NAG-library.

To find $\hat{\hat{m}}$, see the derivation of m^{**} on page 169 and replace path 5 by path 6.

<u>Numerical exercises</u>
The numerical exercises only concern the value of $\hat{\hat{m}}$. The first set of parameters is similar to the last parameter set in the numerical exercises for the case $i<(1\text{-}f)r$; the only difference is the value of i (and a value for b must be added):

$e=2$ $a=0.04$ $f=0.4$ $g=0.07$ $i=0.06$ $r=0.09$ $t_0=10$ $t_1=50$
$k=2$ $l=3$ $w=2/3$ $b=2$

For $m\geq 0.22$ the string 2-6-2 is no longer possible. Only for very large values of m $t_{6,7}$ tends to zero. For $m=2$ (!) $t_{6,7}\approx 7.3$ and $t_{7,6}\approx 713$! Values for the parameters for which the situation is less extreme were not found. For instance, for the following parameter set:

$e=4$ $a=0.04$ $f=0.4$ $g=0.05$ $i=0.06$ $r=0.09$ $t_0=10$ $t_1=50$
$k=2$ $l=3$ $w=3$ $b=2$

Already for $m=0.15$ the string 2-6-2 is no longer feasible. But again, $t_{6,7}$

decreases gradually, but very slowly if m grows. For instance, for m=0.15: $t_{6,7} \approx 40$ and $t_{7,6} \approx 53$. For m=2: $t_{6,7} \approx 0.45$ and $t_{7,6} \approx 875$.

APPENDIX 3

ON THE SHADOW PRICE INTERPRETATION OF THE MULTIPLIERS OF PURE STATE CONSTRAINTS IN OPTIMAL CONTROL PROBLEMS

A3.1 Introduction

The interpretation of costate variables as shadow prices in Chapter 6 asks for an interpretation of the multipliers of pure state constraints. This appendix uses rather general Kuhn-Tucker conditions and general sensitivity results to derive a mathematically precise formulation of a convenient shadow price interpretation for the multipliers of pure state constraints. These general results are presented in sections A3.4, A3.5 and A3.6, the desired result is derived in section A3.7. Sections A3.2 and A3.3 give the class of models to be considered and an outline of the proof. The notation in this appendix is independent of the notation in the rest of this thesis.

A3.2 The class of models to be considered

The following class of models will be considered:

<u>Model or problem II</u>

$$\max_{u} \int_0^T e^{-it} F(x,u,t)dt + e^{-iT} S(x(T),T) \tag{A3.1}$$

$$\dot{x}(t) = f(x,u,t), \quad x(0)=x_0 \tag{A3.2}$$

$$h(x,t) \geq 0 \tag{A3.3}$$

$$u(t) \in U \text{ for a.e. } t \in [0,T] \tag{A3.4}$$

The functions $F:\mathbb{R}^n \times \mathbb{R}^m \times \mathbb{R} \to \mathbb{R}$, $f:\mathbb{R}^n \times \mathbb{R}^m \times \mathbb{R} \to \mathbb{R}^n$, $S:\mathbb{R}^n \times \mathbb{R} \to \mathbb{R}$ and $h:\mathbb{R}^n \times \mathbb{R} \to \mathbb{R}^s$ are (for the time being) assumed to be continuously differentiable. U is a closed convex set in $\mathbb{R}^m$ with nonempty interior. It is assumed that U can be written as: $U=\{u \in \mathbb{R}^m: g(u) \leq 0\}$, $g:\mathbb{R}^m \to \mathbb{R}^k$. The control variable is to be chosen from L_∞^m [0,T], the space of $\mathbb{R}^m$-valued measurable, essentially bounded functions on [0,T], which is a Banach space with norm (e.g. Luenberger [1969], p.37):

$$\|u\|_\infty := \operatorname*{ess\,sup}_{0 \leq t \leq T} \|u(t)\| = \operatorname*{infimum}_{v(t)=u(t) \text{ a.e.}} [\sup |v(t)|] \tag{A3.5}$$

A3.3 An outline of the proof

One could generalise model II by letting the functions F, f, S, and h depend on another variable a, where a belongs to some Banach space. For $a=0$, this generalised problem equals model II. Next one could examine how the value of the objective function changes when $a \neq 0$. In other words, one could look at the sensitivity of the optimal value function to changes (perturbations) in one or more of the functions appearing in the problem. A well known sensitivity result concerns a relaxation or tightening of an inequality constraint in linear programming problems. That sensitivity result is derived using the Kuhn-Tucker conditions. Since one expects that an interpretation of the multipliers of the pure state constraints has got something to do with the effect of perturbations of those constraints, something similar might work for the problem at hand.

Therefore the optimal control problem II will be formulated as an optimisation problem on some Banach space and then the general Kuhn-Tucker conditions for such a problem will be used to derive the desired sensitivity result. The biggest problem is to translate these results back to the familiar optimal control terminology.

A3.4 A general sensitivity result

This section closely follows Lempio & Maurer [1980].

Let X,Y,A be real Banach spaces and let $H: X \times A \to \mathbb{R}$ and $G: X \times A \to Y$ be mappings. For each fixed $a \in A$, consider the problem P_a:

$$\begin{aligned} &\text{minimise } H(x,a) \\ &\text{subject to } x \in C \text{ and } G(x,a) \in K, \end{aligned} \tag{A3.6}$$

where C in X and K in Y are nonempty closed convex sets. Assume that K is a closed convex cone with vertex at the origin. For $a=0$, problem P_a is called the unperturbed problem. For each a, define the feasible set

$$\Sigma(a) = \{x \in C \mid G(x,a) \in K\} \tag{A3.7}$$

and the optimal value function

$$V(a) = \inf \{H(x,a) \mid x \in \Sigma(a)\} \tag{A3.8}$$

Assume that H is diffferentiable and G is continuously differentiable in the sense of Fréchet at $(\bar{x},\bar{a})$, where $\bar{x}$ is a solution of P_a for $a=\bar{a}$. $\bar{x}$ is called <u>regular</u> if $0 \in \text{int}\, \{G(\bar{x},\bar{a}) + G_x(\bar{x},\bar{a})(C-\bar{x})-K\}$. If $\bar{x}$ is regular, there exists a Lagrange multiplier $l \in Y'$ (Y' denotes the dual space of Y) satisfying the Kuhn-Tucker conditions:

$$L_x(\bar{x},\bar{a},l)(x-\bar{x}) \geq 0 \text{ for all } x \in C \tag{A3.9}$$

$$l(G(\bar{x},\bar{a})) = 0,\ l(y) \leq 0 \text{ for all } y \in K \tag{A3.10}$$

where $L(x,a,l) = H(x,a) + l(G(x,a))$.

For the sensitivity result another condition is needed, the <u>strong stability condition</u>:

Let $d \in A$ be fixed. The strong stability condition holds, if for every $\varepsilon > 0$ there exist $\bar{x}$ optimal, $\delta > 0$, $c \geq 0$ and a curve $x:[0,\delta] \to X$ with

- $x(t) \in \Sigma(\bar{a}+td)$
- $\|x(t)-\bar{x}\| \leq ct$
- $H(x(t),\bar{a}+td) \leq V(\bar{a}+td)+t\varepsilon$

for all $t \in [0,\delta]$. The strong stability condition holds <u>at</u> $\bar{x}$ if $\bar{x}$ can be chosen above independently of ε

The sensitivity result which will be used is (Lempio & Maurer [1980], Corollary 3.5):

<u>Theorem 1</u>

Let x_0 be a solution of the unperturbed problem. If:

- x_0 is regular
- the set of all Lagrange multipliers associated with x_0 is a singleton
- the strong stability condition holds at x_0 for all $a \in A$

Then the Gateaux-differential $\partial V(0;b)$ of V at point zero with increment b exists and equals the Gateaux-differential of the function $a \to L(x_0,a,l)$ at zero with increment b:

$$\partial V(0;b) = L_a(x_0,0,l;b). \tag{A3.11}$$

A3.5 Problem II written as a problem P_a

There are many ways to write an optimal control problem as an optimisation problem P_a (cf. Jacobson, Lele and Speyer [1971], Maurer [1979], Machielsen [1987], Luenberger [1969], Kirsch, Warth and Werner [1978]). The method used here is similar to Kirsch, Warth and Werner, Maurer, and Machielsen. The symbols in the previous section are now specified as follows:

Let $X = W^n_\infty[0,T] \times L^m_\infty[0,T]$

$Y = L^n_\infty[0,T] \times C^s[0,T]$

$C = \{ (x,u) \in X \mid u(t) \in U \ \forall t \in [0,T] \}$

$K = \{0\} \times C^s[0,T]_+$

$W^n_\infty[0,T] = \{x \mid x:[0,T] \to \mathbb{R}^n \text{ absolute continuous and } \dot{x} \in L^n_\infty[0,T]\}$

$L^m_\infty[0,T] = \{x \mid x:[0,T] \to \mathbb{R}^m, \text{ x measurable and essentially bounded}\}$

$C^s[0,T]_+ = \{x \mid x:[0,T] \to \mathbb{R}^s, \text{ x continuous and } x(t) \geq 0 \text{ for all } t \in [0,T]\}$

Now X and Y are Banach spaces with the following norms (e.g. Kirsch, Warth and Werner, p.91-92):

$$\|x,u\|_X := \max \{\|x\|_\infty, \|\dot{x}\|_\infty, \|u\|_\infty\}$$

$$\|v,w\|_Y := \max \{\|v\|_\infty, \|w\|_\infty\}$$

Furthermore, let

$$H(x,u,a) = \int_0^T e^{-it} F(x,u,t,a)dt + e^{-iT} S(x(T),T,a)$$

$$G(x,u,a) = (\dot{x}(t) - f(x,u,t,a), h(x,t,a))$$

For the time being, A is not specified.

With these definitions, problem P_a is almost problem II. The only difference is that problem II is a maximisation problem, whereas P_a was formulated as a minimisation problem. For a maximisation problem the inequalities in (A3.9) and (A3.10) are reversed. Note that the differential equation (A3.2) is written as an "=0" constraint. This makes it possible to treat x and u as independent variables.

A3.6 The Kuhn-Tucker conditions and Theorem 1 for problem II

Let $(\bar{x},\bar{u})$ be an optimal solution of problem II. In other words, $(\bar{x},\bar{u})$ is an optimal solution of problem II, written as a problem P_a, with $a=0$ (problem II is the 'unperturbed' problem). To apply the Kuhn-Tucker conditions it is necessary that $(\bar{x},\bar{u})$ is regular. This also implies that problem II is a so-called "normal" (see, for instance, Feichtinger and Hartl [1986], p.24) optimal control problem. Maurer ([1979], Assumption 3.1) and Machielsen ([1987] , Theorem 3.6) give sufficient conditions for regularity. Here it is assumed that all conditions of Theorem 1 are satisfied. Now the function

L in the Kuhn-Tucker conditions looks as follows:

$$L(x,u,a,l_1,l_2,a) = {}_0\int^T e^{-it}F(x,u,t,a)dt + e^{-iT}S(x(T),T,a) +$$

$$l_1(\dot{x}(t)-f(x,u,t,a)) + l_2(h(x,t,a)) \qquad \text{(A3.12)}$$

In general it is hard to find representations for the Lagrange multipliers l_1 and l_2. Especially the representation for l_1 is extremely complicated. It turns out that the very fact that l_1 is a Lagrange multiplier makes it possible to find a representation. In other words, writing out the first Kuhn-Tucker condition (A3.9) leads to such a representation. The details can be found in Kirsch, Warth and Werner and Machielsen. The result is (from now on Greek symbols stand for row vectors):

$$l_1(y) = -{}_0\int^T \lambda(t)y(t)dt \qquad \text{for every } y \in L^n_\infty [0,T], \qquad \text{(A3.13)}$$

where λ is a function of bounded variation.

The representation of l_2 is much easier, since it is well known that the dual space of the space of continuous functions on an interval is the space of functions of bounded variation on that interval, normalised in one point. So:

$$l_2(y) = -{}_0\int^T y(t)^T d\tilde{\upsilon}(t)^T \quad \text{for every } y \in C^S[0,T], \qquad \text{(A3.14)}$$

where $\tilde{\upsilon}:[0,T]\to\mathbb{R}^S$ is a function of bounded variation, normalised by $\tilde{\upsilon}(T)=0$.

The Kuhn-Tucker condition (A3.10) states that $l_2(y)\geq 0$ for all non-negative continuous functions and that $l_2(h(\overline{x},t,0))=0$. It is easily seen that this leads to the conclusion that $\tilde{\upsilon}$ is non-increasing and $\tilde{\upsilon}_i$ is constant on intervals where $h_i(\overline{x},t,0)>0$. In most applications one can say even more about $\tilde{\upsilon}$, namely that $\tilde{\upsilon}$ is continuously differentiable on the interior of boundary intervals of h (a boundary interval of h_i is an interval on which h_i is active; a boundary interval of h is an interval on which all h_i are active). Maurer and Machielsen give sufficient conditions for this:

Let p_i be the lowest number for which $\frac{\partial}{\partial u}\frac{d^{p_i}}{dt^{p_i}}h_i \neq 0$. p_i is called the <u>order</u> of the constraint h_i.

Let $p \equiv \max p_i$

Let I_i be the set of active points of the state constraint h_i.

Let $\hat{h}^p(x,u,t) := \begin{bmatrix} h_1^{p_1}(x,u,t) \\ \\ h_s^{p_s}(x,u,t) \end{bmatrix}$

Let $[t_1,t_2]$ be an interval on which all constraints h_i are active.

Assume that:

- rank $\hat{h}_u^p(\bar{x},\bar{u},t) = s$ almost everywhere on $I_1 \cup \ldots\ldots \cup I_s$.
- F,f,S and h^p are C^{p+r} functions with respect to all arguments and $r \geq 0$
- $\bar{u}$ is a C^{p+r} function on $[t_1,t_2]$ and $\bar{u}(t) \in$ int U for all $t \in (t_1,t_2)$

Then λ and $\tilde{\upsilon}$ are C^{r+1} functions on (t_1,t_2).

Note that this theorem applies to boundary intervals of h, that is, intervals where all pure state constraints are active. However, as Machielsen notes (p.50), cases where some but not all state constraints are active are similar. In those cases all assumptions and results correspond to the case that all inactive components of h are omitted completely. It can easily be seen that this statement can be applied to model II at least for $r=0$, so that υ_i is a C^1 function on intervals where h_i is active, and we define:

$$\upsilon(t) = -\frac{\partial}{\partial t}\tilde{\upsilon}(t) \text{ for all } t \text{ where } \tilde{\upsilon} \text{ is differentiable.} \tag{A3.15}$$

Now υ is piecewise continuous and, since $\tilde{\upsilon}$ is non-increasing, υ is non-negative.

The Lagrangian function L (see (A3.12)) can now be written as:

$$L(x,u,a,\lambda,\tilde{\upsilon}) = \int_0^T e^{-it}F(x,u,t,a)dt + e^{-iT}S(x(T),T,a) +$$

$$\int_0^T \lambda(t)f(x,u,t,a)dt - \int_0^T \lambda(t)\dot{x}(t)dt +$$

$$\int_0^T \upsilon(t)h(x,a,t)dt + \Sigma\ \eta(t_j)h(x\ ,a,t_j), \tag{A3.16}$$

where the summation is over all entry- and exit points of boundaries and contact points[1] and $\eta(t) \equiv \tilde{\upsilon}(t^-) - \tilde{\upsilon}(t^+) \geq 0$. For completeness sake I give

---

[1]For a definition of entry and exit points, see Appendix 1, p.151. A contact point of a constraint h_i is a timepoint τ with the following property: there is an $\varepsilon > 0$ such that $h_i(\tau)=0$ and $h_i(t) \neq 0$ for $t \in (\tau-\varepsilon,\tau+\varepsilon)$,

the well known differential equation for the costate vector, which follows directly from the representation of l_1 (which I have not given; cf. Machielsen or Kirsch, Warth and Werner): λ is piecewise continuously differentiable and

$$\dot{\lambda}(t) = -e^{-it}F_x(\bar{x},\bar{u},t,0) - \lambda(t)f_x(\bar{x},\bar{u},t,0) - \upsilon(t)h_x(\bar{x},t,0) \tag{A3.17}$$

for points where λ is differentiable. Jumps of λ may occur at entry- or exit points of boundaries or contact points, and for these jumps:

$$\lambda(t^+) - \lambda(t^-) = -\eta(t)h_x(\bar{x}(t),t,0) \tag{A3.18}$$

A3.7 The shadow price interpretation of υ

The central result of Theorem 1 (section A3.4) is: $\partial V(0;b)=L_a(x_0,0,l;b)$. Maurer applies this result to an optimal control problem to find the shadow price interpretation for λ and to analyse a perturbation of the form: $h_i(x,t)\leq a$, $\forall t$, $a\in \mathbb{R}$. He finds: $L_a(\bar{x},\bar{u},0,l) = \tilde{\upsilon}(0)$. To find a shadow interpretation for $\upsilon_i(t)$, h_i should be perturbed locally in the following way:

Let $A=L^1_\infty[0,T]$. A momentary perturbation of h_i can be mimicked as follows (this tric is borrowed from Léonard [1987]):

Let $h_i(x,t,a) = h_i(x(t),t,a(t)) = h_i(x(t),t)-a(t)$

$$\text{Let } b\in A \text{ be: } \begin{cases} b=0 & \text{for } 0\leq t<\tau \\ b=\gamma\varepsilon^{-1} & \text{for } \tau\leq t<\tau+\varepsilon,\ \gamma<0 \\ b=0 & \text{for } \tau+\varepsilon\leq t\leq T \end{cases} \tag{A3.19}$$

For $\varepsilon\to0$ the perturbation $h_i(x,t,b)\geq0$ resembles a momentary relaxation of the state constraint $h_i(x,t)\geq0$ (see figure 3 of chapter 6).

From Theorem 1: $\partial V(0;b) = L_a(\bar{x},\bar{u},0,\lambda,\tilde{\upsilon};b)$,

where the right hand side is the Gateaux differential of the function $a\to L(\bar{x},\bar{u},a,\lambda,\tilde{\upsilon})$ at zero with increment b. Since a only appears, by assumption, in $h_i(x,t,a)$, to find $\partial V(0,b)$ just compute the Gateaux differential at zero with increment b of the function (see (A3.16)):

$$a\to \int_0^T \upsilon_i(t)h_i(x,t,a)dt + \Sigma\ \eta(t_i)h_i(x,t,a) \tag{A3.20}$$

---

property: there is an $\varepsilon>0$ such that $h_i(\tau)=0$ and $h_i(t)\neq0$ for $t\in(\tau-\varepsilon,\tau+\varepsilon)$, $t\neq\tau$.

This Gateaux differential is just what one expects it to be. It is allowed to change the order of differentiation and integration resp. summation and then to apply 'ordinary' differentiation. A formal justification for this can be found in Luenberger [1969], p.173, example 2. Things go well because h_i is continuous and b and υ_i are piecewise continuous. The result is:

$$\begin{aligned}\partial V(0;b) &= \int_0^T \frac{\partial}{\partial a(t)} h_i(x,a,t)\upsilon_i(t)b(t)dt + \Sigma\ \eta(t_j)\frac{\partial}{\partial a(t_j)} h_i(x,a,t_j)b(t_j) \\ &= \int_0^T -\upsilon_i(t)b(t)dt - \Sigma\ \eta(t_j)b(t_j) \\ &= \int_\tau^{\tau+\varepsilon} -\upsilon_i(t)\tfrac{\gamma}{\varepsilon}\ dt - \Sigma\ \eta(t_j)\tfrac{\gamma}{\varepsilon} \qquad \text{(A3.21)}\end{aligned}$$

where the last summation is over the entry-, exit- and contact points in the interval $[\tau,\tau+\varepsilon]$. Now assume that τ is not an entry-, exit-, or contact point. Then for small ε one can say that there are no exit- or entry points in $[\tau,\tau+\varepsilon]$. Therefore (A3.21) is equivalent to:

$$\partial V(0;b) = -\gamma \int_\tau^{\tau+\varepsilon} \upsilon_i(t)/\varepsilon\ dt \qquad \text{(A3.22)}$$

Define $K_i(t) = \int_0^t \upsilon_i(s)\ ds$. Then

$$\lim_{\varepsilon\to 0} \partial V(0;b) = \lim_{\varepsilon\to 0} -\gamma\{K_i(\tau+\varepsilon)-K_i(\tau)\}/\varepsilon = -\gamma\dot{K}_i(\tau) = -\gamma\upsilon_i(\tau) \qquad \text{(A3.23)}$$

Remember that for $\varepsilon\to 0$ the perturbation $h_i(x,t,b)\geq 0$ mimics a momentary relaxation of $h_i(x,t)\geq 0$ at time τ. Now (A3.23) state that $\upsilon_i(\tau)$ can be seen as the rate at a which gain (in terms of contributions to the objective function) could be made if the pure state constraint $h_i(x,t)\geq 0$ would be momentarily relaxed at time τ. In this sense, υ_i can be seen as the shadow price of the constraint $h_i(x,t)\geq 0$.

APPENDIX 4

NECESSARY AND SUFFICIENT CONDITIONS FOR AN OPTIMAL CONTROL PROBLEM WITH AN ENDOGENEOUSLY DETERMINED "LAG-STRUCTURE"

A4.1 Introduction

This appendix derives a variant of the 'Maximum Principle', which can be used to solve the vintage models of chapters 7 and 8. The model presented in the next section is intended to be as general as possible. The notation in this appendix is not related to the notation in the rest of this thesis.
Section A4.2 gives the model which is the basis for this appendix and which includes the models of chapters 7 and 8 as special cases. Section A4.3 discusses the tric which is essential in the heuristic derivation of the necessary conditions in section A4.4. In section A4.5 these 'necessary conditions' are augmented with some concavity conditions and it is proved that this augmented set of conditions is sufficient for optimality.

A4.2 The model

$$\max_{u,s} \int_0^\infty e^{-it} F\{Q(t),x(t),u(t),t\}\, dt \tag{A4.1}$$

$$Q(t) = \int_{v^{-1}(t)}^{t} G(u(\tau),t,\tau)\, d\tau \tag{A4.2}$$

$$\dot{x}(t) = f\{Q(t),x(t),u(t),t\}, \text{ for all } t \geq 0 \tag{A4.3}$$

$$\dot{v}(t) = s(t), \text{ for all } t \geq n_0 \tag{A4.4}$$

$$g_a\{Q(t),x(t),v(t),u(t),s(t),t\} \geq 0 \text{ for all } t \geq 0 \tag{A4.5}$$

$$g_b\{v(t),s(t)\} \geq 0 \text{ for all } n_0 \leq t < 0 \tag{A4.6}$$

$$h_a\{Q(t),x(t),v(t)\} \geq 0, \text{ for all } t \geq 0 \tag{A4.7}$$

$$h_b\{v(t)\} \geq 0 \text{ for all } n_0 \leq t < 0 \tag{A4.8}$$

$x(0)$ is given and $v(n_0)=0$ (A4.9a)

the values of the components of u explicitly appearing in (A4.2) are given for all t with $n_0 \leq t < 0$ (A4.9b) where F: $\mathbb{R}\times\mathbb{R}^n\times\mathbb{R}^m\times\mathbb{R}\to\mathbb{R}$, f: $\mathbb{R}\times\mathbb{R}^n\times\mathbb{R}^m\times\mathbb{R}\to\mathbb{R}^n$, G: $\mathbb{R}^m\times\mathbb{R}\times\mathbb{R}\to\mathbb{R}$, g_a: $\mathbb{R}\times\mathbb{R}^n\times\mathbb{R}\times\mathbb{R}^m\times\mathbb{R}\times\mathbb{R}\to\mathbb{R}^s$, g_b: $\mathbb{R}\times\mathbb{R}\to\mathbb{R}^k$ are assumed to be continuously differentiable in all their arguments and $h_a:\mathbb{R}\times\mathbb{R}^n\times\mathbb{R}\to\mathbb{R}^q$, $h_b:\mathbb{R}\to\mathbb{R}^l$ are assumed to be twice continuously differentiable in all their arguments.

Constraints of type (A4.2) are the reason to develop a variant of the Maximum Principle. The standard Maximum Principle can not cope with such constraints. The fact that Q appears as an argument of g_a and h_a complicates the matter considerably.

The state variables of the problem are Q, v , and x, where x is a n-dimensional vector. This vector of state variables is denoted by x_e (the extended state vector):

$$x_e = (Q,x,v) \tag{A4.10}$$

The control variables are s (the first derivative of v), and u, where u is an m-dimensional vector. The vector of control variables is denoted by:

$$u_e = (u,s) \tag{A4.11}$$

Now Q, x, and u are defined on the interval $[0,\infty)$ and v and s are defined on the interval $[n_0,\infty)$, where $n_0 < 0$.

Since the monotonicity of v is required later on, the restriction $s>0$ is needed. But for notational simplicity only 'greater than or equal to'-constraints are considered. However, adding 'strictly greater than'-constraints would not change the arguments. Note that s and v do not appear as arguments of F, f and G, and that the constraints g_b and h_b only involve s and v.

A4.3 The tric

The central feature of the approach in this appendix, which makes it possible to use 'calculus of variations' to derive necessary conditions and which is also the reason why the monotonicity of v is crucial, is as follows:

Consider v^{-1} as an arbitrary function (so nót as the inverse function of some function v). An essential part of the tric is to append the constraint (A4.2) to the integrand in (A4.1) and then to change the order

---

[1]Note that v in this appendix corresponds to V in chapters 7 and 8 and thus s in this appendix corresponds to B in chapters 7 and 8.

of integration in the double integral. To be more precise, multiply (A4.2) with a multiplier $\lambda_1(t)$ and then integrate the result with regard to t; this gives the following double integral[2]:

$$\int_0^{\infty} e^{-it}\lambda_1(t) \left\{ \int_{v^{-1}(t)}^{t} G\{u(\tau),t,\tau\}\, d\tau \right\} dt \tag{A4.12}$$

Changing the order of integration yields:

$$\int_{n_0}^{\infty} \left\{ \int_{\tau}^{v(\tau)} e^{-it}\lambda_1(t) G\{u(\tau),t,\tau\}\, dt \right\} d\tau \tag{A4.13}$$

<u>if</u>

$$G\{u(\tau),t,\tau\}=0 \text{ for } (t,\tau)\in \{ (t,\tau) \mid n_0<\tau<t<0 \}, \tag{A4.14}$$

as can be seen in the figure below:

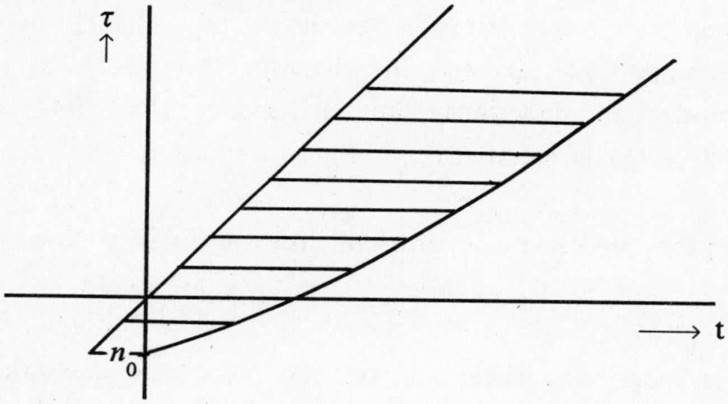

Figure 1: The area of integration

It depends on the problem whether the restriction on G is a serious one. In chapters 7 and 8, $G\{u(\tau),t,\tau\}$ stands for the number of capital goods installed at time τ or the number of employees working on capital goods installed at time τ. The number of capital goods installed at time $\tau<0$ is fixed by (A4.9b) and it is consequently not a part of the optimisation problem. So (A4.14) is a harmless restriction. Another crucial and possibly serious assumption concerning G is needed:

$$G\{u(\tau),t,\tau\} = G_1\{u(\tau)\}G_2\{t,\tau\} \tag{A4.15}$$

The reason for this assumption is that I want to be able to 'pull u out of the inner integral' in (A4.13). This will enable me to differentiate the

---

[2]In this appendix Greek letters denote row vectors, Latin letters denote column vectors.

double integral with regard to u:

$$\int_{n_0}^{\infty} \left\{ \int_{\tau}^{v(\tau)} e^{-it}\lambda_1(t)G\{u(\tau),t,\tau\}\, dt \right\} d\tau =$$

$$\int_{n_0}^{\infty} G_1\{u(\tau)\} \left\{ \int_{\tau}^{v(\tau)} e^{-it}\lambda_1(t)G_2\{t,\tau\}\, dt \right\} d\tau =$$

$$\int_{n_0}^{\infty} G_1\{u(t)\} \left\{ \int_{t}^{v(t)} e^{-i\tau}\lambda_1(\tau)G_2\{\tau,t\}\, d\tau \right\} dt, \tag{A4.16}$$

where the last equality is the result of the interchanging of t and τ. Now one sees that the last double integral in (A4.16) can easily be differentiated with regard to u(t), whereas (A4.12) could not. This will be crucial in the next section. Note that it is enough to know λ_1 on the interval $[0,\infty)$ (and nót on $[n_0,\infty)$) because of assumption (A4.14). Assumption (A4.15) might be serious. In chapters 7 and 8 it rules out certain types of production functions, but it seems that for the usual production functions, (A4.15) is satisfied.

A4.4 Derivation of the necessary conditions for optimality for a special case

This section gives a heuristic derivation of the necessary conditions using a calculus of variations approach for the model consisting of (A4.1)-(A4.4), (A4.9) and the following control constraints:

$$s_{min} \leq s \leq s_{max}, \text{ for all } t \geq n_0, \text{ with } s_{min} > 0 \tag{A4.17}$$

$$u_{min} \leq u \leq u_{max}, \text{ for all } t \geq 0, \text{ component-wise} \tag{A4.18}$$

Define

$$J(x_e,u_e) = \int_0^{\infty} e^{-it}\, F\{Q(t),x(t),u(t),t\}\, dt \tag{A4.19}$$

Now for each (x_e,u_e) satisfying (A4.2)-(A4.4), (A4.9), and (A4.17)-(A4.18) and for all continuous functions λ_1,λ_2: $[0,\infty)\to\mathbb{R}$ and λ_3 : $[n_0,\infty)\to\mathbb{R}$:

$$J(x_e,u_e) = \int_0^{\infty} e^{-it} \Big[F\{Q(t),x(t),u(t),t\} +$$

$$+ \lambda_1(t) \Big\{ \int_{v^{-1}(t)}^{t} G\{u(\tau),t,\tau\}\, d\tau - Q(t) \Big\} +$$

$$+ \lambda_2(t) \Big\{ f\{Q(t),x(t),u(t),t\} - \dot{x}(t) \Big\} \Big] dt +$$

$$+ \int_{n_0}^{\infty} e^{-it} \lambda_3(t) \Big\{ s(t) - \dot{v}(t) \Big\} dt^3 \qquad \text{(A4.20)}$$

Integrating by parts the terms involving $\dot{x}$ and $\dot{v}$ and rearranging yields

$$J(x_e,u_e) = \int_0^{\infty} e^{-it} \Big[F\{Q(t),x(t),u(t),t\} - \lambda_1(t)Q(t)$$

$$+ \lambda_2(t)f\{Q(t),x(t),u(t),t\} + \lambda_3(t)s(t) + x(t)\dot{\lambda}_2(t) - i\lambda_2(t)x(t)$$

$$+ v(t)\dot{\lambda}_3(t) - i\lambda_3(t)v(t) + \lambda_1(t) \Big\{ \int_{v^{-1}(t)}^{t} G\{u(\tau),t,\tau\}\, d\tau \Big\} \Big] dt$$

$$+ \int_{n_0}^{0} e^{-it} \Big[\lambda_3(t)s(t) + v(t)\dot{\lambda}_3(t) - i\lambda_3(t)v(t) \Big] dt$$

$$- \lim_{t\to\infty} e^{-it} \Big\{ x(t)\lambda_2(t) + v(t)\lambda_3(t) \Big\} + x(0)\lambda_2(0) + v(n_0)\lambda_3(n_0)$$

$$\text{(A4.21)}$$

Now using the 'tric' to rewrite the double integral gives:

---

[3]Note that for $t < 0$, we are actually compounding instead of discounting.

$$J(x_e,u_e) = \int_0^{\infty} e^{-it} \Big[F\{Q(t),x(t),u(t),t\} - \lambda_1(t)Q(t)$$

$$+ \lambda_2(t)f\{Q(t),x(t),u(t),t\} + \lambda_3(t)s(t) + x(t)\dot{\lambda}_2(t) - i\lambda_2(t)x(t)$$

$$+ v(t)\dot{\lambda}_3(t) - i\lambda_3(t)v(t)$$

$$+ G_1(u(t))\Big\{ \int_t^{v(t)} e^{-i(\tau-t)}\lambda_1(\tau)G_2\{\tau,t\}\, d\tau\Big\} \Big]\, dt$$

$$+ \int_{n_0}^{0} e^{-it}\Big[\lambda_3(t)s(t) + v(t)\dot{\lambda}_3(t) - i\lambda_3(t)v(t)$$

$$+ G_1(u(t))\Big\{ \int_t^{v(t)} e^{-i(\tau-t)}\lambda_1(\tau)G_2\{\tau,t\}\, d\tau\Big\} \Big]\, dt$$

$$- \lim_{t\to\infty} e^{-it}\Big\{ x(t)\lambda_2(t) + v(t)\lambda_3(t) \Big\} + x(0)\lambda_2(0) + v(n_0)\lambda_3(n_0)$$

(A4.22)

Next assume that (x_e^*,u_e^*) is an optimal solution for our problem. Define

$$(Q(t),x(t)) = (Q^*(t)+\delta Q(t),x^*(t)+\delta x(t)) \text{ for all } t\geq 0,$$
$$v(t) = v^*(t)+\delta v(t) \text{ for all } t\geq n_0$$
$$u(t) = u^*(t)+\delta u(t) \text{ for all } t\geq 0 \qquad \text{(A4.23)}$$
$$s(t) = s^*(t)+\delta s(t) \text{ for all } t\geq n_0,$$

where $(x_e,u_e) = (Q(t),x(t),v(t),u(t),s(t))$ satisfies (A4.2)-(A4.4), (A4.9), (A4.17)-(A4.18).

Then the following inequality must hold:

$$J(x_e,u_e) \leq J(x_e^*,u_e^*) \qquad \text{(A4.24)}$$

Now make a Taylor expansion of $J(x_e,u_e)$ in the neighbourhood of (x_e^*,u_e^*) and ignore the terms of second and higher order (note that at this point assumption (A4.15) and the subsequent argument are crucial). The result is (use (A4.9b) to conclude that δu vanishes on $[n_0,0)$):

$$\delta J \equiv J(x_e,u_e) - J(x_e^*,u_e^*) =$$

$$\int_0^\infty e^{-it}\Big[F_Q\{Q^*,x^*,u^*,t\}\delta Q(t) + F_x\{Q^*,x^*,u^*,t\}\delta x(t)$$

$$+ F_u\{Q^*,x^*,u^*,t\}\delta u(t) - \lambda_1(t)\delta Q(t) + \lambda_2(t)f_Q\{Q^*,x^*,u^*,t\}\delta Q(t)$$

$$+ \lambda_2(t)f_x\{Q^*,x^*,u^*,t\}\delta x(t) + \lambda_2(t)f_u\{Q^*,x^*,u^*,t\}\delta u(t) + \lambda_3(t)\delta s(t)$$

$$+ \dot{\lambda}_2(t)\delta x(t) - i\lambda_2(t)\delta x(t) + \dot{\lambda}_3(t)\delta v(t) - i\lambda_3(t)\delta v(t)$$

$$+ G_{1u}(u^*(t))\Big\{ \int_t^{v^*(t)} e^{-i(\tau-t)}\lambda_1(\tau)G_2\{\tau,t\}\, d\tau\Big\}\delta u(t)$$

$$+ G_1(u^*(t))e^{-i(v^*(t)-t)}\lambda_1(v^*(t))G_2\{v^*(t),t\}\delta v(t) \Big]\, dt$$

$$+ \int_{n_0}^{0} e^{-it}\Big[\lambda_3(t)\delta s(t) + \dot{\lambda}_3(t)\delta v(t) - i\lambda_3(t)\delta v(t)$$

$$+ G_1(u^*(t))e^{-i(v^*(t)-t)}\lambda_1(v^*(t))G_2\{v^*(t),t\}\delta v(t) \Big]\, dt$$

$$-\lim_{t\to\infty} e^{-it}\Big\{\lambda_2(t)\delta x(t) + \lambda_3(t)\delta v(t)\Big\} + \lambda_2(0)\delta x(0) + \lambda_3(n_0)\delta v(n_0) \qquad \text{(A4.25)}$$

Note that (A4.9a) gives: $\delta x(0)=\delta v(n_0)=0$. Using this in (A4.25) and rearranging terms gives:

$$\delta J = \int_0^{\infty} e^{-it} \Big[\Big\{F_Q\{Q^*,x^*,u^*,t\} - \lambda_1(t) + \lambda_2(t)f_Q\{Q^*,x^*,u^*,t\}\Big\}\delta Q(t)$$

$$+ \Big\{F_x\{Q^*,x^*,u^*,t\} + \lambda_2(t)f_x\{Q^*,x^*,u^*,t\} + \dot{\lambda}_2(t) - i\lambda_2(t)\Big\}\delta x(t)$$

$$+ \Big\{\dot{\lambda}_3(t) - i\lambda_3(t) + G_1(u^*(t))e^{-i(v^*(t)-t)}\ \lambda_1(v^*(t))G_2\{v^*(t),t\}\Big\}\delta v(t)$$

$$+ \Big[F_u\{Q^*,x^*,u^*,t\} + \lambda_2(t)f_u\{Q^*,x^*,u^*,t\}$$

$$+ G_{1u}(u^*(t))\Big\{ \int_t^{v^*(t)} e^{-i(\tau-t)}\lambda_1(\tau)G_2\{\tau,t\}\ d\tau\Big\}\Big]\delta u(t)$$

$$+ \lambda_3(t)\delta s(t) \Big]\ dt$$

$$+ \int_{n_0}^{0} e^{-it}\Big[\lambda_3(t)\delta s(t) + \Big\{\dot{\lambda}_3(t) - i\lambda_3(t)$$

$$+ G_1(u^*(t))e^{-i(v^*(t)-t)}\lambda_1(v^*(t))G_2\{v^*(t),t\}\Big\}\delta v(t) \Big]\ dt$$

$$-\lim_{t\to\infty} e^{-it}\Big\{\lambda_2(t)\delta x(t) + \lambda_3(t)\delta v(t)\Big\} \tag{A4.26}$$

For every feasible (x_e,u_e), the right hand side of (A4.26) must be non-positive according to (A4.24). Now choose the functions λ_1, λ_2 and λ_3 in such a way that the coefficients of $\delta Q(t)$,$\delta x(t)$ and $\delta v(t)$ are zero. Next observe that δu, and δs can be chosen independently, but not completely free because of (A4.17) and (A4.18). This implies that to ensure that the right hand side of (A4.26) is non-positive for all feasible modifications $(\delta u,\delta s)$ (that is, modifications that maintain (A4.17) (resp. (A4.18)), u^* and s^* must be chosen in such a way that:

$$\begin{aligned} &u^* = u_{min} \text{ if the coefficient of } \delta u \text{ is negative;} \\ &u^* = u_{max} \text{ if the coefficient of } \delta u \text{ is positive;} \\ &u_{min} \le u^* \le u_{max} \text{ if the coefficient of } \delta u \text{ is zero,} \end{aligned} \tag{A4.27}$$

and a similar condition for s^*. To write all these conditions down in a

'Maximum Principle'-like way, define:

$$\mathbb{H}_a(x_e,u_e,\lambda,t) = F\{Q,x,u,t\} + \lambda_2(t)f\{Q,x,u,t\} + \lambda_3(t)s(t) + G_1\{u(t)\} \int_t^{v(t)} \lambda_1(\tau)e^{-i(\tau-t)}G_2(\tau,t)\,d\tau, \text{ for all } t\geq 0. \quad (A4.28)$$

$$\mathbb{H}_b(v,s,\lambda,t) = \lambda_3(t)s(t) + G_1\{u(t)\} \int_0^{v(t)} \lambda_1(\tau)e^{-i(\tau-t)}G_2(\tau,t)\,d\tau, \text{ for } n_0\leq t<0 \quad (A4.29)^4$$

Moreover, define:

$$\mathbb{L}_a(x_e,u_e,\lambda,\mu,t) = \mathbb{H}_a + \mu_1(u-u_{min}) + \mu_2(u_{max}-u) + \mu_3(s-s_{min}) + \mu_4(s_{max}-s), \text{ for all } t\geq 0 \quad (A4.30)$$

$$\mathbb{L}_b(v,s,\lambda,\mu,t) = \mathbb{H}_b + \mu_3(s-s_{min}) + \mu_4(s_{max}-s), \; n_0\leq t<0 \quad (A4.31)$$

Now the condition that λ_1,λ_2 and λ_3 are chosen in such a way that the coefficients of δQ, δx and δv are zero can be rephrased as:

$$\lambda_1(t) = \partial/\partial Q\; \mathbb{L}_a(x_e^*,u_e^*,\lambda,\mu,t), \text{ for all } t\geq 0 \quad (A4.32)$$

$$\dot{\lambda}_2(t) = i\lambda_2(t) - \partial/\partial x\; \mathbb{L}_a(x_e^*,u_e^*,\lambda,\mu,t), \text{ for all } t\geq 0 \quad (A4.33)$$

$$\dot{\lambda}_3(t) = i\lambda_3(t) - \partial/\partial v\; \mathbb{L}_a(x_e^*,u_e^*,\lambda,\mu,t), \text{ for all } t\geq 0 \quad (A4.34)$$

$$\dot{\lambda}_3(t) = i\lambda_3(t) - \partial/\partial v\; \mathbb{L}_b(v^*,s^*,\lambda,\mu,t), \; n_0\leq t<0 \quad (A4.35)$$

$$\lim_{t\to\infty} e^{-it}\left\{\lambda_2(t)\delta x(t) + \lambda_3(t)\delta v(t)\right\} \geq 0 \quad (A4.36)$$

Condition (A4.27) and its analogue for s can now be rephrased as:

$$u_e^*(t) \text{ maximises } \mathbb{H}_a(x_e^*,u_e,\lambda,t) \text{ subject to (A4.18) for all } t\geq 0 \quad (A4.37)$$

$$s^*(t) \text{ maximises } \mathbb{H}_a(v^*,s,\lambda,t) \text{ and } \mathbb{H}_b(v^*,s,\lambda,t) \text{ subject to (A4.17), for all } t\geq n_0 \quad (A4.38)$$

And so:

---

[4]Note that for $t<0$, the lower bound of the integral is 0 instead of t. This is correct because of assumption (A4.14).

$$\partial/\partial u\ \mathbb{L}_a(x_e^*,u_e^*,\lambda,\mu,t) = 0 \text{ for all } t\geq 0$$

$$\mu_1(u-u_{min})=0,\ \mu_1\geq 0,\quad \mu_2(u_{max}-u)=0,\ \mu_2\geq 0 \text{ for all } t\geq 0 \tag{A4.39}$$

$$\partial/\partial s\ \mathbb{L}_a(x_e^*,u_e^*,\lambda,\mu,t) = 0 \text{ for all } t\geq 0$$

$$\mu_3(s-s_{min})=0,\ \mu_3\geq 0,\quad \mu_4(s_{max}-s)=0,\ \mu_4\geq 0 \quad \text{for all } t\geq 0 \tag{A4.40}$$

$$\partial/\partial s\ \mathbb{L}_b(x_e^*,u_e^*,\lambda,\mu,t) = 0,\ n_0\leq t<0$$

$$\mu_3(s-s_{min})=0,\ \mu_3\geq 0,\quad \mu_4(s_{max}-s)=0,\ \mu_4\geq 0,\ n_0\leq t<0 \tag{A4.41}$$

Of course this derivation is far from rigorous. I will not try to make it more rigorous. Instead I 'guess', assuming that for a more general problem the necessary conditions will be similar to (A4.32)-(A4.41), the necessary conditions for the original problem (A4.1)-(A4.9), and then prove that under some additional concavity assumptions, these conditions are sufficient.

A4.5 Sufficient conditions for the general model

For the general problem the Hamiltonian functions are the same as in (A4.28)-(A4.29), but the Lagrangian functions are different, because of the restrictions (A4.5)-(A4.8). So define:

$$\mathbb{L}_a(x_e,u_e,\lambda,\mu_a,\upsilon_a,t) = \mathbb{H}_a + \mu_a(t)g_a(x_e,u_e,t) + \upsilon_a(t)h_a(x_e,t) \tag{A4.42}$$

$$\mathbb{L}_b(v,s,\lambda,\mu_b,\upsilon_b,t) = \mathbb{H}_b + \mu_b(t)g_a(v,s,t) + \upsilon_b(t)h_b(v,t) \tag{A4.43}$$

To prove the sufficiency result a constraint qualification is needed. In fact *two* constraint qualifications are needed, one for $t\geq 0$ and one for $n_0\leq t<0$. The constraint qualification for $t\geq 0$ is:

The matrix

$$\begin{bmatrix} \partial g_{a1}/\partial u_e & g_{a1} & \cdots & 0 \\ \vdots & \vdots & & \vdots \\ \partial g_{as}/\partial u_e & 0 & \cdots & g_{as} \end{bmatrix} \qquad \text{(A4.44)}$$

has maximal row rank.

The constraint qualification for $\eta_0 \leq t < 0$ is:

The matrix

$$\begin{bmatrix} \partial g_{b1}/\partial s & g_{b1} & \cdots & 0 \\ \vdots & \vdots & & \vdots \\ \partial g_{bk}/\partial s & 0 & \cdots & g_{bk} \end{bmatrix} \qquad \text{(A4.45)}$$

has maximal row rank.

Now combining our knowledge of the special case and our knowledge about 'standard' problems with pure and mixed state constraints is sufficient to formulate a sufficiency theorem for the general model.

<u>Theorem one</u>

Let (x_e^*, u_e^*) be a feasible solution of (A4.2)-(A4.9) and let constraint qualification (A4.44) be satisfied for all $t \geq 0$ and constraint qualification (A4.45) for all t with $\eta_0 \leq t < 0$. Moreover, let there be piecewise continuously differentiable functions λ_1, λ_2: $[0,\infty) \to \mathbb{R}$ and a piecewise continuously differentiable function λ_3: $[\eta_0, \infty) \to \mathbb{R}$, piecewise continuous functions μ_a: $[0,\infty) \to \mathbb{R}^s$, υ_a: $[0,\infty) \to \mathbb{R}^s$, μ_b: $[\eta_0, 0) \to \mathbb{R}^k$, υ_b: $[\eta_0, 0) \to \mathbb{R}^k$, for each point $\tau \geq 0$ where λ is discontinuous a vector $\eta_a(\tau) \in \mathbb{R}^q$ and for each point $\tau < 0$ where λ_3 is discontinuous a vector $\eta_b(\tau) \in \mathbb{R}^1$, such that for all points where u_e^* and λ are continuous:

$$u_e^*(t) = \underset{\{u_e \mid g_a(x_e^*,u_e)\geq 0\}}{\operatorname{argmax}} \mathbb{H}_a(x_e^*,u_e,\lambda,t), \text{ for all } t\geq 0 \tag{A4.46a}$$

$$s^*(t) = \underset{\{s \mid g_b(v^*,s)\geq 0\}}{\operatorname{argmax}} \mathbb{H}_b(v^*,s,\lambda,t), \; n_0\leq t<0 \tag{A4.46b}$$

$$\partial/\partial u_e \, \mathbb{L}_a(x_e^*,u_e^*,\lambda,\mu_a,\upsilon_a,t) = 0 \text{ for all } t\geq 0 \tag{A4.47a}$$

$$\partial/\partial s \, \mathbb{L}_b(v^*,s^*,\lambda_3,\mu_b,\upsilon_b,t) = 0, \; n_0\leq t<0 \tag{A4.47b}$$

$$\lambda_1(t) = \partial/\partial Q \, \mathbb{L}_a(x_e^*,u_e^*,\lambda,\mu_a,\upsilon_a,t), \text{ for all } t\geq 0 \tag{A4.48}$$

$$\dot{\lambda}_2(t) = i\lambda_2(t) - \partial/\partial x \, \mathbb{L}_a(x_e^*,u_e^*,\lambda,\mu_a,\upsilon_a,t), \text{ for all } t\geq 0 \tag{A4.49}$$

$$\dot{\lambda}_3(t) = i\lambda_3(t) - \partial/\partial v \, \mathbb{L}_a(x_e^*,u_e^*,\lambda,\mu_a,\upsilon_a,t), \text{ for all } t\geq 0 \tag{A4.50}$$

$$\dot{\lambda}_3(t) = i\lambda_3(t) - \partial/\partial v \, \mathbb{L}_b(v^*,s^*,\lambda,\mu_b,\upsilon_b,t), \; n_0\leq t<0 \tag{A4.51}$$

$$\mu_a\geq 0, \; \mu_a g_a=0, \; \upsilon_a\geq 0, \; \upsilon_a h_a=0, \; t\geq 0 \tag{A4.52a}$$

$$\mu_b\geq 0, \; \mu_b g_b=0, \; \upsilon_b\geq 0, \; \upsilon_b h_b=0, \; n_0\leq t<0 \tag{A4.52b}$$

$$\lim_{t\to\infty} e^{-it}\left\{\lambda_2(t)\{x(t)-x^*(t)\} + \lambda_3(t)\{v(t)-v^*(t)\}\right\} \geq 0 \tag{A4.53}$$

At points $\tau\in [0,\infty)$ where h_a is active, λ_2 and λ_3 may jump:

$$\lambda_2(\tau^-) = \lambda_2(\tau^+) + \eta_a(\tau)\{\partial/\partial x \; h_a\}$$

$$\lambda_3(\tau^-) = \lambda_3(\tau^+) + \eta_a(\tau)\{\partial/\partial v \; h_a\} \tag{A4.54a}$$

At points $\tau\in [n_0,0)$ where h_b is active, λ_3 may jump:

$$\lambda_3(\tau^-) = \lambda_3(\tau^+) + \eta_b(\tau)\{\partial/\partial v \; h_b\} \tag{A4.54b}$$

$$\eta_a(\tau)\geq 0, \quad \eta_a(\tau)h_a(x_e^*,\tau) = 0 \tag{A4.55a}$$

$$\eta_b(\tau)\geq 0, \quad \eta_b(\tau)h_b(v^*,\tau) = 0 \tag{A4.55b}$$

Finally, let $\mathbb{H}_a^o(x_e,\lambda,t)= \max_{\{u_e \mid g_a(x_e,u_e)\geq 0\}} \mathbb{H}_a(x_e,u_e,\lambda,t)$ be concave in x_e for every (λ,t), $t\geq 0$; let $\mathbb{H}_b^o(v,\lambda_3,t)= \max_{\{s \mid g_b(v,s)\geq 0\}} \mathbb{H}_b(v,s,\lambda,t)$ be concave in v for every (λ_3,t), $n_0 \leq t < 0$; let $g_a(x_e,u_e,t)$ be quasi-concave in (x_e,u_e) for every $t \geq 0$; let $g_b(v,s,t)$ be quasi-concave in (v,s) for every t in $[n_0,0)$; let $h_a(x_e,t)$ be quasi-concave in x_e for every $t \geq 0$; let $h_b(v,t)$ be quasi-concave in v for every t in $[n_0,0)$. Then (x_e^*,u_e^*) is an optimal solution.

The proof of this theorem follows very closely the proof of theorem 7.1 of Feichtinger and Hartl [1986], which is based on Seierstadt and Sydsaeter [1977]. For that reason I will now formulate a theorem which is similar to theorem 7.2 of Feichtinger and Hartl.

<u>Theorem 2</u>

Let (x_e^*,u_e^*) be a feasible solution of (A4.2)-(A4.9) and let there be piecewise continuously differentiable functions λ_1,λ_2: $[0,\infty)\to\mathbb{R}$ and a piecewise continuously differentiable function λ_3: $[n_0,\infty)\to\mathbb{R}$, so that for every feasible solution (x_e,u_e):

1) $\mathbb{H}_a(x_e^*,u_e^*,\lambda,t)-\mathbb{H}_a(x_e,u_e,\lambda,t) \geq -\lambda_1(t)\{Q(t)-Q^*(t)\} +$

$$\{\dot{\lambda}_2(t)-i\lambda_2(t)\}\{x(t)-x^*(t)\} + \{\dot{\lambda}_3(t)-i\lambda_3(t)\}\{v(t)-v^*(t)\},\ t\geq 0 \qquad \text{(A4.56a)}$$

$$\mathbb{H}_b(v^*,s^*,\lambda,t)-\mathbb{H}_b(v,s,\lambda,t) \geq \{\dot{\lambda}_3(t)-i\lambda_3(t)\}\{v(t)-v^*(t)\},\ n_0\leq t<0 \qquad \text{(A4.56b)}$$

for almost every t.

2) $\{\lambda_2(\tau^-)-\lambda_2(\tau^+)\}\{x(\tau)-x^*(\tau)\} + \{\lambda_3(\tau^-)-\lambda_3(\tau^+)\}\{v(\tau)-v^*(\tau)\}\geq 0$, for every point $\tau>0$ where (λ_2,λ_3) is discontinuous. (A4.57a)

3) $\{\lambda_3(\tau^-)-\lambda_3(\tau^+)\}\{v(\tau)-v^*(\tau)\}\geq 0$, for every point $\tau \in (n_0,0]$ where λ_3 is discontinuous.[5] (A4.57b)

4) $$\lim_{t\to\infty} e^{-it}\left\{\lambda_2(t)\{x(t)-x^*(t)\} + \lambda_3(t)\{v(t)-v^*(t)\}\right\} \geq 0 \qquad \text{(A4.58)}$$

Then (x_e^*,u_e^*) is optimal.

---

[5]Note that this may include $\tau=0$

<u>Proof</u>

Let (x_e,u_e) be an arbitrary feasible solution. Define:

$$\Delta = \int_0^{\infty} e^{-it}F\{Q^*,x^*,u^*,t\}\ dt - \int_0^{\infty} e^{-it}F\{Q,x,u,t\}\ dt \qquad \text{(A4.59)}$$

Since (x^*_e,u^*_e) and (x_e,u_e) are feasible solutions, if follows that:

$$\Delta = \int_0^{\infty} e^{-it}\Big[F\{Q^*,x^*,u^*,t\}\ dt + \lambda_1(t)\Big\{\int_{v^{-1}(t)}^{t} G\{u^*(\tau),t,\tau\}\ d\tau\Big\}$$

$$+ \lambda_2(t)\Big\{f\{Q^*(t),x^*(t),u^*(t),t\}\Big\}\Big]\ dt + \int_{n_0}^{\infty} e^{-it}\ \lambda_3(t)s^*(t)\ dt$$

$$- \int_0^{\infty} e^{-it}\Big[F\{Q,x,u,t\}\ dt + \lambda_1(t)\Big\{\int_{v^{-1}(t)}^{t} G\{u(\tau),t,\tau\}\ d\tau\Big\}$$

$$+ \lambda_2(t)\Big\{f\{Q(t),x(t),u(t),t\}\Big\}\Big]\ dt - \int_{n_0}^{\infty} e^{-it}\ \lambda_3(t)s(t)\ dt$$

$$- \int_0^{\infty} e^{-it}\Big[\lambda_1(t)\{Q^*(t)-Q(t)\} + \lambda_2(t)\{\dot{x}^*(t)-\dot{x}(t)\}\Big]\ dt$$

$$- \int_{n_0}^{\infty} e^{-it}\ \lambda_3(t)\{\dot{v}^*(t)-\dot{v}(t)\}\ dt \qquad \text{(A4.60)}$$

After performing the 'tric' of section A4.3, and using the definition of $\mathbb{H}_a$ and $\mathbb{H}_b$, this is equal to:

$$\Delta = \int_0^{\infty} e^{-it}\Big[\mathbb{H}_a(x^*_e,u^*_e,\lambda,t)-\mathbb{H}_a(x_e,u_e,\lambda,t)\Big]\ dt$$

$$+ \int_{n_0}^{0} e^{-it}\Big[\mathbb{H}_b(v^*,s^*,\lambda,t)-\mathbb{H}_b(v,s,\lambda,t)\Big]\ dt$$

$$- \int_0^{\infty} e^{-it}\Big[\lambda_1(t)\{Q^*(t)-Q(t)\} + \lambda_2(t)\{\dot{x}^*(t)-\dot{x}(t)\}\Big]\ dt$$

$$- \int_{n_0}^{\infty} e^{-it}\ \lambda_3(t)\{\dot{v}^*(t)-\dot{v}(t)\}\ dt \qquad \text{(A4.61)}$$

Using (A4.56) gives:

$$\Delta \geq \int_0^\infty e^{-it}\Big[-\lambda_1(t)\{Q(t)-Q^*(t)\} + \{\dot\lambda_2(t)-i\lambda_2(t)\}\{x(t)-x^*(t)\}$$

$$+ \{\dot\lambda_3(t)-i\lambda_3(t)\}\{v(t)-v^*(t)\}\Big]\, dt$$

$$+ \int_{n_0}^{0} e^{-it}\{\dot\lambda_3(t)-i\lambda_3(t)\}\{v(t)-v^*(t)\}\, dt$$

$$- \int_0^\infty e^{-it}\Big[\lambda_1(t)\{Q^*(t)-Q(t)\} + \lambda_2(t)\{\dot x^*(t)-\dot x(t)\}\Big]\, dt$$

$$- \int_{n_0}^\infty e^{-it}\, \lambda_3(t)\{\dot v^*(t)-\dot v(t)\}\, dt \qquad \text{(A4.62)}$$

Now the terms involving Q and Q^* cancel in the right hand side of (A4.62) and the remaining part can be rewritten to arrive at:

$$\Delta \geq \int_0^\infty \frac{d}{dt}\Big\{e^{-it}\lambda_2(t)\{x(t)-x^*(t)\}\Big\}\, dt$$

$$+ \int_{n_0}^\infty \frac{d}{dt}\Big\{e^{-it}\lambda_3(t)\{v(t)-v^*(t)\}\Big\}\, dt \qquad \text{(A4.63)}$$

Taking into account possible jumps of λ_2 and λ_3, the right hand side of (A4.63) equals:

$$\lim_{t\to\infty} e^{-it}\Big\{\lambda_2(t)\{x(t)-x^*(t)\} + \lambda_3(t)\{v(t)-v^*(t)\}\Big\} +$$

$$\sum_{\tau>0} e^{-i\tau}\{\lambda_2(\tau^-)-\lambda_2(\tau^+)\}\{x(\tau)-x^*(\tau)\} - \lambda_2(0)\{x(0)-x^*(0)\}$$

$$+ \sum_{\tau\geq n_0} e^{-i\tau}\{\lambda_3(\tau^-)-\lambda_3(\tau^+)\}\{v(\tau)-v^*(\tau)\} - \lambda_3(n_0)\{v(n_0)-v^*(n_0)\} \qquad \text{(A4.64)}$$

Using $x(0)=x^*(0)$ and $v(n_0)=v^*(n_0)$, (A4.57) and (A4.58) gives: $\Delta \geq 0$. □

This theorem as well as the lemmas 7.3 and 7.4 of Feichtinger and Hartl [1986] will be used to prove theorem 1. For convenience the lemmas are given here without proof as lemmas 1 and 2.

Lemma 1

Let ϕ be a quasi-concave and differentiable function on a convex set $D(\phi)$. Let there be a vector z^* and a scalar ρ such that

$$\phi(z^*)\geq 0,\ \rho\geq 0,\ \rho\phi(z^*)=0$$

Then for all $z\in D(\phi)$ with $\phi(z)\geq 0$:

$$\rho\phi_z(z^*)(z-z^*)\geq 0$$

Lemma 2

Let ϕ be a concave function on a convex set $D(\phi)$.

Then there is for every $z^*\in D(\phi)$ a row vector $a=a(z^*)$, such that for all $z\in D(\phi)$:

$$\phi(z)-\phi(z^*)\leq a(z-z^*).$$

a is called a supergradient of ϕ.

Proof of theorem 1

Define

$$A_a(t) = \{x_e \mid \exists u_e \text{ with } g_a(x_e,u_e,t)\geq 0\},\ \text{for every } t\geq 0 \qquad \text{(A4.65a)}$$

$$A_b(t) = \{v \mid \exists s \text{ with } g_b(v,s,t)\geq 0\},\ \text{for every t in } [n_0,0) \qquad \text{(A4.65b)}$$

From the quasi-concavity of g_a and g_b it follows that $A_a(t)$ and $A_b(t)$ are convex sets. Now $\mathbb{H}_a^O$ is concave on $A_a(t)$ and $\mathbb{H}_b^O$ is concave on $A_b(t)$, so there are (by Lemma 2) supergradients (row vectors) $w_a(t)\in\mathbb{R}^{n+2}, t\geq 0$ and $w_b(t)\in\mathbb{R}$, $n_0\leq t<0$, such that:

$$\mathbb{H}_a^O(x_e,\lambda,t)-\mathbb{H}_a^O(x_e^*,\lambda,t) \leq w_a(t)[x_e-x_e^*(t)],\ \text{for all } x_e\in\mathbb{R}^{n+2} \qquad \text{(A4.66a)}$$

$$\mathbb{H}_b^O(v,\lambda,t)-\mathbb{H}_b^O(v^*,\lambda,t) \leq w_b(t)[v-v^*(t)],\ \text{for all } v\in\mathbb{R} \qquad \text{(A4.66b)}$$

From the definition of $\mathbb{H}^O$ this implies:

$$\mathbb{H}_a(x_e,u_e,\lambda,t)-\mathbb{H}_a(x_e^*,u_e^*,\lambda,t) \leq w_a(t)[x_e-x_e^*(t)],\ \text{for all } (x_e,u_e) \text{ that satisfy } g_a(x_e,u_e,t)\geq 0 \qquad \text{(A4.67a)}$$

$$\mathbb{H}_b(v,s,\lambda,t)-\mathbb{H}_b(v^*,s^*,\lambda,t) \leq w_b(t)[v-v^*(t)],\ \text{for all } (v,s) \text{ that satisfy } g_b(v,s,t)\geq 0 \qquad \text{(A4.67b)}$$

Therefore, for every $t\geq 0$, $(x_e^*(t),u_e^*(t))$ is an optimal solution for the static optimisation problem

$$\max_{x_e, u_e} \; \mathbb{H}_a(x_e,u_e,\lambda,t)-w_a(t)x_e, \text{ subject to } g_a(x_e,u_e,t)\geq 0,$$

and for every t, $n_0 \leq t < 0$, $(v^*(t),s^*(t))$ is an optimal solution for the static optimisation problem

$$\max_{v,s} \; \mathbb{H}_b(v,s,\lambda,t)-w_b(t)v, \text{ subject to } g_b(v,s,t)\geq 0.$$

And thus, because constraint qualifications (A4.44) and (A4.45) are satisfied, there exists for every $t \geq 0$ a multiplier $\hat{\mu}_a(t)$, and for every t, $n_0 \leq t < 0$, a multiplier $\hat{\mu}_b(t)$, such that we have the following Kuhn-Tucker conditions:

$$\mathbb{H}_{ax_e}(x_e^*(t),u_e^*(t),\lambda,t)-w_a(t) + \hat{\mu}_a(t)g_{ax_e}(x_e^*,u_e^*,t) = 0 \qquad \text{(A4.68a)}$$

$$\mathbb{H}_{bv}(v^*(t),s^*(t),\lambda,t)-w_b(t) + \hat{\mu}_b(t)g_{bv}(v^*,s^*,t) = 0 \qquad \text{(A4.68b)}$$

$$\mathbb{H}_{au_e}(x_e^*(t),u_e^*(t),\lambda,t) + \hat{\mu}_a(t)g_{au_e}(x_e^*,u_e^*,t) = 0 \qquad \text{(A4.69a)}$$

$$\mathbb{H}_{bs}(v^*(t),s^*(t),\lambda,t) + \hat{\mu}_b(t)g_{bs}(v^*,s^*,t) = 0 \qquad \text{(A4.69b)}$$

$$\hat{\mu}_a(t)\geq 0,\; \hat{\mu}_a(t)g_a(x_e^*,u_e^*,t) = 0 \qquad \text{(A4.70a)}$$

$$\hat{\mu}_b(t)\geq 0,\; \hat{\mu}_b(t)g_b(v^*,s^*,t) = 0 \qquad \text{(A4.70b)}$$

The constraint qualification ensures that $\hat{\mu}_a(t)$ and $\hat{\mu}_b(t)$ are uniquely determined. Therefore it follows form (A4.47a) and (A4.69a) that $\hat{\mu}_a(t)=\mu_a(t)$ for all $t\geq 0$ and from (A4.47b) and (A4.69b) that $\hat{\mu}_b(t)=\mu_b(t)$ for all $t\in[n_0,0)$.

Combining this with (A4.68) and the adjoint equations (A4.48)-(A4.51) gives:

$$w_a(t) = \Big[(\lambda_1(t)-\upsilon_a(t)h_{aQ}(x_e^*,t),\; i\lambda_2(t)-\dot{\lambda}_2(t)-\upsilon_a(t)h_{aX}(x_e^*,t),$$
$$i\lambda_3(t)-\dot{\lambda}_3(t)-\upsilon_a(t)h_{aV}(x_e^*,t)\Big], \text{ for all } t\geq 0 \qquad \text{(A4.71a)}$$

$$w_b(t) = i\lambda_3(t)-\dot{\lambda}_3(t)-\upsilon_b(t)h_{bV}(v^*,t), \text{ for all t in } [n_0,0) \qquad \text{(A4.71b)}$$

Substituting (A4.71a) in (A4.67a) and (A4.71b) in (A4.67b) gives:

$$\mathbb{H}_a(x_e,u_e,\lambda,t)-\mathbb{H}_a(x_e^*,u_e^*,\lambda,t) \leq \lambda_1(t)\{Q(t)-Q^*(t)\}$$

$$+ \{i\lambda_2(t)-\dot{\lambda}_2(t)\}\{x(t)-x^*(t)\} + \{i\lambda_3(t)-\dot{\lambda}_3(t)\}\{v(t)-v^*(t)\}$$

$$- \upsilon_a(t)h_{aQ}(x_e^*,t)\{Q(t)-Q^*(t)\} -\upsilon_a(t)h_{aX}(x_e^*,t)\{x(t)-x^*(t)\}$$

$$- \upsilon_a(t)h_{aV}(x_e^*,t)\{v(t)-v^*(t)\}, \text{ for all } t\geq 0 \qquad \text{(A4.72a)}$$

$$\mathbb{H}_b(v,s,\lambda,t)-\mathbb{H}_b(v^*,s^*,\lambda,t) \leq \{i\lambda_3(t)-\dot{\lambda}_3(t)\}\{v(t)-v^*(t)\}$$

$$- \upsilon_b(t)h_{bV}(x_e^*,t)\{v(t)-v^*(t)\}, \; n_0\leq t<0 \qquad \text{(A4.72b)}$$

The quasi-concavity of h_a and h_b and (A4.52) ensure that the terms involving the partial derivatives of h_a and h_b are non-negative (Lemma 1). And thus (A4.72) implies (A4.56) of Theorem 2. Condition (A4.57) of Theorem 2 follows from (A4.54) and another application of Lemma 1, using (A4.55) and the quasi-concavity of h_a and h_b. Finally, since (A4.53) is equal to (A4.58), all assumptions of Theorem 2 are satisfied and it can be concluded that (x_e^*,u_e^*) is optimal, which concludes the proof of Theorem 1. □

APPENDIX 5
VARIOUS DERIVATIONS

Appendix A5.1 The details of section 7.4

A5.1.1 Existence of a steady state solution in section 7.4.1

Substituting the values of λ_1, λ_2, λ_4 and λ_5 in (7.26), and using $\mu_i=0$, i=1,..,6, and $\upsilon_2=0$ gives:

$$\frac{c(t)}{1-f}\left\{1-f\int_t^{t+v} e^{-i(\tau-t)}d(\tau-t)\ d\tau\right\}$$

$$=\int_t^{V(t)} e^{-(i+a)(\tau-t)}\left\{\frac{\partial S}{\partial K}(\tau)-(l(t)/k)w(\tau)\right\}d\tau \qquad \text{(A5.1)}$$

Substituting (7.40) into (A5.1) gives:

$$\frac{c(t)}{1-f}\left\{1-f\int_t^{t+v} e^{-i(\tau-t)}d(\tau-t)\ d\tau\right\}$$

$$=\int_t^{V(t)} e^{-(i+a)(\tau-t)}(w(\tau)/k)\{\ l(N(\tau))-l(t)\ \}\ d\tau \qquad \text{(A5.2)}$$

Substituting the steady state values for w, V, N, c and l gives:

$$\frac{c^*}{1-f}\left\{1-f\int_t^{t+v} e^{-i(\tau-t)}d(\tau-t)\ d\tau\right\}$$

$$=\int_t^{t+T^*} e^{-(i+a)(\tau-t)}(l(0)w^*/k)e^{h\tau}\left\{\ e^{-h(\tau-T^*)}-e^{-ht}\ \right\}\ d\tau \qquad \text{(A5.3)}$$

Changing the integration variable in both integrals, this equals:

$$\frac{c^*}{1-f}\left\{1-f\int_0^{v} e^{-i\tau}\ d(\tau)\ d\tau\right\}$$

$$=\int_0^{T^*} e^{-(i+a)\tau}(l(0)w^*/k)e^{h\tau}\left\{\ e^{-h(\tau-T^*)}-1\ \right\}\ d\tau \qquad \text{(A5.4)}$$

The right hand side of (A5.4) is easily integrable. The result is equation (7.57) in chapter 7.

A5.1.2 Derivation of (7.57)

Given the assumptions concerning the final path in section 7.4.2 it is clear that on the final path (7.26) amounts to:

$$\frac{c(t)}{1-f}\left\{ 1 - f \int_t^{t+v} e^{-i(\tau-t)} d(\tau-t)\ d\tau\right\}$$

$$= \int_t^{V(t)} e^{-(i+a)(\tau-t)} \left\{ \frac{\partial S}{\partial K}(\tau) - (l(t)/k)w(\tau) \right\} d\tau \tag{A5.5}$$

Differentiating both sides and using the scrapping condition (7.44) gives:

$$\frac{\partial S}{\partial K}(t) = \left\{1 - f \int_0^{v} e^{-i\tau} d(\tau)\ d\tau\right\} \{(i+a)c(t)-\dot{c}(t)\}/(1-f) +$$

$$(l(t)/k)w(t) - e^{(i+a)t} \int_t^{V(t)} e^{-(i+a)\tau} w(\tau)\dot{l}(t)/k\ d\tau \tag{A5.6}$$

With assumptions (7.50) and (7.51) in mind, substituting $l(t)=l(0)e^{-ht}$, $w(t)= w^{*}e^{ht}$, and $c(t)=c^{*}$ into (A5.6) gives:

$$\partial S/\partial K(t) = \left\{1 - f \int_0^{v} e^{-i\tau} d(\tau)\ d\tau\right\} \{(i+a)c^{*}\}/(1-f) +$$

$$(w^{*}l(0)/k) - (w^{*}l(0)/k) \frac{h}{i+a-h} \{ e^{-(i+a-h)(V(t)-t)} - 1 \} \tag{A5.7}$$

Using the scrapping condition (7.54) gives:

$$\left\{1 - f \int_0^{v} e^{-i\tau} d(\tau)\ d\tau\right\} \{(i+a)c^{*}\}/(1-f) + (w^{*}l(0)/k) -$$

$$(w^{*}l(0)/k) \frac{h}{i+a-h}\{e^{-(i+a-h)(V(t)-t)} - 1\} = (w^{*}l(0)/k)e^{h(t-N(t))} \quad \Leftrightarrow$$

$$\left\{1 - f \int_0^{v} e^{-i\tau} d(\tau)\ d\tau\right\} \{(i+a)c^{*}\}/(1-f) =$$

$$(w^{*}l(0)/k)\left\{ e^{h(t-N(t))} - 1 + \frac{h}{i+a-h} \{ e^{-(i+a-h)(V(t)-t)} - 1 \} \right\} \quad \Leftrightarrow$$

$$\left\{1 - f \int_0^{v} e^{-i\tau} d(\tau)\ d\tau\right\} \frac{i+a}{1-f} (i+a-h) \frac{c^{*}k}{w^{*}l(0)} + i+a =$$

$$(i+a-h)e^{h(t-N(t))} + he^{-(i+a-h)(V(t)-t)} \tag{A5.8}$$

The last equality in (A5.8) is identical to (7.64).

A5.1.3 Convergence of the upper and lower bounds on M and T

The following equations (equations (7.64)-(7.71)) are available:

$$\varphi = \beta e^{hT(t)} + he^{-\beta M(t)} \tag{A5.9}$$

$$M(t) = T(t+M(t)) \tag{A5.10}$$

$$M(t) = -1/\beta \ \ln\{ (\varphi-\beta e^{hT(t)})/h \} \tag{A5.11}$$

$$1/h \ \ln\frac{\varphi-h}{\beta} < T(t) < 1/h \ \ln\frac{\varphi}{\beta} \tag{A5.12}$$

$$\varphi-h = \beta(1+\delta) \text{ with } \delta>0 \tag{A5.13}$$

$$1/h \ \ln\frac{\varphi-h}{\beta} < M(t) < 1/h \ \ln\frac{\varphi}{\beta} \tag{A5.14}$$

$$T(t) = 1/h \ \ln\{ (\varphi-he^{-\beta M(t)})/\beta \} \tag{A5.15}$$

From (A5.15) it follows:

$$dT/dM = \beta/(\varphi-he^{-\beta M(t)}) \ e^{-\beta M(t)} \tag{A5.16}$$

From (A5.13) it follows that the right hand side of (A5.16) is positive.Combining (A5.15) and (A5.16) gives new bounds on T(t):

$$(1/h) \ \ln \left[\frac{1}{\beta} \left[\varphi-h\exp\left\{-(\beta/h)\ln(\frac{\varphi-h}{\beta})\right\} \right] \right] < T(t) <$$

$$(1/h) \ \ln \left[\frac{1}{\beta} \left[\varphi-h\exp\left\{-(\beta/h)\ln(\frac{\varphi}{\beta})\right\} \right] \right] \qquad \Leftarrow\Rightarrow$$

$$(1/h) \ \ln \left[\frac{1}{\beta} \left[\varphi-h\left\{\frac{\varphi-h}{\beta}\right\}^{-\beta/h} \right] \right] < T(t) <$$

$$(1/h) \ \ln \left[\frac{1}{\beta} \left[\varphi-h\left\{\frac{\varphi}{\beta}\right\}^{-\beta/h} \right] \right] \tag{A5.17}$$

Using (A5.10), it is clear that M(t) must also satisfy (A5.17) and using (A5.15) this gives new bounds on T(t). Comparing (A5.12) and (A5.17) and writing out the next upper and lower bound reveals that it is possible to characterise the sequence of lower and upper bounds on T(t) and M(t), for $t\rightarrow\infty$, as follows:

$$\text{Lower bounds } \frac{1}{h}\ln(x_n):\ x_0 = \frac{\varphi-h}{\beta},\quad x_{n+1} = \left\{ \varphi-h(x_n)^{-\beta/h} \right\}/\beta$$

$$\text{Upper bounds } \frac{1}{h}\ln(y_n):\ y_0 = \frac{\varphi}{\beta},\quad y_{n+1} = \left\{ \varphi-h(y_n)^{-\beta/h} \right\}/\beta \tag{A5.18}$$

Note that the recursive formula is the same for the lower and upper bounds. Only the initial values differ. Define:

$$w_0=1,\ w_{n+1}=(x_n)^{-\beta/h},\ n=0,1,... \tag{A5.19}$$

Combining (A5.18) and (A5.19) gives:

$$x_n = (\varphi-hw_n)/\beta \tag{A5.20}$$

$$w_0=1,\ w_{n+1}=\left\{(\varphi-hw_n)/\beta\right\}^{-\beta/h},\ n=0,1,... \tag{A5.21}$$

Similarly define (z_n):

$$z_0=0,\ z_{n+1}=\left\{(\varphi-hz_n)/\beta\right\}^{-\beta/h},\ n=0,1,... \tag{A5.22}$$

$$y_n = (\varphi-hz_n)/\beta \tag{A5.23}$$

The question is whether the sequences of lower and upper bounds converge. Sufficient condition for an affirmative answer is the convergence of the sequences (w_n) and (z_n).

Using (A5.13), it can be seen that both rows lie in the interval [0,1]. It is then easily seen that, for all n:

$$w_{n+1}>w_n \iff \left\{(\varphi-hw_n)/\beta\right\}^{-\beta/h} > \left\{(\varphi-hw_{n-1})/\beta\right\}^{-\beta/h} \iff$$

$$(\varphi-hw_n)/\beta < (\varphi-hw_{n-1})/\beta \iff w_n>w_{n-1} \iff ......\iff w_1>w_0 \tag{A5.24}$$

Similarly:

$$z_{n+1}>z_n \iff z_1>z_0 \tag{A5.25}$$

Thus the row (w_n) is monotonically decreasing and the row (z_n) is monotonically increasing. Since each bounded monotonic row has a limit, it follows:

$$w_n \rightarrow \overline{w},\qquad z_n \rightarrow \overline{z} \tag{A5.26}$$

Define:

$$g(x) = \left\{(\varphi-hx)/\beta\right\}^{-\beta/h} \tag{A5.27}$$

Then $w_{n+1}=g(w_n)$ and $z_{n+1}=g(z_n)$. Since g is a continuous function, (A5.26) implies:

$$g(\overline{w})=\overline{w},\quad g(\overline{z})=\overline{z} \tag{A5.28}$$

$\overline{w}$ and $\overline{z}$ must lie in [0,1]. From (A5.27) it is easily seen that $g(0)\neq 0$ and $g(1)\neq 1$. So $\overline{w}$ and $\overline{z}$ must lie in (0,1). In other words, $\overline{w}$ and $\overline{z}$ are solutions of the equation $h(y) \equiv g(y)-y=0$ in the interval (0,1). Using (A5.13) it is easily seen that h is strictly decreasing on the interval (0,1), so the equation $h(y)=0$ will have at most one solution in the interval (0,1). This implies $\overline{w} = \overline{z}$.

So now it follows from (A5.18) that the sequence of lower bounds as well as the sequence of upper bounds on M(t) and T(t), $t \to \infty$, converges to:

$$\frac{1}{h} \ln\left\{ \frac{\varphi - h\overline{w}}{\beta} \right\}, \text{ with } g(\overline{w}) = \overline{w}. \tag{A5.29}$$

This implies that M(t) and T(t) must equal (A5.29), for $t \to \infty$. Moreover, (A5.29) must equal the steady state value T^*. This can be checked with (A5.9). For $M(t)=T(t)=T^*$, (A5.9) is:

$$\varphi = \beta e^{hT^*} + he^{-\beta T^*} \tag{A5.30}$$

Substituting (A5.29) for T^* in the right hand side of (A5.30) gives:

$$\beta\left\{\frac{\varphi - h\overline{w}}{\beta}\right\} + h\exp\left\{ -\frac{\beta}{h} \ln\left\{ \frac{\varphi - h\overline{w}}{\beta} \right\} \right\}$$

$$= \varphi - h\overline{w} + h \left\{ \frac{\varphi - h\overline{w}}{\beta} \right\}^{-\beta/h}$$

$$= \varphi - h\overline{w} + hg(\overline{w}) = \varphi - h\overline{w} + h\overline{w} = \varphi$$

Appendix A5.2 The optimal policy of section 8.2.2

The optimal policy in section 8.2.2 is:

use I(t) to close the gap between $\partial S/\partial K(t)$ and $(\partial S/\partial K)^*$ as quickly as possible (A5.31a)

use B(N(t)) to close the gap between $\partial S/\partial K(t)$ and $w(t)l(N(t))/k$ as quickly as possible (A5.31b)

This rule is examined for the same initial situations as in section 8.2.2, but now more precisely, and the difficulties in case the initial capital goods stock is large are illustrated.
It is assumed in this appendix that $I(t) > 0$ for $t \in [n_0, 0)$.

1) Suppose $\partial S/\partial K(0) > (\partial S/\partial K)^*$ and $\partial S/\partial K(0) > w(0)l(N(0))/k$.
For this initial situation the optimal policy was described in section 8.2.2. However, a few points need some clarification.
In section 8.2.2 it is implicitly assumed that the capital goods stock grows if the firms invests as much as possible. Using (8.19) this implies that I must be, at least, larger than aK. Therefore the following reasonable assumption is made :

if the capital goods stock is below the 'desired' level K^*, then:

$$S(K(t)) - wL(t) - ac^* K(t) > 0, \qquad \text{(A5.32)}$$

irrespective of the vintage structure of K and thus irrespective of L. Equation (A5.32) implies that if I is on its upper bound (see (8.8)), then $I > aK$.
Part of the optimal policy is "maintain $\partial S/\partial K = (\partial S/\partial K)^*$ and continue $B = B_{max}$ until $w(t)l(N(t))/k$ reaches $(\partial S/\partial K)^*$". It is not obvious that this is possible. Maintaining $\partial S/\partial K = (\partial S/\partial K)^*$ implies keeping K constant. Using (8.19) this means:

$$I(t) = aK(t) + e^{-a(t-N(t))} I(N(t)) \dot{N}(t). \qquad \text{(A5.33)}$$

In the first place this implies that I(t) and $\dot{N}(t)$ cannot be chosen independently. In the second place it has to be checked whether I(t) in (A5.33) lies inside the control region. It is clear that $I(t) \geq 0$, since $\dot{N}$ is always positive. Moreover, the upper bound on B, B_{max}, is arbitrarily high, which implies that the lower bound on $\dot{N}$, $1/B_{max}$ is arbitrarily low. If the optimal policy is to scrap as little as possible, implying $\dot{N}(t) = 1/B_{max}$, then the right hand side of (A5.33) is arbitrarily close to $aK(t)$. Now assumption (A5.32) guarantees that $I(t) \leq \{S(K) - wL\}/c^*$.

Another part of the optimal policy is "maintain $\partial S/\partial K = w(t)l(N(t))/k$ and continue to invest as much as possible untill $\partial S/\partial K$ reaches $(\partial S/\partial K)^*$". Maintaining $\partial S/\partial K(t) = w(t)l(N(t))/k$ implies (differentiating both sides): $(-1/e)(\partial S/\partial K)(\dot{K}(t)/K(t)) = h(1-\dot{N}(t))(\partial S/\partial K)$. And thus, using (8.19):

$$I(t) - aK(t) - e^{-a(t-N(t))} I(N(t))\dot{N}(t) = -eh(1-\dot{N}(t))K(t) \quad \Leftrightarrow$$

$$\dot{N}(t)\left\{ehK(t) + e^{-a(t-N(t))} I(N(t))\right\} = I(t) + (eh-a)K(t). \tag{A5.34}$$

The right hand side of (A5.34) must to positive, to guarantee that $\dot{N}(t)$ is positive. Since the firm is investing as much as possible and K is still lower than K^*, assumption (A5.32) guarantees that the right hand side of (A5.34) is positive. For the proposed policy to be feasible, it must be assumed that the boundaries on $\dot{N}(t)$ ($1/B_{max}$ and $1/B_{min}$) are such that $\dot{N}(t)$ in (A5.34) lies in the control region.

2) Suppose: $\partial S/\partial K(0) > (\partial S/\partial K)^*$ and $\partial S/\partial K(0) < w(0)l(N(0))/k$.

It is now demonstrated that the proposed optimal policy fulfils the optimality conditions. Firstly note that λ_3 is continuous. Secondly, suppose that μ_5 and μ_6 are zero on some interval starting at $t = n_0$. Equation (8.12) then implies that λ_3 and $\dot{\lambda}_3$ equal zero on this interval. In particular, $\lambda_3(z) = \dot{\lambda}_3(n_0) = 0$. Together with (8.15) and the assumption that $I(z) > 0$, this gives: $\partial S/\partial K(0) = w(0)l(N(0))/k$. So it can be concluded that if $\partial S/\partial K(0) \neq w(0)l(N(0))/k$, $\mu_5 \neq 0$ or $\mu_6 \neq 0$ on the path starting at $t = n_0$. In other words, on the path starting at $t = n_0$, B equals B_{min} or B_{max}.

Now suppose the firm decides nót to scrap the unprofitable vintages, in order to grow as quickly as possible: $B(t) = B_{max}$, $\mu_5 > 0$ on some interval beginning at n_0. If the firm invests as much as possible for t close to zero (implying, according to assumption (A5.32), that K increases and $\partial S/\partial K$ decreases), then this leads to a contradiction: as before, $B(t) = B_{max}$ for $t \geq n_0$ implies that $w(t)l(N(t))/k$ will increase for $t \geq 0$. Since $\partial S/\partial K$ decreases for $t \geq 0$, $\partial S/\partial K(t) - w(t)l(N(t))/k$ will be negative for on some interval beginning at $t = 0$. From (8.15) it follows:

$$d/dt(e^{-it}\lambda_3(t)) =$$

$$-I(t)e^{-(i+a)(V(t)-t)}\{\partial S/\partial K(V(t) - w(V(t))l(t)/k\}\{1+\mu_2(V(t))\} \tag{A5.35}$$

Since $I(t) > 0$ and and $\partial S/\partial K(V(t) < w(V(t))l(t)/k$ on some interval beginning at

n_0, $e^{-it}\lambda_3(t)$ increases on this interval. Moreover, as long as $B(t)=B_{max}$ for $t \ge n_0$, $\lambda_3=\mu_5>0$, and thus $e^{-it}\lambda_3(t)$ is positive and increasing. At a certain point of time the path with $B=B_{max}$ will have to end; on the path that follows, μ_6 will be zero. Since λ_3 is continuous, this implies that in the coupling point with the next path λ_3 has to be zero, and thus $e^{-it}\lambda_3$ has to be zero. But we saw that on the path with $B=B_{max}$ $e^{-it}\lambda_3$ is positive and increasing! This leads to a contradiction.

An alternative solution is to adhere to the decision rule (8.21) even though the aims in (8.21) are conflicting for the given initial conditions. So the firm will start scrapping at a maximal rate, even though this slows down the growth of K. As in the first example, the optimal policy is to close the gaps between $\partial S/\partial K$ and $(\partial S/\partial K)^*$ and $w(t)l(N(t))/k$ respectivily; and, if a gap is closed, to keep it closed.

Checking if this policy satisfies the optimality conditions in particular implies verifying if $\mu_i(t) \ge 0$ for all i and all t. However, this involves solving the integral equation (8.11) and the differential equation (8.15), and this is in general not possible. However, for specific solutions we can try to circumvent the problem of solving these equations. For instance, in Figure 8.1 it is assumed that the initial conditions are as in the second example above. Furthermore it is assumed that $\partial S/\partial K(t)$ reaches $w(t)l(N(t)/k$ for $t=t^1$. This implies, according to the decision rule, that $B(t)=B_{min}$, $\lambda_3=-\mu_5$ for $t<N(t^1)$. Define $\tau=N(t^1)$. It is clear from Figure 8.1 that the right hand side of (A5.35) is positive for $t<\tau$. This implies that $e^{-it}\lambda_3$ is increasing. Imposing the boundary condition $\lambda_3(\tau)=0$, this yields that λ_3 is negative for $t<\tau$. Consequently, $\mu_5(t)=-\lambda_3(t)>0$ for $t<t$ and $\mu_5(t)=0$ for $t \ge \tau$.

Next it must be verified whether $\mu_2 \ge 0$ for all $t \ge 0$. It is assumed that $\partial S/\partial K$ reaches $(\partial S/\partial K)^*$ at $t=t^2$. Note that for $t \ge 0$ (see Figure 8.1):

$$w(t)l(N(t)/k=l(0)w^*/ke^{hT(t)} \ge \partial S/\partial K(t) \ge (\partial S/\partial K)^* = l(0)w^*/ke^{hT^*}.$$

This implies that $T(t) \ge T^*$ for $t \ge 0$. Consequently, $M(t) \ge T^*$ for $t \ge 0$ (use (7.71)). Moreover, since (8.11) must be satisfied on the final path:

$$c^* = \int_t^{t+T^*} e^{-(i+a)(\tau-t)} \{ \partial S/\partial K(\tau) - w(\tau)l(t)/k \} d\tau \text{ for } t \ge t^2 \Longrightarrow$$

$$c^* = \int_0^{T^*} e^{-(i+a)\tau} \{ (\partial S/\partial K)^* - w^*l(0)/ke^{h\tau} \} d\tau \tag{A5.36}$$

For $t \ge 0$:

$$\mu_2(t)c^* = \int_0^{M(t)} e^{-(i+a)\tau} \{ \partial S/\partial K(t+\tau) - w^* l(0)/ke^{h\tau} \} d\tau - c^* \qquad (A5.37)$$

Since $M(t) \geq T^*$ for all $t \geq 0$ and $\partial S/\partial K(t+\tau) \geq (\partial S/\partial K)^*$ for all $t \geq 0$ and $\tau \geq 0$, the integral in the right hand side of (A5.37) is larger than the integral in the right hand side of (A5.36). And thus, $\mu_2(t) \geq 0$ for all $t \geq 0$. Moreover, since $\partial S/\partial K(t) = (\partial S/\partial K)^*$ for all $t \geq t^2$ and M is continuous, μ_2 is continuous in t^2.

In section 8.2.2 it has been stated that the 'decision rule' does not apply to initial conditions which involve a high capital goods stock.

Suppose $\partial S/\partial K(0) < (\partial S/\partial K)^*$

This implies that the initial capital goods stock is 'too large'. The 'decision rule' requires $I(t)=0$, from $t=0$ onwards. Suppose that at a certain point of time $\partial S/\partial K(t)$ becomes equal to $w(t)l(N(t))/k$, while $\partial S/\partial K$ is still smaller than $(\partial S/\partial K)^*$. Now the decision rule requires: maintain $\partial S/\partial K(t) = w(t)l(N(t))/k$ and use I to close the gap between $\partial S/\partial K(t)$ and $(\partial S/\partial K)^*$. As before, this implies (see (A5.34)):

$$\dot{N}(t)\left\{ehK(t) + e^{-a(t-N(t))}I(N(t))\right\} = I(t) + (eh-a)K(t).$$

To guarantee that $\dot{N}(t)$ is positive, $I(t)+(eh-a)K(t)$ has to be positive. Closing the gap between $\partial S/\partial K(t)$ and $(\partial S/\partial K)^*$ as quickly as possible asks for $I=0$. However, if $eh-a<0$, this would lead to a negative $\dot{N}(t)$. Now there are three possibilities:

1) setting $\dot{N}(t)$ on its lower bound and maintaining (A5.34) gives an I in the interior on the control region; moreover, K decreases. This way the firm could reach the final path. However, this policy implies that at the moment that $\partial S/\partial K(t)$ reaches $w(t)l(N(t))/k$, $\mu_2(t)$ must reach zero, or μ_2 and λ_1 jump. I did not succeed in checking whether the necessary conditions are satisfied in this case.

2) setting $\dot{N}(t)$ on its lower bound and maintaining (A5.34) gives an I in the interior on the control region; however, K *increases*.

3) setting $\dot{N}(t)$ on its lower bound and maintaining (A5.34) gives an I which is larger than the upper bound on I.

In cases 2) and 3) I do not know how to derive the optimal solution.

The conclusion is that I am not able to find the optimal solution if the initial capital goods stock is large. The main problem is that the decision rule, which applies to a small capital goods stock, cannot be applied in all cases. Especially, if one of the two 'gaps' in rule (8.21) is closed, it is often impossible to keep it closed, while closing the remaining 'gap'.

Appendix A5.3 The pattern of investments in section 8.4.2

For $t \leq t_0$:

$$\partial S/\partial K(t) = (1-1/e)\left\{e^{-gt}K(t)/k\right\}^{-1/e} \tag{A5.38}$$

This implies for the steady state value of K(t):

$$K(t) = ke^{gt}\left\{(\partial S/\partial K)^*/(1-1/e)\right\}^{-e} \tag{A5.39}$$

Define:

$$K^* = k\left\{(\partial S/\partial K)^*/(1-1/e)\right\}^{-e} \tag{A5.40}$$

Remember (8.19):

$$\dot{K}(t) = -aK(t) + I(t) - I(N(t))\dot{N}(t)e^{-a(t-N(t))} \tag{A5.41}$$

Substituting $N(t)=t-T^*$, $\dot{N}(t)=1$ and (A5.38) in (A5.41) gives:

$$I(t) = (g+a)K^*e^{gt} + I(t-T^*)e^{-aT^*} \quad \text{for all } t\in[0,t_0) \tag{A5.42}$$

Given $I(t), t<0$, this determines $I(t)$ for all $t\in[0,t_0)$. It is easily seen that if $t_0=\infty$, $I(t)\to(g+a)K^*e^{gt}/(1-e^{-(g+a)T^*})$. If it is assumed that $I(t)=(g+a)K^*e^{gt}/(1-e^{-(g+a)T^*})$ for all $t<0$, then:

$$I(t) = (g+a)K^*e^{gt}/(1-e^{-(g+a)T^*}) \quad \text{for all } t\in[0,t_0) \tag{A5.43}$$

Define:

$$I_1^* = (g+a)K^*/(1-e^{-(g+a)T^*}) \tag{A5.44}$$

Note that I_1^* is positive.
Then:

$$I(t) = I_1^*e^{gt} \quad \text{for all } t\in[0,t_0) \tag{A5.45}$$

For $t\in(t_0,t_1)$:

$$\partial S/\partial K(t) = (1-1/e)\left\{e^{(m-g)t}e^{-mt_0}K(t)/k\right\}^{-1/e} \tag{A5.46}$$

Suppose that (A5.46) would be valid for all t. Then we could try to find the steady state value for I(t). Analogous to (A5.43), this would be:

$$I(t) = (g+a-m)K^*e^{(g-m)t}/(1-e^{-(g+a-m)T^*}) \tag{A5.47}$$

Define:

$$I_2^* = (g+a-m)e^{-mt_0}K^*/(1-e^{-(g+a-m)T^*}) \tag{A5.48}$$

Then (A5.47) is:

$$I(t) = e^{(g-m)t}I_2^* \qquad \text{(A5.49)}$$

Note that I_2^* is positive.

For $t<t_0$ (A5.45) is valid. Together with (A5.41), (A5.46), and the fact that $\partial S/\partial K(t)=(\partial S/\partial K)^*$ and $N(t)=t-T^*$, this determines I(t) for $t\in[t_0,t_0+T^*)$:

$$I(t) = I_1^* e^{-(g+a)T^*}e^{gt} + I_2^*(1-e^{-(g+a-m)T^*})e^{(g-m)t}, \text{ for } t\in[t_0,t_0+T^*) \qquad \text{(A5.50)}$$

Define the number Λ such that:

$$t_0+\Lambda T^* < t_1 < t_0+(\Lambda+1)T^* \qquad \text{(A5.51)}$$

Note that, given the steady state values for $\partial S/\partial K$ and N, (A5.50) determines I(t) for $t\in[t_0+T^*,t_0+2T^*)$, etcetera. Careful calculation shows:

$$I(t) = I_1^* e^{-(n+1)(g+a)T^*}e^{gt} + I_2^*(1-e^{-(n+1)(g+a-m)T^*})e^{(g-m)t}$$

$$\text{for } t_0+nT^* < t < t_0+(n+1)T^*,\ n=0,1,\ldots,\Lambda-1 \text{ and } t_0+\Lambda T^* < t < t_1 \qquad \text{(A5.52)}$$

Here we used that $1+x+x^2+.....+x^n=(1-x^{n+1})/(1-x)$.

Substitution of (A5.44) and (A5.48) in (A5.52) reveals that I(t) is positive if $a+g>m$ and that the right hand side of (A5.52) is increasing if $a+g<m$. Also from (A5.52) (and (A5.43)) it can be derived that I jumps downward for $t=t_0+nT^*$, $n=0,1,..,\Lambda-1$ and that the magnitude of the jump equals

$$e^{gt_0}e^{-naT^*}mK^* \qquad \text{(A5.53)}$$

Finally, from (A5.52) it can be derived that $\lim_{t\downarrow t_0+nT^*} I(t)$ is a decreasing function of n.

(A5.52) gives the values for I(t) for $t<t_1$. For $t\geq t_1$:

$$\partial S/\partial K(t)=(1-1/e)(e^{-gt}e^{m(t_1-t_0)}K(t)/k)^{-1/e} \qquad \text{(A5.54)}$$

For $t\geq t_1$ we still have $\partial S/\partial K(t)=(\partial S/\partial K)^*$ and $N(t)=t-T^*$. Consequently:

$$K(t) = e^{-m(t_1-t_0)}K^*e^{gt} \text{ for all } t\geq t_1 \qquad \text{(A5.55)}$$

$$I(t) = (g+a)K(t) + e^{-aT^*}I(t-T^*) \qquad \text{(A5.56)}$$

Combining (A5.55), (A5.56) and (A5.52) gives:

$$I(t) = I_1^* e^{gt}\left\{ e^{-m(t_1-t_0)} (1-e^{-(g+a)T^*}) + e^{-(\Lambda+1)(g+a)T^*} \right\} +$$

$$I_2^* e^{(g-m)t}\left\{ e^{-(g+a-m)T^*} (1-e^{-\Lambda(g+a-m)T^*})\right\}, \text{ for } t_1 < t < t_0+(\Lambda+1)T^*$$

(A5.57)

$$I(t) = I_1^* e^{gt}\left\{ e^{-m(t_1-t_0)} (1-e^{-(g+a)T^*}) + e^{-(\Lambda+2)(g+a)T^*} \right\} +$$

$$I_2^* e^{(g-m)t}\left\{ e^{-(g+a-m)T^*} (1-e^{-(\Lambda+1)(g+a-m)T^*})\right\},$$

$$\text{for } t_0+(\Lambda+1)T^* < t < t_1+T^* \qquad \text{(A5.58)}$$

We can use (A5.57) and (A5.58) to calculate I(t) for $t_1+T^* < t < t_1+2T^*$, etcetera. This gives:

$$I(t) = I_1^* e^{gt}\left\{ e^{-m(t_1-t_0)} (1-e^{-(k+1)(g+a)T^*}) + e^{-(\Lambda+1+k)(g+a)T^*} \right\} +$$

$$I_2^* e^{(g-m)t}\left\{ e^{-(k+1)(g+a-m)T^*} (1-e^{-\Lambda(g+a-m)T^*})\right\},$$

$$\text{for } t_1+kT^* < t < t_0+(\Lambda+1+k)T^*,\ k=0,1,\ldots. \qquad \text{(A5.59)}$$

$$I(t) = I_1^* e^{gt}\left\{ e^{-m(t_1-t_0)} (1-e^{-(k+1)(g+a)T^*}) + e^{-(\Lambda+2+k)(g+a)T^*} \right\} +$$

$$I_2^* e^{(g-m)t}\left\{ e^{-(k+1)(g+a-m)T^*} (1-e^{-(\Lambda+1)(g+a-m)T^*})\right\},$$

$$\text{for } t_0+(\Lambda+1+k)T^* < t < t_1+(k+1)T^*,\ k=0,1,\ldots. \qquad \text{(A5.60)}$$

Using (A5.59) and (A5.60) it can be shown that I(t) increases for $t > t_1$ when $g+a-m < 0$, and that $I(t) > 0$ for $t > t_1$ when $g+a > m$. Using (A5.59), (A5.60) and (A5.52) it can be seen that I jumps upward for $t=t_1+kT^*$, $k=0,1,\ldots$ and that the magnitude of the jump equals

$$e^{gt_1}K^* e^{-kaT^*} e^{-m(t_1-t_0)} m \qquad \text{(A5.61)}$$

Using (A5.59) and (A5.60) it can be seen that I jumps downward for $t=t_0+(\Lambda+1+k)T^*$, $k=0,1,\ldots.$ and that the magnitude of the jump equals

$$e^{gt_0} e^{-(\Lambda+1+k)aT^*} mK^* \qquad \text{(A5.62)}$$

Finally, from (A5.50), (A5.44) and (A5.48) it follows that:

$$\lim_{t \downarrow t_0} I(t) = e^{gt_0} K^* \left\{ g+a-m + (g+a)e^{-(g+a)T^*}/(1-e^{-(g+a)T^*}) \right\} \quad \text{(A5.63)}$$

So:

$$\lim_{t \downarrow t_0} I(t) \geq 0 \Leftarrow\Rightarrow m > g + a + (g+a)e^{-(g+a)T^*}/(1-e^{-(g+a)T^*}) \Leftarrow\Rightarrow$$

$$m > (g+a)/(1-e^{-(g+a)T^*}) \quad \text{(A5.64)}$$

Appendix A5.4 Discussion of 'zero investment'-periods

This appendix discusses the problems that arise if there are 'zero investment'-periods. Suppose $I(t)=0$ for $t\in(\alpha,\beta)$ and $I(t)\neq 0$ for $t\notin(\alpha,\beta)$. It is no restriction to assume that $V(\alpha)>\beta$, since otherwise the firm would no longer exist at $t=\beta$ (all capital goods would be scrapped). For $t\in(V(\alpha),V(\beta)]$ the oldest existing vintage is the vintage installed at time β. So holding on to the given interpretation of N implies that $N(t)=\beta$ for $t\in(V(\alpha),V(\beta)]$. According to the same interpretation, $N(V(\alpha))$ equals α. Thus maintaining our interpretation of N for 'zero investment'-periods implies that N is discontinuous at $t=V(\alpha)$.

To apply the Maximum Principle of Appendix 4, continuity of N is required. Fortunately there seems to be a way out of this problem. Note that V(t) for $t\in(\alpha,\beta)$ has no interpretation. Let us assume that we simply *require* that V is stricly increasing on (α,β) and continuous on $[\alpha,\beta]$. This implies that $V^{-1}(t)$ exists for $t\in(V(\alpha),V(\beta))$ and that V^{-1} is a strictly increasing function on $(V(\alpha),V(\beta))$ and continuous on $[V(\alpha),V(\beta)]$ (note that now V^{-1} no longer equals N on $(V(\alpha),V(\beta))$!).

Of course it has to be checked whether this does violate the statement in section 7.2.3 that replacing N by V^{-1} does not affect the model. If $I(N(t)>0$, it is clear that $N(t)=V^{-1}(t)$. If there are 'zero investment'-periods, one can reason as follows:

Above it was noted that for all $t\in(V(\alpha),V(\beta)]$, $N(t)=\beta$. And thus:

$$K(t) = \int_{N(t)}^{t} e^{-a(t-\tau)} I(\tau)\, d\tau = \int_{\beta}^{t} e^{-a(t-\tau)} I(\tau)\, d\tau \qquad \text{(A5.65)}$$

Since V is required to be continuous and strictly increasing on (α,β), it follows that $V^{-1}(t)\in(\alpha,\beta)$ for $t\in(V(\alpha),V(\beta))$. Also $I=0$ on (α,β), so in particular $I=0$ on $(V^{-1}(t),\beta)$, for each $t\in(V(\alpha),V(\beta))$. This implies:

$$\int_{V^{-1}(t)}^{t} e^{-a(t-\tau)} I(\tau)\, d\tau = \int_{\beta}^{t} e^{-a(t-\tau)} I(\tau)\, d\tau = K(t) \qquad \text{(A5.66)}$$

for all $t\in(V(\alpha),V(\beta))$, where the second equality in (A5.66) follows from (A5.65). So indeed it does not affect the model if N(t) is replaced by $V^{-1}(t)$ even if there are 'zero investment'-periods.

It is important to note once again that: V(t) has no interpretation for $t\in(\alpha,\beta)$; N(t) is defined, *for all t*, as the birth date of the oldest capital goods still in use at time t; N(t) does not equal $V^{-1}(t)$ for $t\in(V(\alpha),V(\beta))$.

It has been established that N can be replaced by V^{-1}, even if there are 'zero investment'-periods. The above analysis revealed that in fact it does not matter which values V takes on during these 'zero investment'-periods. This is confirmed by the fact that, at first glance, the optimality conditions do nót determine V during 'zero investment'-periods (see (8.15)). Does a second glance confirm this first glance?

As in section 8.4.3 define:

$$s_1(t) = \int_t^{V(t)} e^{-(i+a)(\tau-t)} \{\partial S/\partial K(\tau)-w(\tau)l(t)/k\}\, d\tau - c^* \tag{A5.67}$$

It is clear that: $s_1(\alpha)=s_1(\beta)=0$. Define $s_2(t)=e^{-(i+a)t}s_1(t)$. Then $s_2(\alpha)=s_2(\beta)=0 \Rightarrow \int_\alpha^\beta \dot{s}_2(t)\, dt = 0$. It is clear that:

$$\dot{s}_2(t) = e^{-(i+a)t}\left\{\dot{s}_1(t)-(i+a)s_1(t)\right\} \tag{A5.68}$$

After substitution of the derivative of s_1 in (A5.68), it can be easily seen that $\int_\alpha^\beta \dot{s}_2(t)\, dt = 0$ is equivalent to:

$$\int_\alpha^\beta e^{-(i+a)t}\Big\{\partial S/\partial K(t)-w(t)l(t)/k-(a+i)c^*-\partial S/\partial K(V(t))+w(V(t))l(t)/k$$

$$- \int_t^{V(t)} e^{-(i+a)(\tau-t)}\, w(\tau)\dot{l}(t)/k\}d\tau\Big\}\, dt = 0 \tag{A5.69}$$

Note that (A5.69) is derived *without using the scrapping condition.*

Now suppose that we are investigating the optimal string consisting of the steady state path for $t\notin(\alpha,\beta)$ and a 'zero investment'-period (α,β) (as we did in section 8.4.3). This implies for instance: $\partial S/\partial K(\alpha)=\partial S/\partial K(\beta)=(\partial S/\partial K)^*$. Equivalently:

$$\int_\alpha^\beta \frac{d}{dt}\partial S/\partial K(t)\, dt = 0 \tag{A5.70}$$

On (α,β), (8.15) implies (since $N(t)<\alpha$ for all $t\in(\alpha,\beta)$ and the scrapping condition is valid for $t<\alpha$):

$$\partial S/\partial K(t) = w(t)l(N(t))/k \tag{A5.71}$$

$$\int_{N(t)}^{\alpha} e^{-a(t-\tau)}I(\tau)d\tau = K(t) = kQ(t)$$

$$= k\pi(t)\{p(t)\}^{-e} = k\pi(t)\{k/(1-1/e)\}^{-e}\{\partial S/\partial K(t)\}^{-e} \tag{A5.72}$$

where $\pi(t)=e^{gt}$ for $t \leq t_0$, $\pi(t)=e^{(g-m)t+mt_0}$ for $t_0<t<t_1$, and $\pi(t)=e^{gt-m(t_1-t_0)}$ for $t \geq t_1$.

Assuming that $I(t)=e^{gt}I_1^*$ for $t \leq \alpha$ (see Appendix 5.3), (A5.71) and (A5.72) constitute two (integral) equations with two unknowns, $\partial S/\partial K(t)$ and N(t). Differentiating (A5.71) and (A5.72) and eliminating N(t) gives the following differential equation for $\partial S/\partial K$:

$$k\pi(t)\{k/(1-1/e)\}^{-e}\ (\partial S/\partial K)^{-e} \left\{ \{a+\dot{\pi}(t)/\pi(t)\}(\partial S/\partial K)\ -\ e(\mathbf{d/dt})(\partial S/\partial K) \right\} =$$

$$= I_1^*\ e^{gt} \left\{(1/h)(\mathbf{d/dt})(\partial S/\partial K)-(\partial S/\partial K)\right\} \left\{c_1/(c_2(0)w^*)(\partial S/\partial K)\right\}^{-(a+g)/h} \qquad \text{(A5.73)}$$

It is clear that, although I cannot solve this differential equation for $\partial S/\partial K$, after substitution of the solution of (A5.73), (A5.70) only has two unknowns, α and β. So we now have two integral equations, (A5.69) and (A5.70), with the unknowns α,β and the function V on (α,β). The question is whether (A5.69) and (A5.70) have only one solution for α,β and V or not. If there is only one solution, then my 'first glance' was not correct: $V(t), t\in(\alpha,\beta)$ is determined by the optimality conditions, as well as the length of the 'zero investment'-period, *without* using the scrapping condition for $V(t), t\in(\alpha,\beta)$. If α can be chosen freely and (A5.69) and (A5.70) can then be solved for β and $V(t), t\in(\alpha,\beta)$, then my first glance was correct.

Unfortunately, I do not know how to decide on the number of solutions of (A5.69) and (A5.70). There exist a number of theorems on the solutions of integral equations, but these theorems do not apply, as far as I know, to (A5.69) and (A5.70).

REFERENCES

Appelbaum, E., R.G. Harris, "Optimal Capital Policy With Bounded Investment Plans". International Economic Review 19 (1978), 103-114.

Arrow, K.J."Optimal Capital Policy with Irreversible Investment" in J.N. Wolfe (ed.), Value, capital and growth. Chicago, 1968.

Arrow, K.J., and M. Kurz, "Optimal Growth With Irreversible Investment in a Ramsey Model". Econometrica 38 (1970), 331-344.

Auerbach, A.J., "Wealth Maximization and the Cost of Capital". Quarterly Journal of Economics 93 (1979), 433-446.

Auerbach, A.J., "Taxes, Firm Financial Policy and the Cost of Capital: An Empirical Analysis". Journal of Public Economics 23 (1984), 27-57.

Bensoussan, A., E.G. Hurst Jr., B. Näslund, Management Applications of Modern Control Theory. Amsterdam, 1974.

Bensoussan, A., P. Kleindorfer, C.S. Tapiero, Applied Stochastic Control in Econometrics and Management Science. Amsterdam, 1980.

Bensoussan, A., J. Lesourne, "Optimal Growth of a Self-financing Firm in an Uncertain Environment" in: A. Bensoussan, P. Kleindorfer, C.S. Tapiero, Applied Stochastic Control in Econometrics and Management Science. Amsterdam, 1980.

Bernanke, B.S., "Irreversibility, Uncertainty, and Cyclical Investment". Quarterly Journal of Economics 98 (1983), 85-106.

Blaug, M., The Methodology of Economics. Cambridge, 1980.

Bliss, C.J., "On putty-clay". Review of Economic Studies 35 (1968), 105-133.

Broer, D.P., Neoclassical Theory and Empirical Models of Aggregate Firm Behaviour. Dordrecht, 1987.

Browder, F.E., "Does Pure Mathematics Have a Relation to the Sciences?". American Scientist 64 (1976), 542-549.

Butter, F.A.G. den, "De optimale economische levensduur van kapitaalgoederen in een jaargangenmodel met vaste kapitaalcoefficient". Maandschrift Economie 40 (1976), 396-405.

Carvalho, F., "Alternative Analyses of Short and Long Run in Post Keynesian Economics". Journal of Post Keynesian Economics 7 (1984), 214-234.

Debreu, G., "Theoretical Models: Mathematical Form and Economic Content". Econometrica 54 (1986), 1259-1270.

Dorfman, R., "An Economic Interpretation of Optimal Control Theory". American Economic Review 59 (1969), 817-831.

Feichtinger, G. (ed.), Optimal Control Theory and Economic Analysis. Amsterdam, 1982.

Feichtinger, G. (ed.), Optimal Control Theory and Economic Analysis 2. Amsterdam, 1985.

Feichtinger, G. (ed.), Optimal Control Theory and Economic Analysis 3. Amsterdam, 1988.

Feichtinger, G., R.F. Hartl, "Optimal Pricing and Production in an Inventory Model". European Journal of Operational Research 19 (1985), 45-56.

Feichtinger, G., R.F. Hartl, Optimale Kontrolle ökonomischer Prozesse. Berlin, 1986.

Feichtinger, G., M. Luptacik, "Optimal Employment and Wage Policies of a Monopolistic Firm". Journal of Optimization Theory and Applications 53 (1987), 59-85.

Goorbergh, W.M. van den, Een macro-economische theorie van de werkgelegenheid. Leiden, 1978.

Goorbergh, W.M. van den, R.J. de Groof, H.W.G.M. Peer, Hoofdlijnen van de Moderne Groeitheorie. Leiden, 1979.

Hahn, F., Equilibrium and Macroeconomics. Oxford, 1984.

Hartl, R.F., "A Dynamic Activity Analysis for a Monopolistic Firm". Optimal Control Applications and Methods 9 (1988), 253-272.

Hartl, R.F., S.P. Sethi, "Optimal Control of a Class of Systems With Continuous Lags: Dynamic Programming Approach And Economic Interpretations". Journal of Optimization Theory and Applications 43 (1984), 73-88.

Hartog, H. den, "Empirical Vintage Models for the Netherlands: A Review in Outline". De Economist 132 (1984), 326-349.

Hartog, H. den, Klundert, Th. van de, H.S. Tjan, "Winstmaximalisatie, marktvorm en economische levensduur van kapitaalgoederen: een antwoord aan Den Butter". Maandschrift Economie 40 (1976), 406-413.

Hartog, H. den, H.S. Tjan, "Investeringen, lonen, prijzen en arbeidsplaatsen". Occasional Paper, C.P.B., Den Haag, 1974.

Hayashi, F., "Corporate Finance Side of the Q Theory of Investment". Journal of Public Economics 27 (1985), 261-280.

Intriligator, M.D., Mathematical Optimization and Economic Theory. Englewood Cliffs, 1971.

Jacobson, D.H., M.M. Lele and J.L. Speyer, "New Necessary Conditions of Optimality for Control Problems With State Variable Inequality

Constraints". Journal of Mathemathical Analysis and Applications 35 (1971), 255-284.

Johansen, L., "Substitution versus Fixed Production Coefficients in the Theory of Economic Growth: A Synthesis". Econometrica 27 (1959), 157-176.

Kamien, M.I., N.L. Schwartz, Dynamic Optimization: The Calculus of Variations and Optimal Control in Economics and Management. New York, 1981.

Kirsch, A., W. Warth, J. Werner, Notwendige Optimalitätsbedingungen und ihre Anwendung. Berlin, 1978.

Klant, J.J., The Rules of the Game. Cambridge, 1984.

Koopmans, T.C., Three Essays on the State of Economic Science. New York, 1957.

Kort, P.M., "Optimal Dynamic Investment Policy Under Financial Restrictions and Adjustment Costs". European Economic Review 32 (1988), 1669-1776.

Kort, P.M., Optimal Dynamic Investment Policies of a Value Maximizing Firm. Berlin, 1989.

Krouse, C.G., W.Y. Lee, "Optimal Equity Financing of the Corporation". Journal of Financial and Quantitative Analysis 8 (1973), 539-564.

Leban, R., "Employment and Wage Strategies of the Firm Over a Business Cycle". Journal of Economic Dynamics and Control 4 (1982), 371-394.

Leban, R., J. Lesourne, "The Firm's Investment and Employment Policy Through a Business Cycle". European Economic Review 13 (1980), 43-80.

Leban, R., J. Lesourne, "Adaptive Strategies of the Firm Through a Business Cycle". Journal of Economic Dynamics and Control 5 (1983), 201-234.

Leland, H.E., "Alternative Long-run Goals and the Theory of the Firm: Why Profit Maximization May Be a Better Assumption Than You Think" in P.T. Liu, Dynamic Optimization and Mathematical Economics. New York, 1980.

Lempio, F., H. Maurer, "Differential Stability in Infinite-dimensional Nonlinear Programming". Applied Mathematics and Optimization 6 (1980), 139-152.

Léonard, D., "Co-state Variables Correctly Value Stocks at Each Instant". Journal of Economic Dynamics and Control 11 (1987), 117-122.

Lesourne, J., Modèles de croissance des enterprises. Paris, 1973.

Lesourne, J., A. Dominguez, "Employment Policy of a Self-financing Firm Facing a Risk of Bankruptcy". Journal of Economic Dynamics and Control 5 (1983), 325-358.

Lesourne, J., R. Leban, "Control Theory and the Dynamics of the Firm: A

Survey". OR Spektrum 4 (1982), 1-14.

Loon, P.J.J.M. van, A Dynamic Theory of the Firm: Production, Finance and Investment. Berlin, 1983.

Loon, P.J.J.M. van, "Investment Grants and Alternatives to Stimulate Industry and Employment" in: G. Feichtinger, Optimal Control Theory and Economic Analysis 2. Amsterdam, 1985.

Ludwig, T., Optimale Expansionspfade der Unternehmung. Wiesbaden, 1978.

Luenberger, D.G., Optimization by Vector Space Methods. New York, 1969.

Maccini, L.J., "The Interrelationship Between Price and Output Decisions and Investment Decisions; Micro Foundations and Aggregate Implications". Journal of Monetary Economics 13 (1984), 41-65.

Machielsen, K.C.P., Numerical Solution of Optimal Control Problems with State Constraints by Sequential Quadratic Programming in Function Space. Dissertation Technical University of Eindhoven, 1987.

Majumdar, M., M. Nermuth, "Dynamic Optimization in Non-convex Models with Irreversible Investment: Monotonicity and Turnpike Results". Zeitschrift für Nationalökonomie 42 (1982), 339-362.

Malcomson, J.M., "Corporate Tax Policy and the Service Life of Capital Equipment. Review of Economic Studies 48 (1981), 311-316.

Malcomson, J.M., "Optimal Replacement Policy and Approximate Replacement Rules". Applied Economics 11 (1979), 405-414.

Malcomson, J.M., "Replacement and the Rental Value of Capital Equipment Subject to Obsolescence. Journal of Economic Theory 10 (1975), 24-41.

Marris, R., "An Introduction to Theories of Corporate Growth" in: R. Marris, A. Wood (eds.), The Corporate Economy (Growth, Competititon, and Innovative potential). London, 1971.

Maurer, H., "Differential Stability in Optimal Control Problems". Applied Mathematics and Optimization 5 (1979), 283-295.

Maurer, H., "First Order Sensitivity of the Optimal Value Function in Mathematical Programming and Optimal Control". Working Paper, Institut für Numerische und Instrumentelle Mathematik, Universität Münster, 1984.

Mirowski, P. (ed.), The Reconstruction of Economic Theory. Boston, 1986.

Mirowski, P., "Shall I Compare Thee to a Minkowski-Ricardo-Leontief-Metzler Matrix of the Mosak-Hicks Type?". Economics and Philosophy 3 (1987), 67-96.

Mitra, T., "Sensitivity of Optimal Programs with Respect to Changes in Target Stocks: The Case of Irreversible Investment". Journal of

Economic Theory 29 (1983), 172-184.

Mitra, T., D. Ray, "Efficient and Optimal Programs When Investment Is Irreversible: A Duality Theory". Journal of Mathematical Economics 11 (1983), 81-113.

Musgrave, A., "'Unreal Assumptions' in Economic Theory: The F-Twist Untwisted", Kyklos 34 (1981), 377-387.

Nickell, S.J., "A Closer Look at Replacement Investment". Journal of Economic Theory 10 (1975), 54-88.

Nickell, S.J., "On the Role of Expectations in the Pure Theory of Investments". Review of Economic Studies 41 (1974), 1-19.

Nickell, S.J., "Fixed Costs, Employment and Labour Demand Over The Cycle". Economica 45 (1978a), 329-345.

Nickell, S.J., The Investment Decisions of Firms. Cambridge, 1978b.

Peterson, D.W., "The Economic Significance of Auxiliary Functions in Optimal Control". International Economic Review 14 (1973), 234-252.

Pindyck, R.S., "Irreversible Investment, Capacity Choice, and the Value of the Firm". American Economic Review 78 (1988), 969-985.

Pitchford, J.D., "Two State Variable Problems" in: J.D. Pitchford, S.J. Turnovsky (eds.), Applications of Control Theory to Economic Analysis. Amsterdam, 1977.

Rossana, J.R., "A Model of the Demand for Investment in Inventories of Finished Goods and Employment". International Economic Review 25 (1984), 731-741.

Salop, S.C., "Wage Differentials in a Dynamic Theory of the Firm". Journal of Economic Theory 6 (1973), 321-344.

Sato, R., Theory of Technical Change and Economic Invariance; Application of Lie Groups. New York, 1981.

Schmidt, R.H., "Methodology and Finance". Theory and Decision 14 (1982), 391-413.

Schijndel, G.J.C.Th. van, Dynamic Firm and Investor Behaviour under Progressive Personal Taxation. Berlin, 1988.

Seierstad, A., K. Sydsæter, "Sufficient Conditions in Optimal Control Theory". International Economic Review 18 (1977), 367-391.

Seierstad, A., K. Sydsæter, Optimal Control Theory with Economic Applications. Amsterdam, 1987.

Senchack, A.J., "The Firm's Optimal Financial Policies: Solution, Equilibrium, and Stability". Journal of Financial and Quantitative Analysis 10 (1975), 543-555.

Sengupta, J.K., Optimal Desicions Under Uncertainty: Methods, Models and Management. Berlin, 1985.

Sethi, S.P., "Optimal Equity and Financing Model of Krouse and Lee: Corrections and Extensions". Journal of Financial and Quantitative Analysis 13 (1978a), 487-505.

Sethi, S.P., "A Survey of Management Science Applications of the Deterministic Maximum Principle". TIMS Studies in the Management Sciences 9 (1978b), 7-31.

Sethi, S.P., G.L. Thompson, Optimal Control Theory: Applications to Management Science. Boston, 1981.

Simon, H.A., "Rational Decision Making in Business Organizations". American Economic Review 69 (1979), 493-513.

Solow, R.M., "Economic History and Economics". American Economic Review 75 (2) (1985), 328-331.

Solow, R.M., "Investment and Technical Progress" in K.J. Arrow, S. Karlin, P. Suppes (eds.), Mathematical Methods in the Social Sciences. Stanford, 1959.

Steigum, E., "A Financial Theory of Investment Behaviour". Econometrica 51 (1983), 637-645.

Stiglitz, J.E., H Uzawa, Readings in the Modern Theory of Economic Growth. Cambridge, Massachusetts, 1969.

Sydsæter, K., "Optimal Control Theory and Economics: Some Critical Remarks on the Literature". Scandinavian Journal of Economics 80 (1978), 113-117.

Tapiero, C.S., "Time, Dynamics and the Process of Management Modelling". TIMS Studies in the Management Sciences 9 (1978), 7-31.

Tapiero, C.S., Applied Stochastic Models and Control in Management. Amsterdam, 1988.

Teece, D.J., S.G. Winter, "The Limits of Neoclassical Theory in Management Education". American Economic Review 74 (2) (1984), 116-121.

Tu, P.N.V., Introductory Optimization Dynamics. Berlin, 1984.

Van Long, N., H. Siebert, "Lay-off Restraints and the Demand for Labor". Zeitschrift für die gesamte Staatswissenschaft 139 (1983), 612-624.

Vermaat, A.J., Over de wiskunde in de economie. Haarlem, 1970.

Virmany, A., "A Dynamic Model of the Firm". Journal of Political Economy 84 (1976), 603-613.

Vroman, S.B., "Behavior of the Firm in a Market for Heterogeneous Labor". Journal of Economic Dynamics and Control 11 (1987), 313-329.

Wan, H.Y., Economic Growth. New York, 1971.

Weintraub, E.R., General Equilibrium Analysis; Studies in Appraisal. Cambridge, 1985.

Witteloostuijn, A. van, "Maximising and Satisficing: Opposite or Equivalent Concepts?". Journal of Economic Psychology 9 (1988), 289-313.

Vol. 261: Th. R. Gulledge, Jr., N.K. Womer, The Economics of Made-to-Order Production. VI, 134 pages. 1986.

Vol. 262: H.U. Buhl, A Neo-Classical Theory of Distribution and Wealth. V, 146 pages. 1986.

Vol. 263: M. Schäfer, Resource Extraction and Market Structure. XI, 154 pages. 1986.

Vol. 264: Models of Economic Dynamics. Proceedings, 1983. Edited by H.F. Sonnenschein. VII, 212 pages. 1986.

Vol. 265: Dynamic Games and Applications in Economics. Edited by T. Başar. IX, 288 pages. 1986.

Vol. 266: Multi-Stage Production Planning and Inventory Control. Edited by S. Axsäter, Ch. Schneeweiss and E. Silver. V, 264 pages. 1986.

Vol. 267: R. Bemelmans, The Capacity Aspect of Inventories. IX, 165 pages. 1986.

Vol. 268: V. Firchau, Information Evaluation in Capital Markets. VII, 103 pages. 1986.

Vol. 269: A. Borglin, H. Keiding, Optimality in Infinite Horizon Economies. VI, 180 pages. 1986.

Vol. 270: Technological Change, Employment and Spatial Dynamics. Proceedings 1985. Edited by P. Nijkamp. VII, 466 pages. 1986.

Vol. 271: C. Hildreth, The Cowles Commission in Chicago, 1939–1955. V, 176 pages. 1986.

Vol. 272: G. Clemenz, Credit Markets with Asymmetric Information. VIII, 212 pages. 1986.

Vol. 273: Large-Scale Modelling and Interactive Decision Analysis. Proceedings, 1985. Edited by G. Fandel, M. Grauer, A. Kurzhanski and A.P. Wierzbicki. VII, 363 pages. 1986.

Vol. 274: W.K. Klein Haneveld, Duality in Stochastic Linear and Dynamic Programming. VII, 295 pages. 1986.

Vol. 275: Competition, Instability, and Nonlinear Cycles. Proceedings, 1985. Edited by W. Semmler. XII, 340 pages. 1986.

Vol. 276: M.R. Baye, D.A. Black, Consumer Behavior, Cost of Living Measures, and the Income Tax. VII, 119 pages. 1986.

Vol. 277: Studies in Austrian Capital Theory, Investment and Time. Edited by M. Faber. VI, 317 pages. 1986.

Vol. 278: W.E. Diewert, The Measurement of the Economic Benefits of Infrastructure Services. V, 202 pages. 1986.

Vol. 279: H.-J. Büttler, G. Frei and B. Schips, Estimation of Disequilibrium Models. VI, 114 pages. 1986.

Vol. 280: H.T. Lau, Combinatorial Heuristic Algorithms with FORTRAN. VII, 126 pages. 1986.

Vol. 281: Ch.-L. Hwang, M.-J. Lin, Group Decision Making under Multiple Criteria. XI, 400 pages. 1987.

Vol. 282: K. Schittkowski, More Test Examples for Nonlinear Programming Codes. V, 261 pages. 1987.

Vol. 283: G. Gabisch, H.-W. Lorenz, Business Cycle Theory. VII, 229 pages. 1987.

Vol. 284: H. Lütkepohl, Forecasting Aggregated Vector ARMA Processes. X, 323 pages. 1987.

Vol. 285: Toward Interactive and Intelligent Decision Support Systems. Volume 1. Proceedings, 1986. Edited by Y. Sawaragi, K. Inoue and H. Nakayama. XII, 445 pages. 1987.

Vol. 286: Toward Interactive and Intelligent Decision Support Systems. Volume 2. Proceedings, 1986. Edited by Y. Sawaragi, K. Inoue and H. Nakayama. XII, 450 pages. 1987.

Vol. 287: Dynamical Systems. Proceedings, 1985. Edited by A.B. Kurzhanski and K. Sigmund. VI, 215 pages. 1987.

Vol. 288: G.D. Rudebusch, The Estimation of Macroeconomic Disequilibrium Models with Regime Classification Information. VII, 128 pages. 1987.

Vol. 289: B.R. Meijboom, Planning in Decentralized Firms. X, 168 pages. 1987.

Vol. 290: D.A. Carlson, A. Haurie, Infinite Horizon Optimal Control. XI, 254 pages. 1987.

Vol. 291: N. Takahashi, Design of Adaptive Organizations. VI, 140 pages. 1987.

Vol. 292: I. Tchijov, L. Tomaszewicz (Eds.), Input-Output Modeling. Proceedings, 1985. VI, 195 pages. 1987.

Vol. 293: D. Batten, J. Casti, B. Johansson (Eds.), Economic Evolution and Structural Adjustment. Proceedings, 1985. VI, 382 pages. 1987.

Vol. 294: J. Jahn, W. Krabs (Eds.), Recent Advances and Historical Development of Vector Optimization. VII, 405 pages. 1987.

Vol. 295: H. Meister, The Purification Problem for Constrained Games with Incomplete Information. X, 127 pages. 1987.

Vol. 296: A. Börsch-Supan, Econometric Analysis of Discrete Choice. VIII, 211 pages. 1987.

Vol. 297: V. Fedorov, H. Läuter (Eds.), Model-Oriented Data Analysis. Proceedings, 1987. VI, 239 pages. 1988.

Vol. 298: S.H. Chew, Q. Zheng, Integral Global Optimization. VII, 179 pages. 1988.

Vol. 299: K. Marti, Descent Directions and Efficient Solutions in Discretely Distributed Stochastic Programs. XIV, 178 pages. 1988.

Vol. 300: U. Derigs, Programming in Networks and Graphs. XI, 315 pages. 1988.

Vol. 301: J. Kacprzyk, M. Roubens (Eds.), Non-Conventional Preference Relations in Decision Making. VII, 155 pages. 1988.

Vol. 302: H.A. Eiselt, G. Pederzoli (Eds.), Advances in Optimization and Control. Proceedings, 1986. VIII, 372 pages. 1988.

Vol. 303: F.X. Diebold, Empirical Modeling of Exchange Rate Dynamics. VII, 143 pages. 1988.

Vol. 304: A. Kurzhanski, K. Neumann, D. Pallaschke (Eds.), Optimization, Parallel Processing and Applications. Proceedings, 1987. VI, 292 pages. 1988.

Vol. 305: G.-J.C.Th. van Schijndel, Dynamic Firm and Investor Behaviour under Progressive Personal Taxation. X, 215 pages. 1988.

Vol. 306: Ch. Klein, A Static Microeconomic Model of Pure Competition. VIII, 139 pages. 1988.

Vol. 307: T.K. Dijkstra (Ed.), On Model Uncertainty and its Statistical Implications. VII, 138 pages. 1988.

Vol. 308: J.R. Daduna, A. Wren (Eds.), Computer-Aided Transit Scheduling. VIII, 339 pages. 1988.

Vol. 309: G. Ricci, K. Velupillai (Eds.), Growth Cycles and Multisectoral Economics: the Goodwin Tradition. III, 126 pages. 1988.

Vol. 310: J. Kacprzyk, M. Fedrizzi (Eds.), Combining Fuzzy Imprecision with Probabilistic Uncertainty in Decision Making. IX, 399 pages. 1988.

Vol. 311: R. Färe, Fundamentals of Production Theory. IX, 163 pages. 1988.

Vol. 312: J. Krishnakumar, Estimation of Simultaneous Equation Models with Error Components Structure. X, 357 pages. 1988.

Vol. 313: W. Jammernegg, Sequential Binary Investment Decisions. VI, 156 pages. 1988.

Vol. 314: R. Tietz, W. Albers, R. Selten (Eds.), Bounded Rational Behavior in Experimental Games and Markets. VI, 368 pages. 1988.

Vol. 315: I. Orishimo, G.J.D. Hewings, P. Nijkamp (Eds.), Information Technology: Social and Spatial Perspectives. Proceedings, 1986. VI, 268 pages. 1988.

Vol. 316: R.L. Basmann, D.J. Slottje, K. Hayes, J.D. Johnson, D.J. Molina, The Generalized Fechner-Thurstone Direct Utility Function and Some of its Uses. VIII, 159 pages. 1988.

Vol. 317: L. Bianco, A. La Bella (Eds.), Freight Transport Planning and Logistics. Proceedings, 1987. X, 568 pages. 1988.

Vol. 318: T. Doup, Simplicial Algorithms on the Simplotope. VIII, 262 pages. 1988.

Vol. 319: D.T. Luc, Theory of Vector Optimization. VIII, 173 pages. 1989.

Vol. 320: D. van der Wijst, Financial Structure in Small Business. VII, 181 pages. 1989.

Vol. 321: M. Di Matteo, R.M. Goodwin, A. Vercelli (Eds.), Technological and Social Factors in Long Term Fluctuations. Proceedings. IX, 442 pages. 1989.

Vol. 322: T. Kollintzas (Ed.), The Rational Expectations Equilibrium Inventory Model. XI, 269 pages. 1989.

Vol. 323: M.B.M. de Koster, Capacity Oriented Analysis and Design of Production Systems. XII, 245 pages. 1989.

Vol. 324: I.M. Bomze, B.M. Pötscher, Game Theoretical Foundations of Evolutionary Stability. VI, 145 pages. 1989.

Vol. 325: P. Ferri, E. Greenberg, The Labor Market and Business Cycle Theories. X, 183 pages. 1989.

Vol. 326: Ch. Sauer, Alternative Theories of Output, Unemployment, and Inflation in Germany: 1960–1985. XIII, 206 pages. 1989.

Vol. 327: M. Tawada, Production Structure and International Trade. V, 132 pages. 1989.

Vol. 328: W. Güth, B. Kalkofen, Unique Solutions for Strategic Games. VII, 200 pages. 1989.

Vol. 329: G. Tillmann, Equity, Incentives, and Taxation. VI, 132 pages. 1989.

Vol. 330: P.M. Kort, Optimal Dynamic Investment Policies of a Value Maximizing Firm. VII, 185 pages. 1989.

Vol. 331: A. Lewandowski, A.P. Wierzbicki (Eds.), Aspiration Based Decision Support Systems. X, 400 pages. 1989.

Vol. 332: T.R. Gulledge, Jr., L.A. Litteral (Eds.), Cost Analysis Applications of Economics and Operations Research. Proceedings. VII, 422 pages. 1989.

Vol. 333: N. Dellaert, Production to Order. VII, 158 pages. 1989.

Vol. 334: H.-W. Lorenz, Nonlinear Dynamical Economics and Chaotic Motion. XI, 248 pages. 1989.

Vol. 335: A. G. Lockett, G. Islei (Eds.), Improving Decision Making in Organisations. Proceedings. IX, 606 pages. 1989.

Vol. 336: T. Puu, Nonlinear Economic Dynamics. VII, 119 pages. 1989.

Vol. 337: A. Lewandowski, I. Stanchev (Eds.), Methodology and Software for Interactive Decision Support. VIII, 309 pages. 1989.

Vol. 338: J.K. Ho, R.P. Sundarraj, DECOMP: an Implementation of Dantzig-Wolfe Decomposition for Linear Programming. VI, 206 pages. 1989.

Vol. 339: J. Terceiro Lomba, Estimation of Dynamic Econometric Models with Errors in Variables. VIII, 116 pages. 1990.

Vol. 340: T. Vasko, R. Ayres, L. Fontvieille (Eds.), Life Cycles and Long Waves. XIV, 293 pages. 1990.

Vol. 341: G.R. Uhlich, Descriptive Theories of Bargaining. IX, 165 pages. 1990.

Vol. 342: K. Okuguchi, F. Szidarovszky, The Theory of Oligopoly with Multi-Product Firms. V, 167 pages. 1990.

Vol. 343: C. Chiarella, The Elements of a Nonlinear Theory of Economic Dynamics. IX, 149 pages. 1990.

Vol. 344: K. Neumann, Stochastic Project Networks. XI, 237 pages. 1990.

Vol. 345: A. Cambini, E. Castagnoli, L. Martein, P. Mazzoleni, S. Schaible (Eds.), Generalized Convexity and Fractional Programming with Economic Applications. Proceedings, 1988. VII, 361 pages. 1990.

Vol. 346: R. von Randow (Ed.), Integer Programming and Related Areas. A Classified Bibliography 1984–1987. XIII, 514 pages. 1990.

Vol. 347: D. Ríos Insua, Sensitivity Analysis in Multi-objective Decision Making. XI, 193 pages. 1990.

Vol. 348: H. Störmer, Binary Functions and their Applications. VIII, 151 pages. 1990.

Vol. 349: G. A. Pfann, Dynamic Modelling of Stochastic Demand for Manufacturing Employment. VI, 158 pages. 1990.

Vol. 350: W.-B. Zhang, Economic Dynamics. X, 232 pages. 1990.

Vol. 351: A. Lewandowski, V. Volkovich (Eds.), Multiobjective Problems of Mathematical Programming. Proceedings, 1988. VII, 315 pages. 1991.

Vol. 352: O. van Hilten, Optimal Firm Behaviour in the Context of Technological Progress and a Business Cycle. XII, 229 pages. 1991.